I am thrilled to see that Gary Sorrells h ary, trainer of missionaries, and leader ot volume. Part autobiography, part missiology, and part ethnography, in every section Gary tells the story of how God works through unassuming people to do amazing things. Gary has a powerful ability to grasp essential practical lessons that others miss and then translate those lessons into principles that can be insteilled in others. This book represents a significant contribution both to missions history and missions theory.

Dan Bouchelle, D. Min.
President, Missions Resource Network

Who better than Gary Sorrells to tell the thrilling story of how Christ used thirty-one young and naive college graduates to ignite a major mission effort in the Spanish- and Portuguese-speaking Latin world? Gary has given more than forty years of his life to this calling, leading and shaping it into the major ministry effort we know today as Great Cities Missions. His passion for the lost shine through *Make Your Vision Go Viral* from beginning to end. You will be blessed in the telling of this marvelous story of God's work.

Royce Money, Ph.D.
Chancellor, Abilene Christian University

Gary Sorrells has staunchly served the people of South America. In *Making Your Vision Go Viral*, Dr. Sorrells further unfolds a compelling plan for the people of the Portuguese- and Spanish-speaking worlds. This volume offers much food for thought for missions planning.

Clyde N. Austin, Ph.D.
Professor Emeritus, Abilene Christian University
Cross-Cultural Reentry: A Book of Readings

Make Your Vision Go Viral is the inspiring story of a group of college students who acted on a dream to reach the cities of Brazil for Jesus Christ. What springs from their efforts is a story of God's provision and grace that you won't want to miss. This book not only inspires, but it also provides crucial insights into how to turn a deep desire to reach the cities of the world for God into a reality.

Dr. Joseph Bentz, Ph.D.
Author, *Pieces of Heaven*
Professor of English, Azusa Pacific University

If this book contained only half of Gary Sorrells' heart, our cup would surely run over. But lucky us—we get the whole heart and soul of a man's mission and his desire to bring it to others, simply, in truth, and with great faith and affection.

Eva Marie Everson
President, Word Weavers International, Inc.
Director, Florida Christian Writers Conference

With great drama, God has worked through Gary Sorrells to change eternity for the Latin world. I am forever in debt to him and Great Cities Missions for the tools they provided me.

David Duncan, D. Min.
Former Missionary to Vitoria, Brazil
Minister, Memorial Church of Christ, Houston, Texas

Gary Sorrells has written a book that is a must-read. Using his personal story as the literary vehicle, Gary has shared the exciting and successful history of Great Cities Missions as it grew from a single mission team in the 1960s to the dynamic church planting organization it is today.

James F. Brickman
Brigadier General, U.S. Army (Retired)
Chairman, Borad of Trustees, Great Cities Missions

Make Your Vision Go Viral is great! I was reliving most of my lifetime on nearly every page. I was also humbled and inspired by the hundreds of times it says that God, the Holy Spirit, and Jesus were with us and deserve all the credit. How else would we have gotten to this wonderful point? Again, you have covered all the bases and written a truly wonderful work on world missions—urban.

Ellis Long, Ph.D.
Founder, Great Cities Missions

Great Cities Missions knew that it wanted to accomplish for the kingdom of God. And at the helm was a determined "bulldog" of a man, who had an enormous heart for the lost and a vision of what could be. Gary Sorrells, with the help of God, kept the vision clear, direct, and exciting. It was simple, but powerful! This is a great book for people who need inspiration to do what God has called them to do. Dreams do come true!

Kent Allen
Vice President of Advancement
Oklahoma Christian University

I can't think of anyone who has helped churches in Latin America grow more than Gary Sorrells. His church-planting insights helped me and my mission team establish a growing work in Rio de Janeiro, Brazil. This book is essential reading for anyone wanting to see the Kingdom succeed in the Latin world.

Gordon Dabbs, Ph.D.
Preaching Minister
Prestoncrest Church of Christ, Dallas

As usual, Dr. Gary Sorrells has done his homework, reminding the reader of the purposeful preparation, relentless resolve, and comprehensive commitment reqired to carry out the Lord's Great Commission.

Dan Coker, Ph.D.
Veteran Latin American Missionary

This book's ease of reading leads to feeling inspired. You'll enjoy the intertwining of lives, teams, churches, and universities in a harmonious call to partnerships. The details are vivid, the lives are real, the dreams become realities.

Carley H. Dodd, Ph.D.
Professor of Intercultural Communication and Dean of the Graduate School
Abilene Christian University

What a blessing to have such a well-written personal history of Church of Christ missionaries in South America. This book should be in the libraries of all university mission departments, and in the homes of all those who have a heart for missions.

Berrylin McGehee Houston
Jacksonville, Florida

This book is a must-read for anyone considering working in the mission field. Gary's observations on mission work are backed by many years of experience. No wonder Great Cities Missions is such a respected work across Christian missionary networks.

John B. Muns
Trustee, Bell Trust
Dallas, Texas

Gary gives us an up-close, un-cut, and up-lifting look into the compelling lives and dreams of young missionaries who, like our mighty God, chose to "call things that are not as though they were."

Allan Stanglin
Preaching Minister
Central Church of Christ
Amarillo, Texas

For additional copies
of
Make Your Vision Go Viral,
please visit
GreatCities.org
or
Amazon.com

MAKE YOUR VISION GO VIRAL

Taking Christ to Great Cities—A Proven 5-Step Plan That Really Works

Dr. Gary J. Sorrells

Foreword
Dr. Howard Norton

CREATIVE ENTERPRISES STUDIO

Bedford, Texas

Make Your Vision Go Viral

Copyright ©2013 by Gary J. Sorrells

All rights reserved. No portion of this book may be reproduced, stored in a retrieval system, or transmitted in any form or by any means—electronic, mechanical, photocopy, recording, scanning, or other—except for brief quotations in critical reviews or articles, or as specifically allowed by the U. S. Copyright Act of 1976, as amended, without the prior written permission of the publisher.

Published in association with Creative Enterprises Studio, A Premier Publishing Services Group, PO Box 224, Bedford, TX 76095. CreativeEnterprisesLtd.com.

All Scripture quotations are taken from the Holy Bible, New International Version®, NIV®. Copyright © 1973, 1978, 1984, 2011 by Biblica Inc.™ Used by permission of Zondervan. All rights reserved worldwide. www.zondervan.com.

ISBN: 978-0982-61439-6 (Softcover)
ISBN: 978-0989-05210-8 (Hardcover)

Library of Congress Control Number: 2013931074

Cover Design: The Dugan Design Group
Interior Image: Istock Photo
Interior Design: Inside-Out Design & Typesetting, Hurst, TX

Printed in the United States of America
13 14 15 16 17 18   MG   6 5 4 3 2 1

To the 1961 Abilene Christian College Brazil Group,
the phenomenal Central Church of Christ of Amarillo, Texas,
and the visionary Great Cities Missions board of trustees

Contents

Foreword — xi

Acknowledgments — xiii

Introduction — xvii

Part 1—The Vision

1	The Call	3
2	Thirty-One College Kids	11
3	Desert Formation	23
4	Life in a Great City	43
5	Leaving Brazil	65
6	Open for Business	69
7	Recruiting Begins	85
8	Reentry	99

Contents

Part 2—The Five Steps

9	Step One: Trust God	113
10	Step Two: Recruit the Best	119
11	Step Three: Do the Homework	139
12	Step Four: Care with Passion	169
13	Step Five: Build with Zeal	183

Part 3—Looking Back, Looking Forward

14	Celebrate Team Arrivals	203
15	Ten Lessons	245
16	Mission and Pain	253
17	God of the Future	263
	Notes	279
	About the Author	281

FOREWORD

In the Spring Semester of 1969, I returned to the United States for a one-month missionary recruiting trip. Early on, the Sao Paulo Mission Team invested in the idea of inviting young men and women to do mission work in Brazil for short periods of time. We viewed this as a means for young people to gain hands-on missionary experience, provide much-needed assistance to the long-term workers on the field, and hopefully fall in love with mission work and become career missionaries.

I believe that month was one of the most productive times of my life. By the end of the month, six young people had decided to move to Brazil and work for two years as part of the Sao Paulo effort. Each of the six eventually extended their time in Brazil and also dedicated many years to the work of ministry in other parts of the world.

It was during that one-month trip that I met Gary Sorrells on the campus of Abilene Christian University. He had transferred from Lubbock Christian University and was finishing up his bachelor's degree in Bible. My fellow missionary, Glenn Owen, had met Gary on an earlier visit and stoked the missionary fires that Gary's mother had kindled in him years before there was a Sao Paulo Mission Team. Building on the foundation of

FOREWORD

others, I invited Gary to move to Brazil for two years and work with our group of missionaries. At the time, I was thirty-four years old and Gary was twenty-two.

I knew that the work I was doing that spring day was important because it was the Lord's work, but I had no idea concerning the far-reaching effects of that apparently uneventful meeting when the two of us became acquainted for the first time. I told Gary what I was doing in the States and invited him to consider joining us. It didn't take Gary long to make the decision to move to Brazil after graduation in a few weeks.

Gary Sorrells exceeded all of my expectations as a missionary. He had people skills, team spirit, administrative gifts, deep spirituality, perseverance, wisdom, evangelistic zeal, and a great sense of humor. He was ready to lead, accompany, or follow—depending on the task at hand. Few people have had a greater impact on the work in Brazil and other parts of Latin America than Gary Sorrells.

Only God knows Gary's greatest contribution to His kingdom, but I believe it has been his work with Great Cities Missions. In 1980, after his years on the São Paulo Missionary Team, he joined Ellis Long in the Great Cities work. Gary dedicated thirty more years to recruiting, training, and nurturing missionary teams committed to establishing churches in the key cities of the Spanish- and Portuguese-speaking world. Thousands have obeyed the gospel, and hundreds of churches exist as a result.

I had no idea in the Spring Semester of 1969 that I was in the presence of a great man when I met a 22-year-old named Gary Sorrells. He has blessed my life again and again, and he will bless your life through this book that recounts a powerful chapter in modern missionary history.

HOWARD W. NORTON
Past President, Baxter Institute
Tegucigalpa, Honduras

Acknowledgments

Make Your Vision Go Viral, like any large project, has taken a tribe to bring it to completion.

I owe a great debt to the board of trustees of Great Cities Missions who backed wholeheartedly a sabbatical at the end of my tenure as executive director to write and publish the book.

Forever friends Dr. Craig Gladman, Ernie King, Travis McGraw, Beverly Morgan, Randy Owen, Sue Johnson, Al Smith, and Leon Wood with their families played vital behind-the-scenes roles.

I cannot fail to mention the leadership and members of the Amarillo Central Church of Christ, who served as my steadfast partners and foundation for more than thirty years. The ways they have blessed my family and me are innumerable. The congregation's dedication to the great Latin cities for over a half century stands as an unprecedented example before God and the worldwide church.

My wife; daughter, Regina; and son-in-law, Darrell provided endless encouragement.

I am grateful for the confidence of coworkers Dr. Ellis and Doris Long and Dr. Dan Coker in giving me the 1980 invitation to join the team to build Great Cities Missions. Dr. Ellis Long, like our Sao Paulo team

ACKNOWLEDGMENTS

colleague Dr. Howard Norton, encouraged me to take hold of this writing project as one who lived the entire story and not leave it to be resurrected by others from a cold file cabinet.

Make Your Vision Go Viral is the culmination of a life's work with the 1961 Brazil missionary team, the Abilene Christian University campus, the tutelage of Dr. Clyde Austin in the area of missionary team assessment, and the hundreds who served on Great Cities teams during the span of this book. The thousands of new Latin Christ followers, my work with consultants Dr. Ernest Clevenger Jr., Jim Ravanelli, Dr. J. Terry Johnson, and Berrylin Houston are also important to the validity of the storyline.

I must mention the personal impact by Brazilian Christians Dr. Alaor and Miriam Leite, Walter Lapa, Dr. J. Walfredo Thome, and the late Dr. Wilson Castellan. Throughout the execution of the events in this book, one of the above would often illuminate an insight I would have otherwise missed.

It is always a joy to work with Kati Clement, who put in many hours proofreading and formatting the original script, working on preliminary cover designs, and digging through archives for the team photos in the center of the book. To Kati I offer my utmost thanks.

Kay Shelton aided in proofreading and gave her special gift of financial oversight for publication. She was always a behind-the-scenes encourager of the book with praise to keep me going and valuable suggestions along the way. I thank Kay for encouragement of which she was unaware.

A delightful new friend, Mary Hollingsworth, managing director of Creative Enterprises Studio, served as publisher, assuring quality to all aspects of the intricate publishing maze. The Creative Enterprises Studio team of professionals made the book pleasing to the eye and the text more effective.

Acknowledgments

I would be remiss not to recognize that the majority of ideas put forth in *Make Your Vision Go Viral* are ideas with their origin bubbling up around the table of expertise from a staff of my heroes.

Among those deserving notable recognition for concept development during thirty to forty years of friendship are Ron and Georgia Freitas, Bryan and Becky Gibbs, and Ken and Liz Lewis. These couples will recognize much of the input throughout the book.

To these and other colleagues of a lifetime, I offer my profound gratitude.

Introduction

Make Your Vision Go Viral is the story of an all-providing God working through thirty-one college kids who ignited a vision for a continent of great cities. The college students formed into a mission group on the campus of Abilene Christian College in 1957. On June 17, 1961, these extraordinary young people arrived in Sao Paulo, Brazil. In Brazil, the allure of all great cities of the continent caught their imagination. The desire to recruit others, trust God, and be courageous was in their organizational DNA.

In the attempt to be open to God's call on my life, I accepted the invitation to join the Sao Paulo group in their eighth year and embraced their vision to share Jesus with the great cities of South America. I cannot tell their story without referring to my own. During forty-plus years, their story became my story. Our stories unite in Great Cities Missions.

The dream launchers were the Sao Paulo young people from Abilene. But the greater story is the dream—the dream to see teams move to the exploding cities of the Latin world to make the saving power of Jesus known to a wonderful people.

Make Your Vision Go Viral is a story of God's provision. Like the manna of the Israelites in the desert, God's provision is enough for the day.

INTRODUCTION

Weaving its way throughout the narrative is the ever-present challenge of learning to trust the Provider.

Your arena in life may differ from the arena of Brazil and the Latin people, but God is the same God. Your struggle is the human struggle. No matter where you are in life, one thread of this book is to encourage you to answer the question, "Will I cultivate a tenacious trust in the Provider to sustain—no matter what?"

My role in this book is the storyteller. I tell the history both as a partner with the original Abilene Christian team and as a participant who lived forty-one years of a story that began fifty-three years ago.

This book is a narration of history. I found myself so tied to the story of the dream of placing missionary teams in the great cities of the Portuguese- and Spanish-speaking world that I could not tell the story of my life apart from the narrative of the thirty-one college kids who first ignited a vision for great Latin cities.

Therefore, I tell the history against the backdrop of who I am. In hindsight, I can see how God used my heritage, my desert roots, my education, and my church family to prepare me to share a dream of fellow colleagues. I trace my call by God as a small child, sharing my journey to Abilene Christian College and the encounter with God and Sao Paulo team members Glenn Owen, Howard Norton, and Ellis Long—encounters resulting in my arrival in Brazil on November 19, 1969.

On September 10, 1968, a historic meeting took place. The purpose was to design what would evolve into today's ministry, Great Cities Missions. Twenty-four American missionaries living in Brazil attended the strategy session in the city of Sao Paulo.

Jointly, with one voice they pledged to:

1. Organize a ten-year effort to train and place a team of workers in each of a select number of major cities in and bordering Brazil.

Introduction

2. These teams would consist of at least three to six full-time workers from the United States and Brazil.
3. These strategic cities would then serve as centers for spreading the gospel to the surrounding areas.

An important link that moves the narrative from Sao Paulo, Brazil, to other great cities is the deep connection I feel to the people of South America—a connection rooted in my formative years in Sao Paulo and cultivated for over four decades. I felt it appropriate to recount the years spent in Sao Paulo and the transition that brought me to rejoin colleagues Ellis and Doris Long in Abilene. Commissioned by the Sao Paulo team, they arrived on the campus of Abilene Christian University in mid-1976 to open an office for Great Cities Missions—the vehicle for fulfilling the vision of teams representing Jesus in the great cities of the Latin world.

Foreign missions has a difficult time staying on the radar screen of the church. We are living in a time when we give lip service to sharing the faith but allocate very little to assuring progress. We talk in terms of holistic missions, rightly emphasizing the importance of meeting physical needs, but we have difficulty in getting a handle on how to establish a community of believers. It is exciting to support our youth on a mission trip but much more difficult to support an on-field church establishment.

Make Your Vision Go Viral is the account of building a fledgling mission ministry called Great Cities Missions, which is a growing entity birthed by a dream of the Abilene Christian College graduates who moved to Brazil in 1961. As a nonprofit mission entity, it annually places one to three career missionary teams in the Portuguese- and Spanish-speaking great cities of the Latin world. It meets the goals of holistic church planting as it services physical needs while building a community of Christ followers who in turn share their own faith with family and friends.

Introduction

This is the story of the development of systems to recruit, select, train, and care for missionaries and their children through the entire missionary cycle. Great Cities Missions walks with each missionary family from first contact to reentry into their home country upon completion of the mission. It is a ministry attempting to meet the full definition of holistic church planting.

To be a world Christian adds a new dimension to discipleship. It is an attempt to fulfill the final spoken wishes of Jesus prior to His return to God the Father. This book will open avenues for you to understand how to reach people who may not speak your language and may not be within your sphere of influence.

Make Your Vision Go Viral reads like a novel. I invite you to meet an outstanding group of young people who burn with a dream that only God can fulfill. I invite you to look behind the curtain of my own soul as I describe my encounter with God that pulled me into the Sao Paulo team and into my life's work with Great Cities Missions. I will share with you mistakes and successes resulting from serving God in a ministry that has recruited, trained, and cared for 279 missionaries and a flock of children on twenty-nine missionary teams in the great cities of Brazil and the Hispanic world.

I invite you to meet missionary recruits along the way, like Max and Denalyn Lucado, Bryan and Becky Gibbs, Tim and Janet Brumfield, Ron and Georgia Freitas, Ken and Liz Lewis, and Kelley and Julie Grant.

You will see how young people are selected, trained, and supported by coaches and mentors to learn to live and work with team members, while together establishing a church of Jesus followers who worship and reach out from a principal avenue location in major cities to serve as light in a world dark with despair.

Throughout the book, I challenge you to develop a tenacious trust in God. I share some of my own struggles of balancing Satan's attacks on life

INTRODUCTION

while continuing to function daily as a believer in the eternal God who understands those struggles and promises not to give us more than He can help us carry.

The final chapter closes with a vision for the Latin world. It dares you to step up to the plate and make a difference in the eternal destiny of the warm and wonderful people of our planet who speak Portuguese or Spanish as their heart language and who reside in great cities on five continents.

It's a unique story. I invite you to discover the thrill of a group of college grads who believe God will execute remarkable feats in a continent of great cities.

Part 1

THE VISION

1

The Call

When my first-grade teacher asked her class at Hillcrest Elementary School, "What do you want to be when you grow up?" it was not a firefighter or a police officer that caught the imagination of this six-year-old. My hand shot straight up: "I want to be a preacher."

I did not sit on the front row in church. But almost. Even after decades of ministry and following Jesus, I still have no rational explanation as to why sermons caught my attention from a young age.

Church was front and center in our family. I don't have a dynamic heathen conversion story. I was born into a large, extended Christian family. Grandpa Frank Morrow was baptized in House, New Mexico, by "ol' brother Mickey." My mother, her sister, and five brothers were all believers from their childhood days in that same dry-dirt farming community.

Grandma Dora made sure her children knew Jesus. She died two weeks prior to my mother's graduation as valedictorian of her class at House High School.

In reflecting on my Irish Morrow family heritage, I can see that faith in God was tied to that dry-dirt farm. How could a family settle on a piece of nonirrigated acreage with the Dust Bowl days raging and expect to survive? Even when blessed to have something green emerge from the fields,

Grandpa and Grandma Morrow did not live in the age of modern pesticides, nor could they have afforded them. They must have had a sense that God controlled their destiny at His pleasure through the annual rainfall.

My childhood was spent in Carlsbad, New Mexico. I was born only thirty-five years after New Mexico became a state. Dad's mother, Lula Belle Puckett Sorrells, lived there. Her brother, Dr. Owen Puckett, and numerous nieces and nephews lived nearby. The family line of farmers, preachers, teachers, doctors, office holders, a pharmacist, and blue-collar workers traces its family migration over several generations from Illinois to Tennessee to Arkansas to Oklahoma, and finally to southeast New Mexico.

Dad's mother and Dr. Puckett were on the same page with the Morrow family. That meant that our family attended church services and congregation-related activities every time the church door was unlocked.

From my earliest days, I believed the world was full of lost people and God wanted them saved. At the age of eleven, my focus turned to my own lack of obedience. The Bible was full of stories of people who immediately requested baptism upon meeting Jesus. I was a follower, yet I had not entered the waters of baptism.

I told no one but thought about it all week. On Sunday morning the church sang, "Jesus is calling, calling, calling; Jesus is calling today; why should I linger, linger, linger? I will arise and away."[1] It was time to let all know of my trust in Jesus. Through immersion in the grave of baptism, I symbolically entered the death, the burial, and the resurrection of Jesus to remove all past sin and to cover all future sin with His blood. My Christian life could then begin in earnest.

A call from God was not a prime sermon topic at my local church. We were sure God did not speak audibly and that His Holy Spirit dwelled only in the pages of Scripture. Although I have not heard God's audible voice, after a lifetime of study and living I have come to see that God is not a

The Call

boxed commodity. God is present, alive, and well. He can call whomever He wants in a variety of ways.

I have come to see the God revealed in Scripture as the Creator of the universe who invites all people to accept Jesus as their one and only King. God gave me the choice to accept Him at His word or to turn my back on Him and walk away. I believed God's claims. For me, I must trust Him.

In Scripture, I see God select and anoint ordinary people for specific tasks. Who could be more ordinary than David the shepherd boy? I believe God selected me to spend my life as one of His divinely appointed, flawed instruments. As such, from my earliest days until this exact moment, my life has been an exhilarating journey of tenacious trust.

Each summer during my teen years, my parents made sure I could attend the two-week music camp at Lubbock Christian College. It was a significant financial sacrifice for them. Lubbock was 180 miles northeast of Carlsbad, New Mexico. I am very much a New Mexican. Even now, an unexplainable calm comes over me when I cross the state line and enter the New Mexico desert.

In my early teen years, Lubbock Christian College, a newly established school in a West Texas cotton field, caught my attention. The imposing aviation hangar overwhelmed the single brick administration building, a new women's dormitory, and a hodgepodge campus of old army barracks.

College was not a word in our family lore at the beginning of 1960, but along the way I saw I would need a college education to prepare myself for full-time ministry. Through attending music camps at Lubbock Christian, I became familiar with the school. I would begin my college education in Lubbock.

On May 25, 1965, I graduated from Carlsbad Senior High School. The next day, I was ready to leave home and take another step on the path to fulfilling my calling. The morning after high school graduation, I loaded my possessions into my green 1952 Ford Crestline Victoria. It was the two-door hardtop model, a cool accessory for a high school kid. The first stop on my journey was Goodland, Kansas, 480 miles north of Lubbock.

I was excited and ready to be on my own. The plan was to follow Uncle Melvin, one of three preaching uncles; Aunt Edna, his wife, and their five children in their giant white Pontiac station wagon to Kansas to plant a church. I was to be the lone passenger in my car: Uncle Melvin and Aunt Edna were not quite ready to entrust their children to my care. They did not realize how mature I had become overnight, as I was now a high school graduate.

I prepared my old Ford, already in its teenage years, for the trip. An oil change and a wash job on the front lawn deemed it roadworthy. Loaded with a suitcase and the clock radio my parents gave me as a graduation gift, the car was ready. The twelve-hour trip meant leaving New Mexico, traveling into the Texas panhandle, crossing the Oklahoma panhandle, and proceeding to the far northwest corner of Kansas to the town of Goodland, population five thousand.

Like most cars of the day, my Ford had a "4/60 air conditioner"—powered by driving with four windows down at sixty miles per hour. With the windows open and the worn door latches leaving a wide gap in both doors for additional airflow, the heat of early summer was tolerable.

The first Sunday meeting of our little church was in a motel room. I knew I was on the trip only for the summer months prior to entering college. But after a few weeks of odd jobs, hoeing sugar beets, loading bundles of hay, and handing out flyers door-to-door, I was bright enough to see that planting churches was hard work. I could not have imagined at the time that once out of college I would spend the next forty years planting churches.

My greatest admiration goes to my uncle Melvin and his family. I also salute a cousin, Norman Morrow, and a Carlsbad classmate, Don Cude, who have both worked with the Goodland, Kansas, church for many decades.

In the fall of 1965, after my Kansas summer, I enrolled as a freshman at Lubbock Christian College to begin my studies. Since Lubbock Christian was a two-year junior college, I had my sights set on finishing my degree at nearby Abilene Christian College.

At Lubbock Christian, I learned a valuable lesson that I have tried to carry with me through life. I did not have the vocabulary to describe it at the time, but I have come to understand it as my first encounter with mentor teachers. K. C. Moser and Gerald Kendrick were exceptional Bible teachers. Never before had I encountered godly teachers who taught powerfully on Jesus being the center of our lives. It was under the tutelage of these two men that I first began to grasp the significance of the atoning sacrifice of Jesus.

I had always assumed professors were concerned with teaching truth. I still believe that is the case. It was an unexpected treasure to find professors with the courage to question perceived truth in light of Scripture. All of us buy into accepted versions of a religious practice. The idea of making a distinction between current practice and the teachings of Jesus and the apostles was new to me. In making this distinction, I began to understand for the first time the New Testament teaching that salvation is available, not by my good works but only through the grace of God. There is nothing I can do to make God love me more or to cause Him to love me less.

Since those early classes at Lubbock Christian College, my proverbial antenna has always been in search of mentor teachers. They are rare. Yet, thankfully, I have found them in church pulpits, in college classrooms, in books, over coffee breaks, and on resourceful websites. They have helped me know, in a more profound way, God, Jesus His Son, and the Holy Spirit. My mentor teachers have helped me understand my own responsibilities while a resident of Earth.

Previously I mentioned that college was not a common experience in our family. For many in my parents' generation, life was so difficult that college was not an option. Thus, it was hard for them to cast a vision for us of something they had not experienced. I was unprepared for the difficulty of going to college while working to cover my expenses. I thought nothing could be harder; Abilene Christian College was soon to challenge that assumption.

Because I was familiar with Lubbock Christian, it was a good place to start. Abilene Christian College was different. While in high school, I had attended two or three weeklong annual Bible lectureships during the cold month of February. But I knew little about the school.

At Abilene Christian, instead of being limited to just two great Bible teachers, the school had an entire Bible faculty of legendary professors trained at Harvard, Chicago, Duke, and other high-profile universities. I made it my aim to sign up for classes with the professors who were reputed to be the most demanding. Bill Humble, LeMoine Lewis, Neil Lightfoot, and J. W. Roberts lived up to their reputations.

I could not have imagined it possible for a human being to read thousands of pages for multiple classes in one semester. Nor could I have imagined it possible for a kid from New Mexico to write multiple research papers each semester and still balance the number of exams that were a part of every class.

I went to college to study the Bible and found myself required to study English, Shakespeare, history, biology, chemistry, science, art, music, and math. All were required for my degree program; none caught my interest like my biblical studies.

I assumed full-time ministry meant working with a local church. That was the only model I saw growing up. I had heard of missionaries, but in our tradition it was more common for a minister to go somewhere on a mission for two or three years and then return to work at a local church.

The Call

In college, there were missions interest meetings, but I did not attend. Mostly, the few students whose parents were career missionaries promoted such meetings. I don't believe I had ever met a "career missionary."

Leaving the United States for a foreign country was not an existent thought in my mind. That all changed in the spring of 1969.

From its founding days, Abilene Christian was committed to a daily chapel and had an ardent commitment to see all students present. Without the enforced attendance rule, chapel would have been as useful as seatbelts without the law to buckle up. Chapel was a powerful force for shaping our lives.

In the spring of 1969, three men who were to occupy significant roles in my life visited the campus of Abilene Christian. One morning a guest speaker from Sao Paulo, Brazil, spoke at the chapel service. Missionary Glenn Owen painted a picture of millions of lost city dwellers desiring to know the God of the Bible and His Son Jesus. The problem was finding people willing to move to Brazil to teach.

In Churches of Christ, that was about as close to a calling as one could expect. He totally had my attention. I could do that. Why should I not go?

That evening I got into my 1965 baby blue Ford Mustang, sat in the white bucket seat, and drove out to a solitary spot at nearby Fort Phantom Lake. I prayed more intensely than I had ever prayed in my life. As I headed back to town, I was headed for Sao Paulo, Brazil, in my heart. I would be a resident of one of the world's great megacities, completely unknown to me just one day before.

A short time later, Howard Norton, teammate of Glenn Owen, came to campus. By that time I was learning about a group of sixteen families who were students at Abilene Christian College in the late 1950s, and I had made the commitment to move with them as a team to Sao Paulo, Brazil, to plant churches in one of the world's most resourced nations.

Glenn Owen inspired my decision to go, and Howard Norton inspired me to speed up my graduation to arrive in Brazil within the year. Howard also pointed me toward a role at a new church in the Campo Grande neighborhood of Sao Paulo. He served as mentor for my first two years in Sao Paulo. The truth is, Howard continues to serve in that role, because neither of us has let the mentoring role terminate.

That spring, a third team member, Ellis Long, arrived on the Abilene Christian campus to research and write in relation to completing his doctoral studies at Florida State University. Like Glenn and Howard, Ellis confirmed my calling and taught me something new: how to raise the money to sustain my life in Sao Paulo. Ellis taught me how to tell my story by projecting color slides at high speed while following a written text. In hindsight, I had no way of knowing the impact Ellis would have on the future direction of my life.

I spent the summer of 1969 finishing my degree and attempting to find funding for Brazil. On August 21, I walked across the stage at Abilene Christian College to receive my bachelor of arts degree.

Ellis was a better teacher than I was a student. I went from church to church as I put my best effort into fundraising. However, when the day came for my departure to Brazil, I still lacked a quarter of my financial support. I determined to trust God for what was lacking. Once again, little did I know that my tenacious trust for God to deliver would characterize my next forty years.

On November 18, 1969, I boarded a flight in Lubbock, Texas, connected to Braniff International Airlines at Dallas Love Field; and after a short stop in Miami, I departed for Brazil. And my life's assignment, sparked by the Abilene Christian couples, began to unfold in a continent of great cities.

2

Thirty-One College Kids

The families I encountered upon my arrival in Brazil were the most amazing people I had ever known. Each person was unique and talented.

Like most small schools coming to life as the twentieth century began, Abilene Christian College saw more challenges than security. The small church school's bills, faculty, and administration tied to a West Texas agriculture economy equated to snail-pace growth. By 1957, the school was well established yet still struggling to grow. Abilene Christian was a late bloomer, tracing its heritage to the Stone-Campbell family of churches.

The Stone-Campbell Movement

On July 4, 1776, the Continental Congress adopted the United States Declaration of Independence. Twenty-five short years later, at the beginning of the 1800s, independence was still very much on the mind of the populace.

The idea of restoring pure New Testament Christianity with democratic participation of the people and independence from historical governing bodies sparked the Second Great Awakening. Great revivals stormed Kentucky, Tennessee, and southern Ohio.

Presbyterians Barton W. Stone, Thomas Campbell, and his son Alexander were among the prominent figures of the day. Their advocacy and the uniting of their two groups in 1832 eventually led to the Stone-Campbell Restoration Movement.

Two key documents—*The Last Will and Testament of the Springfield Presbytery,* signed by Stone and five others on June 28, 1804, along with Thomas Campbell's *Declaration and Address,* signed on September 8, 1809—led to a fellowship of churches known interchangeably by the names of Disciples of Christ, Christian Churches, or Churches of Christ. The primary mission of these churches was to bring salvation through Jesus to their fellowman and to interpret as accurately as possible God's teachings as revealed in Scripture.

They were unanimous about leaving behind human creeds and denominational structures, and uniting all believers in Jesus as one church. Using Scripture as its guide, this fellowship of churches would grow as disciples of Jesus attempting to live as He lived. It was important for each individual to have the right to interpret Scripture, for the New Testament teaches that every believer belongs to the priesthood of Christ and is directly responsible to Jesus. Sayings like "using Bible names in Bible ways," "speak where the Bible speaks, be silent where the Bible is silent," and "Christian only, not the only Christians," guided the believers on their quest to unity.

For the next three-quarters of a century, the growing demand for uniformity slowly derailed the quest for unity. As descendants of the Eden fall, we are prone to believe our own conclusions are true—whether based on Scripture or our own bias—and insist that others agree. Sometimes we are right, and other times we are wrong. In either case, we assign our conclusions as being what God believes. Finally, we rally around those who believe as we do and force the dissenters out.

By the time of the United State Census of Religious Bodies of 1906, the grand unity aspiration of the Stone-Campbell movement manifested for the first time as three divided, independent groups. The Disciples of Christ, the Independent Christian Church, and the Church of Christ were now separate churches.

The unspoken elephant in the room was the Southerner's bitter pill of the North winning the Civil War. The church divide was surprisingly parallel to the Mason-Dixon Line. To express a political grievance in the form of church doctrine is a mechanism to place God on the right side of the argument. One difference from the northern victor's churches was that southern Churches of Christ affirmed that Scripture did not speak of mission societies. In the view of these churches, mission work was the domain of a local church rather than individuals cooperating through an organized entity. This view became doctrine of the southern churches.

Interestingly enough, this is not a point of view supported by the New Testament. Granted, the Bible does *not* speak of missionary societies. However, it does describe groups of workers spreading the news of what God was doing in the world. The New Testament speaks of individuals working together to expand the kingdom of God.

The support of Jesus and His disciples by a band of wealthy women (Luke 8) is one of many examples. Throughout the Acts of the Apostles and the Epistles, the apostle Paul, his colleagues, and other evangelistic bands crisscrossed the known world telling of the resurrection of Jesus and planting churches. They were not working as members of the same local congregation.

With the 1906 division, the majority of foreign mission activity remained with the Independent Christian Churches and their missionary societies. That meant Churches of Christ were starting over in world missions. For the next thirty-five years, prior to World War II, a few courageous missionaries went to Africa, Asia, Europe, and South America from within Churches of Christ.

Make Your Vision Go Viral

As World War II closed and the troops returned, mission activity was poised to increase. The church had seen the world. With the United States rebuilding devastated nations, there was an increased consciousness within churches and among young missionaries to follow Jesus' commission to go into the entire world.

By 1957, missionaries were frequent speakers on the campus of Abilene Christian College. These returning missionaries planted seeds of inspiration for world missions. Small seeds sprouted and blossomed into the formation of the Sao Paulo, Brazil, mission team.

Abilene Christian College was a startup school in 1906 affiliated with Churches of Christ. In 1957, its students took a major step to place mission work back on the radar screen of local congregations.

Teams and teamwork is a major theme throughout this book. Using a team model is a power for good. This book follows the development of one team from Abilene Christian University and the twenty-nine other teams it generated for Portuguese- and Spanish-speaking cities.

As a child, I fell in love with the idea of teams through the team sport of baseball. The variety of team roles was intriguing. I admired the specific skill set necessary for each position. The skill and talent level of pitchers is evident. It is almost impossible for a major league team to find five starting pitchers who are winners. Catchers are always the workhorses of the team. They are in on every play, backing up first and third base, directing traffic on the field, and are seldom noticed—unless they fail to stop a ball. I loved second base. I still get a rush of adrenaline at seeing a rocket pickoff at second base or a lightning-speed double play.

In 1957, I was ten years old and an ardent follower of the New York Yankees. I would lie on the wood floor in our small living room on Second Street and watch Whitey Ford, Don Larsen, Yogi Berra, Mickey Mantle, and Bobby Richardson. Our first snowy, black-and-white television did not do justice to the images of my heroes. Every player was king of his position yet a member of the team. They were bigger than television could transmit.

What winners they were—until they met Warren Spahn, Hank Aaron, and Eddie Mathews of the Milwaukee Braves in the seventh and final game of the 1957 World Series. The Braves somehow beat the Yankees 5 to 0, a disappointing day for a young baseball fanatic. My team lost. That same year a winning team was in formation.

The more important team that year was the one forming at Abilene Christian College. Each person would play a specific role in the new team game plan. Howard Norton and Don Vinzant, two cousins from Fort Worth, Texas; with their wives, Jane and Carol; shared a dream. They exemplified two great characteristics of youth—high energy and the naïveté to believe that anything is possible. I have heard them tell the story many times:

> We had developed deep friendships at Abilene Christian with some of God's most talented youth. It would be a shame to let graduation end the joy we have in being together with fellow students. Who could have imagined how important our network of fellow students would become in our lives over our college years? Let's invite our friends to join with us after graduation and move to a great city of the world. Together, we can all share the saving Jesus and plant reproducing churches across a major population.

One evening, in the spring of 1957 in Howard and Jane's Abilene Christian apartment located in old army barracks six, the Nortons and Don and Carol committed to God and to each other to go anywhere—yes, *anywhere*—in the world to serve God and the people He would lead them to. Wherever the destination, they agreed to remain together.

At once, the Nortons and Vinzants began to put together a list of fellow students. With the close of the semester and graduation upon them, they had to work fast. Howard and Don divided the list and set out to visit with their friends. A few nights later, fifteen of those friends from student government and from within their classes crowed into the same little barracks apartment. Before leaving, several friends made their commitment to join in the effort.

The first task was to decide where to go. They listened to needs from around the world. Three places caught their attention. Some on the team wanted to go to New York. Jimmy Shu, a Chinese student friend, made the case for Hong Kong. Team member Ted Stewart, speaker of the house of the student body, pushed for South America's largest city—Sao Paulo, Brazil. It was time for the vote. Sao Paulo won out over Hong Kong by one vote.

By May of that year, just prior to breaking up for the summer, the departure date was set for June 1, 1961—four years into the future. The idea started to grow. The team increased to thirty-one men and women.

A New Vision for Churches of Christ

The sheer size of this group and the magnitude of the project caught the attention of churches. The Brazil team provided Churches of Christ a new vision. That vision was one of grand possibilities for reaching a lost world through team missions.

It was staggering to move sixteen families to another continent in the late 1950s. At the same time, the potential was awe-inspiring. The logistics required for this kingdom of God move raised the confidence and expectation for what a fellowship of churches could accomplish. The Brazil group brought to the attention of churches and individuals the extraordinary potential of a united team. The excitement among stateside churches was contagious.

The leadership DNA of this group was evident from the beginning. Team members were natural leaders. In college, they served in student government and as officers in their social clubs. Their college peers voted some team members as their favorite people in various areas of campus life.

There was a lot to accomplish. Every team member set out to learn Portuguese. Four years would give them time to get married, finish degrees, get at least some stateside supervised work experience, find funding, get their parents used to the idea, and begin to have lots of babies—twenty children would accompany their thirty parents and one single man to Brazil. Twenty-two more children were to be born in the new and unfamiliar country.

Immediately, they organized a structure to keep them together over the four years of preparation. They would meet together twice a year, form a working committee structure, and be methodical in exchanging letters and visiting each other's homes. They would also share the vision, design the initial work plan, and raise the money for this unprecedented endeavor. Across the United States, the young missionaries found churches and individuals to finance their vision.

During the four-year preparation leading to the move, churches were delighted to have such talented members serve in their congregations. The actions of these young families made a statement to all: this team of talented leaders was purposely choosing to dedicate their lives to building the worldwide church.

On Thursday afternoon, June 1, 1961, the majority of the team boarded the SS *Del Norte* in Houston. Their traveling group consisted of twenty-six men and women and their eighteen children. The remaining seven members of the team would depart within the year.

The SS *Del Norte*, built in 1946, was America's first post-war ocean liner. As the 120-passenger cargo ship sailed from the Port of Houston, Texas, hundreds of well-wishers lined the docks while raising their voices together to sing "Send the Light, Send the Light." With the notes of the song fading in the distance it was official—they were now missionaries.

Traveling at seventeen nautical miles per hour, seventeen days later they reached the Port of Santos. Team members spent the major portion of the day clearing customs. Hunger set in. A vendor's pile of sandwiches was in sight and jealously guarded by a swarm of flies. Howard Norton succumbed first. Ted Stewart ridiculed the others mercilessly for eating food contaminated by flies. But as the day wore on, Ted went to the sandwich line. Soon everyone followed.

After clearing the Brazilian custom house with the necessary documents for entering a new country, it was time for the last leg of their journey. The thirty-three-mile bus trip from Santos would take them up the steep switchback mountain highway to the city of Sao Paulo, the manufacturing center of South America.

Checking into the Hotel Sao Paulo, they were ready to begin the process of finding housing and settling into their new country. They could now await with anticipation the arrival of the remaining five adults and two children who would join them, making the entire team of fifty-one members present in Brazil.

It was a time when commitment was serious business. Their word was important. All thirty-one students who committed to the team placed their trust in God and arrived in Brazil as they had promised their teammates.

Just think of the prospect of fifty-one people becoming the aroma of Jesus in their new culture. The apostle Paul said God uses his children to "spread the aroma of the knowledge of him everywhere" (2 Corinthians 2:14). Fifty-one men, women, and children would bring a wonderful perfume to the city. The large group of Americans did not enter Sao Paulo unnoticed by the Brazilian people. Even the children played roles in meeting new neighbors. Curious Brazilians wondered why so many Americans moved to their city and their neighborhood. The Brazilian neighbors were more than gracious.

Thirty-One College Kids

In 1968, the team celebrated their seventh anniversary on the mission field. The stateside churches were beginning to see a glimpse of God's accomplishments through the strength and diversity found in a large team.

One of the first team projects was the establishment of a school of the Bible. The idea was to create neutral ground to give people the opportunity to examine the teachings of the Bible, from Genesis to Revelation. As the school grew, it also became a training arm of the churches. During the first seven years of the team's work in Sao Paulo, hundreds of Brazilians studied at the school.

Then there was the writing and the distribution of *What the Bible Says*, a Bible correspondence course used throughout Brazil. In subsequent years, the course found worldwide distribution in many languages. By this time, the Sao Paulo team had also written and produced *The Eternal Purpose* filmstrip series for home Bible study.

From the beginning, the Sao Paulo group thought beyond its chosen city. On August 14, 1961, two months after their arrival, the team debated and penned twenty-five major goals and eighteen subsidiary goals. Ten of those goals dealt directly with expanding the kingdom outside the city of Sao Paulo. The second goal, listed for January 1962, was to begin a campaign to send missionaries to other Brazilian cities.

In 1965, World Radio arrived in Sao Paulo, along with administrator Lowell Perry from Abilene Christian College and his family. Perry moved to Sao Paulo to oversee the purchase of Radio Piratininga's twenty-eight stations. The radio network given to the Sao Paulo team by the World Radio Foundation functioned legally through a local foundation formed by Brazilian Christians, with the missionary team providing input. Glenn Owen, a Sao Paulo team member and a gifted communicator, spoke daily to thousands of listeners on the *Open Your Bible* program. The broadcast reached across Brazil.

World Radio provided the Sao Paulo team with an airplane to follow up with contacts produced through the radio and the correspondence course. The radio, the correspondence course, the airplane, and the followup on contacts resulted in many new churches.

At the seven-year mark, the missionary team owned 126 acres of land for Camp Mount of Olives. It would become one of the finest Christian youth camps in Brazil, sharing Jesus with young people, providing future leadership for churches, and being the catalyst for starting many Christian homes.

Four urban congregations, each with its own land and building, were reaching out to the city. One of the most ambitious church plants was the congregation on the corner of the avenues of Nove de Julho (Ninth of July) and Sao Gabriel.

Nove de Julho Avenue connected the Governor's Palace to the international airport and to the banking center of Sao Paulo. World dignitaries, including Queen Elizabeth and Robert Kennedy, passed in front of the newly purchased property.

Breaking with mission methodology of the day, the team raised money in the United States beyond what the Brazilian church could supply. The goal was to purchase land and construct a beautiful place of worship. The subfoundation of 176 concrete-encased pilings, each measuring twenty-six feet long and weighing 3,307 pounds, was driven into the ground. On top of the pilings, a foundation was set that would support a twelve-story highrise. A basement and two floors housed a worship center, classrooms, fellowship space, offices, a print shop, and a kitchen. If needed, ten floors could be added in the future.

The Sao Paulo team's visibility among stateside churches increased interest in foreign church planting. Operation '68, the most notable of those efforts, was started by three teenage girls who were attending Senior Teen Camp in 1962 at Camp Yamhill, forty-five miles south of Portland, Oregon. Like the Abilene Christian group, they committed themselves to the Lord, to each other, and to the mission field. These young people sought out the commitment of their camp counselors as team members. The goal was for sixty-eight people to arrive on a mission field in 1968. The team quickly grew to five families.

Correspondence began to flow between the Operation '68 group and the Sao Paulo team. The Brazil team recruited in earnest. The Camp Yamhill missionaries cast their vision toward Brazil and focused on the interior city of Belo Horizonte, the capital of the state of Minas Gerais. At that time, Belo Horizonte, a city of two million people, doubled in size every seven years.

The Sao Paulo team met the SS *Argentina Maru* on August 16, 1967, at the Port of Santos. Onboard were seven families of the advanced guard. They were the first of sixteen families bound for Belo Horizonte. Their arrival only fanned the recruiting flame of the Sao Paulo team.

A Historic Meeting

The success of the first seven years laid the foundation for a historic meeting on September 10, 1968. The Sao Paulo group burned with a vision for the South American continent. In those seven years, they visited a few of the continent's great cities. Through television and daily newspapers, they were aware of many more.

The newly arrived Belo Horizonte mission team also saw the potential of the great cities of Brazil. Glover and Marjorie Shipp, members of the original Operation '68 Belo Horizonte team, arrived on August 16, 1967. Glover, ever the visionary, was the original advocate of the name "Brazil Breakthrough."

On Tuesday, September 10, twenty-four missionaries met in Sao Paulo to confirm a mutual vision for the South American continent. "Breakthrough Brazil" was the name given to the vision. Its purpose was "to plan and organize a ten-year effort to train and place a team of workers in each of a selected number of major cities in and bordering Brazil. These teams would consist of at least three to six full-time workers . . . coming from the United States and Brazil. These strategic cities then would serve as centers for spreading the Gospel to the surrounding areas."

It took over ten years for the idea to take off, with the move of Ellis and Doris Long and their children Beth, Kent, and Roy Southern from Sao Paulo to Abilene Christian University in 1976 to open a full-time office for fulfilling the Breakthrough Brazil dream.

What they did not know at the time was that, in addition to those from the United States and Brazil, team members would come from Argentina, Colombia, Cuba, Dominican Republic, Guatemala, Haiti, Honduras, Mexico, Nicaragua, Panama, Paraguay, Peru, Salvador, Uruguay, and Venezuela.

Not knowing of Breakthrough Brazil, I could not have imagined how that little meeting of missionaries was to chart the trajectory of my life's mission under the banner of Great Cities Missions.

3

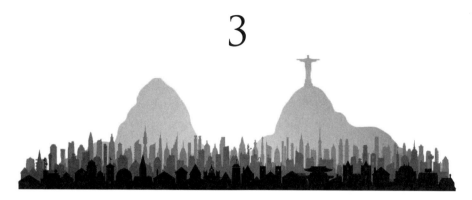

Desert Formation

Since I never liked parties—being an introvert from my wiring—nor the loud explosion of fireworks, I delayed my entrance into the world until the 1947 New Year celebration ended. My parents arrived at the hospital in plenty of time. My birth certificate attests to the fact that Mom checked into the hospital in 1946, one day, twelve hours, and five minutes prior to my arrival. With minimal effort on my part, I could have made the front-page New Year's Baby photo for the *Carlsbad Current Argus*—but I had no interest.

In 1947, on the frontier of New Mexico, the word *hospital* was an overstatement. My hospital—modern for its time—was on the corner of Fox and Halagueno Streets. Today it continues as a small stucco office near the center of town.

On January 2, 1947, Dr. H. D. Pate—affectionately known in town as Old Doctor Pate throughout my childhood—the nurse, Mom, Dad, and I were in our places ready to receive a new resident for Carlsbad and a new citizen for the state of New Mexico. I made my arrival, all nine pounds of me, at 2:35 p.m. The scent of books from the public library across the street must have passed through the open windows that day, becoming a sort of opium for my life.

Make Your Vision Go Viral

Carlsbad Migration

My father, Joe Oscar Sorrells, was born in Antlers, Oklahoma. His dad, James Oscar Sorrells, was born in Izard County, Arkansas, on October 18, 1872, and faced common difficulties of the time: flu, along with many of today's controllable diseases, was often a death warrant for those living in the 1800s.

James Oscar Sorrells knew young Lula Belle Puckett from childhood. When Miss Lula was sixteen or seventeen, they dated for a while. For reasons lost through time, Oscar moved to Moyers, Oklahoma; married a young woman, and four children were born. With the all-too-familiar pain of the times, his wife died young, leaving him to care for three small boys and a little girl.

Miss Lula learned of the situation. An exchange of letters took place, and Oscar returned to Izard County for a visit. They were married on June 22, 1913, in Izard County, Arkansas, in the rural community of LaCrosse. James Oscar immediately took his bride to meet her four new children in Moyers, Oklahoma.

In the early 1900s, keeping families fed and living under one roof topped the family agenda. Homesteading on available land in the West provided hope for a better shot at survival, and even progress beyond just survival. That shot for Oscar and Lula Belle Puckett Sorrells was on their small piece of land near Antlers. Three additional children, Paul, Joe, and Cleo, were born on their little farm.

Grandma Lula was constantly inviting circuit-riding preachers to their little town for evangelism in hopes of beginning a church. Somewhere along the way, Grandpa Oscar entered the baptismal waters but never shared Grandma's interest in a growing church.

In 1936, at age sixty-four, James Oscar Sorrells died of pancreatic cancer. Dad finished high school the next year and moved to Stillwater, Oklahoma, to attend college. Grandma Lula went to Altus to stay with a sister. On Dad's first visit home, his half brother Harley met him on the road to the farm and took him to a café in Antlers. They visited the entire night in the café instead of going to the family home. The next morning, he returned to school. What he did not know at the time was that his stepbrother was preparing to sell the home and its belongings, take the money, and move to California. The all-night coffee visit was a diversion so Dad would not discover his home was prepared for auction. In 1938, Dad left for Carlsbad, New Mexico, in search of a job. His uncle, Dr. Owen E. Puckett, had arrived in Carlsbad twelve years earlier as the newly appointed county health officer. Dr. Puckett would become a formative mentor figure in my own life.

Dad found work with the entrepreneurial Charlie White, who homesteaded 320 acres at the mouth of the canyon entrance to what Congress on May 14, 1930, would designate as Carlsbad Caverns National Park. In 1927, Charlie White had begun building White's Cavern Camp with his home, a gasoline station, and thirteen overnight cabins for visitors. By 1938 it was operating as White's City, and Charlie was adding additional hotel rooms to the garage, grocery store, café, drugstore, and museum he owned. Dad found work on the hotel project, giving the tourist town three hundred rooms by 1940.

Two hundred miles to the northeast of Carlsbad, in the farming community of House, New Mexico, another story was unfolding. After four years of firing boilers at the Roundhouse in Tucumcari, New Mexico, James Franklin Morrow, who migrated to New Mexico with his parents from his birthplace in Oxford, Mississippi, was ready to rejoin his parents and siblings in the farming business. In 1921, he bought the "old Merall place," three-quarters of a section of land, four and a half miles from House, New Mexico.

There was not much of a house on the land in House. One room comprised the living room, the kitchen, and the bedroom for my mom, her older brother, and my grandparents, James Franklin Morrow and Francis Eudora Pannell Morrow. You will note the absence of a bathroom. That was due to a little four-wall, boxlike outhouse—called a "privy" for some strange reason—and for not so strange a reason, it was located some distance from the house.

In winter, cold air and snow penetrated the house's wooden frame. The bachelor heater, fed with cow chips, glowed to keep the airy space warm. The following year brought the Christmas blizzard of 1922. With four inches of snow on top of the bed, water pouring into the room from the ceiling as the bellowing heater melted snow from the roof, Grandpa—or perhaps it was Grandma—reached the limit. Quickly hitching horses to the work sled, the family made its way to seek refuge at the home of Great-grandpa and Great-Grandma Morrow.

My great-grandparents were finishing a new home in town, so Grandpa Frank paid rent on their original homestead for several years before building a house on his own farm in 1930. The new farmhouse became part of family lore. Many family stories from my uncles, aunt, and parents have their setting in and around that farmhouse. Living there for two years shaped my earliest memories.

It was in that farmhouse that my mom, along with her parents and siblings, survived the Great Depression, the Dust Bowl, and periodic droughts. One year, they survived by President Roosevelt's program that paid four dollars a head to shoot their cows. That was one time they beat the government, as one cow was too sick to live through the night anyway. They still received the four dollars.

It was at the farmhouse on May 5, 1937, that my grandmother Dora Morrow died at age forty-one. She left seven children. Her oldest, Owen, was in Terrero, New Mexico, working as a miner for the American Metal Company. From its opening in 1927 through its final closing in 1939, the mine produced zinc, lead, copper, silver, and gold. For Owen it provided a job to help meet family expenses.

Her youngest child was three-year-old Ola Mae, my aunt.

That fall, Mother enrolled in Draughon's Business College in Lubbock, Texas. As Mom began her classes, tragic news struck again. Little sister Ola Mae found a match in the flour bin and managed to strike it, setting her dress on fire. One-third of her body suffered horrible burns. Mom immediately quit school and returned home to care for Ola Mae through many months of hospital stays and daily care.

On September 1, 1939, Germany invaded Poland. Within two days, Britain and France entered the war. By the week's end, Australia, New Zealand, Canada, and South Africa had joined the war against Germany: World War II was underway. In two short years, the bombing of Pearl Harbor would draw the United States fully into the second war of the world.

In 1925, Carlsbad was the discovery site of deep potash veins. Potash, a saltlike substance, is important in the manufacturing of fertilizer. The town is located in the Pecos River Valley on the floor of the Chihuahuan Desert, which covers northern Mexico and fans out into portions of southwest Texas, southeast Arizona, and into southern and central New Mexico. From the opening of the potash mines near Carlsbad in 1940 until the mid-1960s, Carlsbad potash dominated the American market. Mining potash was labor intensive, creating many jobs.

Lack of rain in the Chihuahuan Desert took its toll on dry land farms. Soldiers joining the armed forces for war placed pressure on the labor market. In the early 1940s, the war effort increased and word spread of the need for workers in the new potash industry. Grandpa leased the farm, and, with his seven children, moved to Carlsbad. They were still living in the Chihuahuan Desert, but at least they had water and jobs.

Carlsbad, New Mexico

In 1942, Joe Sorrells found work as an airplane inspector at the Carlsbad Army Field, home of the 386th Army Air Force Base unit. Edith Morrow found work as a sampler at the American Potash mine. They found each other at the Church of Christ at Fox and Lake Streets.

One year later, on July 25, 1943, they married. Dad's uncle, Frank Puckett, officiated. The wedding took place in the living room of another uncle, Dr. Owen E. Puckett. Dad and Mom celebrated their marriage for sixty-two years.

Home

After my birth at Carlsbad Memorial Hospital, I went home to our little rock house on Church Street to join my sister Ellouise and Grandma Lula Sorrells. As I write sixty-five years later, thinking over how intertwined are my life and church, it seems appropriate for my first residence to be on Church Street. The rock house on Church Street was the first home my parents purchased. I would not be there long—the farm was calling.

Carlsbad Army Field, declared inactive at the close of the war, had served its purpose since its establishment in 1942. Dad went to work for Standard Oil, employed by Portwood Oil Company. His job was to deliver gasoline across southeastern New Mexico.

The family farm in House, New Mexico, which was rented out during the war, was in need of attention. Grandpa Morrow returned to operate the farm at the end of 1945. In 1948, our family joined him at the farm. Dad's job with Portwood Oil gave him the flexibility and income the family would need while away from Carlsbad. During the two farm years, my younger brother, Larry, was born in the nearby town of Tucumcari. Keeping family tradition alive, it was the same place where Mom was born in 1919.

Desert Formation

After the farm sold in 1951, our family, Grandpa Morrow, Aunt Ola Mae, and the five Morrow uncles were back in Carlsbad. Dad's mother, an uncle, two aunts, and several cousins were also making Carlsbad their home.

Second Street

We were home but in need of a place to live. With the close of the Carlsbad Army Field, FOR SALE signs made it possible for army buildings to enter civilian life. Our family purchased one of the square box structures and moved it to a lot on Second Street, where Dad placed under it a cinder-block foundation and poured a front porch of concrete and steps for the back door. He divided the four outside walls into two small bedrooms, a bathroom, a living room, and a kitchen, giving us a house for the formation of my childhood.

The house started out rather sparse. To accommodate our Grandma Sorrells's moving in with us, a new kitchen, a second bathroom, and a third bedroom increased the size and functionality of our little white house. During the first years, we would use the garden hose in the late afternoon to wet the street in an attempt to keep the dust down. Eventually, pavement graced Second Street and did away with the afternoon street watering. A wooden privacy fence, a willow tree, two pecan trees, a peach tree, two rose bushes near the front porch, two cedars on each side of the front steps, and hearty Bermuda grass slowly made the barracks a home.

Summers were the best time of the year. Starting in late May, my brother, Larry, and I would place army cots near the willow tree and sleep under the stars all summer. New Mexico is a great place for watching stars. I learned to spot the Big Dipper, Little Dipper, Mars, Venice, and the Milky Way. Each evening, stars were the last images I saw before closing my eyes. A few nights, heavy rain drove us inside, but most nights the cool desert air, our dog, Sparky; the chirping locusts; and the buzzing mosquitoes made for unforgettable summer sleep.

Dad built a sturdy picnic table that lasted throughout my childhood. Many nights in the summer, we would eat in the backyard. Sometimes Mom cooked inside and served the evening meal on the outside table. Other times we would grill hamburgers or hot dogs. In July and August, ripe peaches produced homemade peach ice cream so delicious it could have been marketed.

I've returned countless times to Carlsbad. Unfortunately, after the Second Street house sold in 1968, I have never been back inside it. But a few years ago, I did stop by one Sunday after church. A Spanish-speaking couple owns the house. To my delight, the family was in the backyard at a picnic table with their two little girls getting ready for an outdoor lunch. With my limited Spanish, I explained that my dad built the house and that I was happy they could enjoy it.

From that home on Second Street in Carlsbad's piece of the Chihuahuan Desert, I received the unmerited gifts of family, church, and school. Each played a formative force in my life.

Family

Family was important. Mom's Morrow family lived in the Second Street neighborhood. Dad's Puckett family lived in the more established part of town. In the small town of Carlsbad, distance was not a barrier, and family visits were frequent.

Grandpa Morrow was a boy's dream for a grandfather. Being retired, he had all the time in the world for his grandkids. At least that's the way I saw it. He loved to fish and hunt. Almost from the time Larry and I could walk he would take us fishing on the Pecos River. He untangled miles of fishing line from our back-lashed reels. What patience he had to teach two young boys the need to keep their lines in the water—instead of in the trees—if they expected to catch fish. On many occasions, we would sit for two hours or more without a bite. He would mutter, "Well, I guess it's going to be a little slow today."

Dad started my driver's instruction by letting me sit in his lap and drive home from church. As I grew, I was occasionally permitted to drive a car or a truck—without a driver's license—three blocks between his construction company and our home. I took driver's education when I was fourteen and received my license on my fifteenth birthday.

Being a legal driver, I often drove for Grandpa Morrow. My favorite trips were taking him to Hot Springs, New Mexico—now Truth or Consequences—for his week of hot mineral baths and fishing at Elephant Butte Lake. We would sit together in the giant hot mineral tub, sipping steaming mineral water from a community dipper as water flowed into the tub. Then, we would spend the remainder of the day fishing at the lake. At home, I was restricted to five-cent Dairy Queen ice cream cones once in a while. With Grandpa, it was daily twenty-five-cent milkshakes.

I was in Brazil when he died. The telegram I received on May 19, 1976, read, "Your grandfather passed away yesterday. Dad."

Grandma Sorrells was a consistent presence for good in our lives. She walked with a cane and was at the age of being more sedentary. She was the Norman Rockwell picture of a grandma in her rocking chair with crochet hooks and sewing needles always flying, propelled by fingers that seem to get more accurate with age. She died when I was ten. That was the only time I saw Dad cry. He was forty years old.

A strong influence in my life on Dad's side of the family came from Grandma's brother, Dr. Owen Puckett. Next to my parents, he was the person I most admired during my formative years in the Carlsbad desert. Dr. Puckett was a humble man whom the local newspaper dubbed "a legend in his time."

Owen Edward Puckett was born in Izzard County, Arkansas, in August 1875. He began his work as a general practitioner at Fitzhugh, Arkansas, in

1904 after receiving his degree in medicine from the University of Tennessee. His rounds made on horseback with medicine in his saddlebags, or in the occasional buggy set the tone for his medical practice, which was always caring for his patients and never shunning house calls.

In 1915, he and six brothers, lured to the West with an investment dream, established the Puckett Ranch in Hope, New Mexico. In a family letter, he described the rich grasslands of Hope as being "high as a horse's belly." What the brothers did not count on was the Rio Penasco, a clear stream that fed the ranch lands and thriving orchards, going underground and cutting Hope off from its water supply.

With a twenty-thousand-dollar loss in the ranching venture, Dr. Puckett moved to Carlsbad in 1926 as a full-time health officer. He retired in 1958 after administering over seventy thousand immunizations and twenty-three-hundred diphtheria antitoxin shots during his more than three decades of service as health officer for southeastern New Mexico. The Spanish-speaking residents lovingly referred to him as "Dr. Vacuña," the Spanish word for "vaccination." His work spared thousands from the dreaded diseases of smallpox, diphtheria, whooping cough, typhoid, lockjaw, and polio.

Even though I received all of the doctor's vaccinations and was the recipient of many of his house calls when I had pneumonia and other childhood illnesses, I knew Dr. Puckett as family and as a member of our church. In 1926, he and his wife started a church with two other couples in the Puckett home. It grew into the congregation that still meets on the corner of Fox and Lake Streets. Eventually the Fox and Lake Street church planted five other churches in the city. Dr. Puckett was a godly leader, serving the church as an elder for over fifty years. At every church service, he would make it a point to greet me with a handshake and a twinkle in his eyes. He and Aunt Clevil always sat on the second pew from the front on the south side of the auditorium.

Desert Formation

As family, we visited often in their home. When I got older, I would stop by their house on my own. I was always inspired by time spent in the presence of Dr. Puckett. I remember listening to him dream of a Christian retirement community where God would be at the center of caring for the needs of older adults. Lakeview Christian Home of the Southwest, established in 1960, was the culmination of that dream.

The last time I visited with Dr. Puckett was prior to his death in 1968 at age ninety-three. The conversation turned quickly to church and spiritual matters. He told me about a stroke he had felt in one of his fingers. To him it was a sign the end of life was near. From a lifetime of medical experience, he recognized he only had a short time to live. Our final conversation was about his desire to see the kingdom of God grow and expand throughout the world. He was a powerful, indelible influence on my formation in the New Mexico desert. I think of him often. Reflecting on his life, I see Dr. Puckett as the embodiment of trusting in God's care and plan.

Growing up in a little town had many upsides, but it was not Utopia. Crime did make the *Carlsbad Current Argus*—even abduction and murder. But crime was the exception and not something that had the least effect on the way we approached life. Our family locked the house only when we left town for a trip. At any time during the day, we would announce we were going bike riding. The town was a playground to explore. As long as our parents knew in general terms where we were and what we were doing, they were satisfied. For sure, we had rules to follow and times to come in. As we grew older, our bicycle independence was expanded to cars, school, and to life surrounding our church.

The surprise pregnancy in 1958 brought baby sister Debbie into my eleven-year-old life. All three siblings were delighted with our new sister. We took her everywhere. It was not long until I taught her to ride with me by sitting on the handlebars of my bike and placing her feet on the front fender. There was the time I unexpectedly hit gravel, wrecked the bike, skinned her leg and arm, and then had to bring her home to Mom. When I started driving, Debbie would stand close enough to where my arm could automatically fly in front of her body to keep her from hitting the dashboard in case of a sudden stop. We grew up in a time not burdened with seatbelts and safety seats.

Parallel to the family's move to Second Street, Dad began his work as a carpenter. He went to work for Dobbs and Beach Construction Company. When I was around ten years old, Dad bought the company and operated for a period under its original name then changed it to J. O. Sorrells Construction Company.

Jokingly, I say I did not have a job growing up—I worked as slave labor. My parents with their farming background assumed the construction company was a family business. Mom kept the books, and the two Sorrells sons became the cleanup crew. Through the years, we learned to lay tile, install roofing shingles, use electric saws and drills, do basic carpentry, and always clean up. We filled countless trucks with construction rubble and were familiar with the dump ground—the 1960s term for a landfill.

Our Second Street house was always a home. I cannot repay the debt I owe to my family. I didn't know it at the time, but those formative years of family in the Carlsbad desert would serve as the foundation for my life. My faith, my work ethic, my commitments, my values, my trust, and whatever ability I have to maintain relationships is grounded in those years.

The final weeks of Mom's life, as Alzheimer's disease climaxed with her death, were a family replay from the previous July, when Dad died of pancreatic cancer. Children, grandchildren, and extended family were always near the hospital bed. My two sisters led in the care. I saw the tender side of my brother as he, too, sat by their beds at the time of death. The family received an unsolicited compliment from a nurse when she inquired if we were Hispanic. We were not. But we did share the admirable trait among

Desert Formation

Hispanic families of deep care for one another. We were living an uncommon family love not often seen in our rushed Anglo world.

For my parents' golden wedding anniversary, I wrote the following tribute to them:

Dear Dad and Mom,

July 25, 1943, was the beginning of a home that generated a lifetime of good memories and rich experiences for all of us as Sorrells kids.

My childhood memories are so positive it is impossible to pick out one occasion and declare it as the best experience. High on the list were the Williams Creek trips in Colorado and other family outings as we camped, hunted, fished, and traveled. I have fond memories of our backyard cookouts with peach ice cream.

Then, there are the memories of the church life we shared as family. Our family was always one of the first to arrive and the last to leave. I have good memories of gospel meetings, the church youth group, and the times we spent as a family with other families from the church. As children, all of our lives were enriched because you made the financial sacrifices that allowed us to attend church camps and youth meetings.

Most of all I am thankful for your having provided us with a stable home environment. We have always been able to count on our dad and mom to be there. I felt loved and trusted. You provided us with a healthy atmosphere of freedom and restraint. In reflection, you provided us with everything we needed.

Thanks for being the kind of parents you are. Thank you for the example you provided us as children, for our mates, and for our children. Congratulations on this your fiftieth wedding anniversary. I love you both.

Gary
July 25, 1993

Church

From my birth, church was as an integral part of life, as were family meals and a warm bed to sleep in each night. Church was a family extension of Second Street. Sunday was church service morning and evening. We had Sunday school on Sunday mornings and youth class on Sunday evenings before worship. Wednesday evening was also church night. At least once each year, a weeklong evangelistic meeting provided guest speakers for early morning and evening services. With periodic congregational Sunday lunches, spontaneous invitations to share meals in each other's homes, church was a year-round lifestyle.

When I reached the teenage years, church activities increased. In the dark ages—before youth leaders—parents and other members of the congregation took on the responsibility of providing spiritual formation. Some members felt called to teach our classes, others enjoyed teaching us to sing. With talented singers and asbestos ceilings for acoustics, we were a singing church. One of my Sunday school teachers, A. C. Gibson, was intensely dedicated to understanding and following Scripture.

Our church was helping to support a national worker in the Philippines, and A. C. Gibson showed me a way to help. Each week I would box up Bible school literature and used clothing and take them to the post office for mailing to the Philippines. At that point, I had not planned to work in foreign missions, but I enjoyed doing the Philippine mailings throughout my high school years.

On the more informal side of church life was our youth group. Throughout my junior high and high school years, the church youth were the best of friends. There were twenty families represented in the youth group with no more than two years' difference in our ages and school grade. Often after church services we would go "get a Coke." That meant we would divide into different cars and cruise the town's main street. An important part of the routine was to drop by Becky's Drive-In for a Coke. Other times we would go to friends' homes and listen to Elvis and the Beatles with an abundant supply of chips, dips, and soft drinks.

Like my family, the expectation and encouragement from church adults stand out on my list of formative influences. In a time before society leached community from American life, our congregation enjoyed four hundred worshippers. Church adults made it a point to treat youth with respect. At each gathering, it was natural to shake hands with most adults. Through greeting and exhortation, adult members encouraged us to make good decisions—not that we didn't disappoint them on occasion. Church life, lived in concert with the home on Second Street in Carlsbad's piece of the Chihuahuan Desert, was an undeniably formative force.

School

For the entire twelve years of school in the Carlsbad desert, I would have never placed it on the list of favorite activities. The report cards at the end of each six weeks always read the same: "Gary talks too much in class. He does not work up to his potential." It would have saved teachers evaluation time if the first-grade teacher had only made a rubber stamp of my two star traits and sent it along with me at the end of the year for presentation to the next teacher in line.

Big Chief tablets played a role in my school formation. On various occasions, my task for the weekend was to fill a Big Chief tablet with the words *I will not talk in class*. In the third grade, the school principal, Mr. Cox, received me into his office for the same offense. He was a member of our church. After a lecture and my first three swats with his shiny razor strap, I returned to class much quieter. My parents did not take my visit to Mr. Cox lightly. There was more discipline when Dad came home. Through school—like home—I learned that action has consequences. It was a great lesson learned in the desert.

In 1956 Miss Elizabeth Johnson was my fourth-grade teacher at Hillcrest Elementary. She married her calling. Born in 1899 in the New Mexico Territory, she moved, at age three, with her family to a ranch in Hope, New Mexico. In 1923, only eleven years after New Mexico received statehood, she began teaching school. Also a member of our church family, Miss Johnson had the reputation as the hardest teacher at Hillcrest.

To help students and teachers make the most of classroom time, classes were divided into three levels: high, middle, and low. I was always among the high achievers but nowhere close to the top of the class. Miss Johnson inspired me to achieve. I experienced success in her class. She was renowned for teaching the multiplication tables, and I learned to go through the tables at lightning speed.

Besides gaining confidence in my ability to learn, I began to catch the hint that I might have a trace of leadership ability. She would send me on special errands, and I would gladly complete each task. That year, instead of filling Big Chief tablets, I received the class citizenship award.

The following year, in fifth grade, an incremental responsibility came my way. My fifth-grade teacher asked me to join the safety patrol, composed of fifth and sixth graders, to help younger students cross safely at nine different street crossings. Appointed captain the following year, I was in charge of assignments and blowing the whistle ten minutes before time for the others to take their post. It was a small leadership step. I was learning to lead in the desert.

Junior high in Carlsbad included the seventh, eighth, and ninth grades. Junior high added additional tools to my life kit. Mrs. Lee Komensky taught my first speech class. She had an artistic flair to her personality. Drama being her specialty, the course was more on theater than on speech.

Three original one-act plays were to be performed before our parents. The play I wrote, *A Day at School*, was one of the three. The author of each play served as director. Though crude at best, it was the first time I glimpsed my creative side.

That small tool discovered on the floor of the Chihuahuan Desert turned into one of the most-used instruments of my life. In part, it turned out to be foundational to developing a tenacious trust in God. I have gone through life painting dreams beyond my ability. Yet, somehow, beyond my understanding, God is often there to carry the load.

At age fourteen, I enrolled in driver's education. We learned to drive in a Chevrolet Corvair, which made *Time* magazine's "50 Worst Cars of All Time" list. But what a fun car it was to drive! The motor in the back made steering a dream. The driver's training model had a stick shift on the floor, which prepared me well for my four decades of driving stick-shift cars in South America.

In 1963, when I enrolled in high school, the Carlsbad school board was opening a new high school on a rocky hill overlooking the city. The hill abounded in yucca plants with white blooms, century plants with bright red and pinkish flowers, and desert cactus in a range of varieties.

The new school was a three-story, U-shaped building with plate glass windows opening to the inner court. The building included a fountain and a flowing stream of water through the first-floor courtyard. Small pine trees and flowers dressed up the use of concrete. The Plexiglas canopy-style roof provided shade throughout the day. It was a beautiful structure, ahead of its time in campus architecture. On the desert hill overlooking Carlsbad, I continued my formation. Reflecting on my New Mexico school years, I am somewhat surprised at my own conclusions as to what played formative roles in preparing me for life. While the university taught me to think, the Carlsbad school years helped me discover my unique wiring and gave me tools for navigating life.

Coach Ralph Bowyer, legendary high school football coach of the Carlsbad Cavemen, led his teams to eight state titles. He served as a role model and an influence for good in the lives of countless young athletes.

I enjoyed watching football, but Coach Bowyer's influence in my life had nothing to do with athletics. A faithful Methodist, he had a deep faith in God and touched the lives of hundreds—if not thousands—through a completely different venue. He taught the course titled "Family Living." The course was well known and every seat was taken. I took copious notes in my Family Living notebook. Though I eventually discarded the notes from many other classes, my Family Living notes continue to survive.

Coach Bowyer was a gentle man and an outstanding teacher. His sincerity and goodness were apparent as he taught us to use common courtesy in family life. Because of his influence, my wife has never set a dish on the table that I was not willing to taste.

Also because of Ralph Bowyer, I never assume it's not my task to make the bed and be a teammate with my wife in the daily responsibilities of maintaining some sense of order in our home. I am continually amazed at how often I reflect on the principles learned from a football coach by someone who hated even minimal activity in physical education.

I reached the junior and senior years in high school having completed most of the required courses for graduation. I was killing time in anticipation of college and getting on with life. Unbeknownst to me, I was still to come across two classes tailored to my education in the desert.

Since I had several elective classes, I signed up for Mr. Barney Legion's graphic arts class, which turned out both intriguing and beneficial. I took the class at the junior level. Beginning with photography, we were assigned cameras and photo shoots. Mr. Legion taught us how to develop negatives in the darkroom and how to make prints from the negatives. At the time, I had no idea I would one day be living in Brazil and daily use lessons I learned about photography while in the desert. Reporting through pictures to our supporting partners in the United States was vital to the financial support of the work.

Printing class came next. For centuries, letterpresses, which print directly from hand-set, lead-type onto paper, were used in the printing industry. It was a slow way to print. Each piece of paper had to be hand-fed into the press. Offset printing started to dominate the commercial printing market in the 1950s. The offset process transferred the image from a metal plate to a rubber-padded cylinder then onto the paper. The belt-driven presses would print multiple copies per minute. The faster the press is run, the more copies are produced per minute.

In 1964, the graphic arts program installed its first offset press. It was a fascinating piece of machinery. Mr. Legion was only a half-step ahead of his class. He was learning along with his students. As he learned, he patiently taught us the darkroom procedures for offset printing and the skills for running an automated offset press.

Barney Legion's printing course prepared me to earn my way through college, making twice the amount of money fellow students made. The experience from the beginning printing course, combined with my college years of working in print shops, gave me a skill set I used daily throughout forty years of working in foreign missions. While living in Brazil, I managed the printing needs of the team.

As I began to direct a nonprofit ministry, hardly a day passed without relying on the skills I'd learned in the darkroom, on the design table, and on a printing press. I have always been grateful for the acquired ability to design a page layout that communicates—another vital lesson learned in the desert.

The story of my parents' migration to Carlsbad, New Mexico, in the Pecos River Valley on the floor of the Chihuahuan Desert, interweaves itself into the tapestry of my life. A house on Second Street became my home. Life on Second Street, intertwined with family, church, and school, played an undeniable formative role in my life. I will forever be indebted to my formative years in the desert. Values and skills I learned on the desert floor went with me to Brazil and continued to serve as tools in the building process of Great Cities Missions.

4

LIFE IN A GREAT CITY

It was my first trip on a jetliner. A boy from the New Mexico desert, I was above the clouds. Never before had I seen clouds from the top. It was a remarkable sight. Even today, I smile when I remember my first two rolls of film. Every picture showed the white cloud carpet below.

In 1969, there were no direct flights to Brazil. To reach Sao Paulo I had to leave Lubbock, make transfers in Dallas and Miami, then stop in Lima, Peru, before arriving in Brazil. What a thrill it was to touch down on the Viracopos International Airport tarmac. I was in Brazil! My first thought after exiting Brazil's port of entry with passport, entrance visa, and cleared baggage: *I can't communicate! They really do speak Portuguese in Brazil!*

Howard and Jane Norton were years ahead of me in experience. They and others set out to help me learn to live among the eight million people in the great city of Sao Paulo.

Howard has leadership in abundance at the core of his genes. It would not surprise me if by mental telepathy he began to lead the hospital nursery the moment the nurse placed him in the crib. *Multitalented* does not overstate the case. In the summer of 1952, during his high school years, the American Legion in Fort Worth selected Howard Norton to be a delegate at Lone Star Boys' State in Austin. While there he served as governor of Boys' State. Later that summer, he was one of two delegates selected to represent Boys' State of Texas at Boys' Nation in Washington, DC. During the event, his colleagues elected him president of Boys' Nation.

Howard has led as a student, husband, parent, mentor, missionary, Portuguese speaker, teacher, preacher, professor, editor, journalist, administrator, church elder, and college president. Through each role, he has constantly demonstrated his love for Jesus and His church.

Howard's wife, Jane, like the other Sao Paulo team women, generously shared her many gifts. Gifted in hospitality and deep wisdom, Jane has made a difference in the lives of hundreds of people around the world through her example, mentoring, and teaching. As a young single missionary, I enjoyed numerous evenings with Howard and Jane at her table.

Immediately, I signed up to study Portuguese with Brazilian Lucia Huff. My next task was to learn how to use public transportation. My first attempt at riding a city bus was with a colleague who flagged down a blue bus like a pro, delivering us within a block of our office. What could be easier?

The following day, I was ready to go on my own. I stood there and watched red, green, and yellow buses pass. Then, there it was—a blue bus just like the day before. The next thing I knew, I was riding into uncharted territory. I started shouting, "Alto, alto," a word from elementary Spanish meaning "stop, stop." At least, that is what I remembered from the stop signs in the Mexico border town, Juarez. To my dismay, the word did not work at all, as it means "tall, tall," in Portuguese. I learned several important lessons for a newcomer that day, not the least being that colors differentiate bus companies, not bus routes. As learners of a new language we encountered countless unsolvable problems.

My first assignment was to housesit for Jerry and Barbara Campbell, a missionary family on furlough. Fortunately for me, it was next door to team members Glenn and Marlene Owen.

Life in a Great City

A fun leader, an avid learner with a photographic memory, and a gifted teacher, Glenn was an absolute force as a people magnet. Looking back, it was little wonder he caught my attention at the Abilene Christian chapel assembly.

All team members spoke fluent Portuguese, but Glenn was a gifted linguist, rising above the others. He spoke like an educated native Brazilian.

He loved people, and he called each person by name, whether it was the following day or a decade later. And he wanted everyone he befriended to become a friend of Jesus. At the time of his death in 2001, Glenn had led hundreds to Jesus, had officiated scores if not hundreds of marriages, and helped untold numbers of people to know more about God's love throughout South America, North America, and Europe.

Glenn's life partner in ministry, Marlene, is also a leader. A wonderful and godly person in her own right, Marlene has influenced many people for good. I teach mission teams that one advantage of working on a team is "your fruit is my fruit." That statement could not be truer in the case of Marlene and Glenn. She was God's gift to Glenn and, in turn, Glenn was God's gift to Marlene. Glenn's fruit was Marlene's fruit. Together they will present an abundant harvest to God.

Now, let me get back to my housesitting responsibility on Sao Jose Street, next door to the Owens. In the multiple details of leaving for a three-month furlough to the United States, Jerry and Barbara Campbell missed an important item—stopping the daily milk delivery for their family of five. Each morning, milk would arrive by way of a horse-drawn milk wagon. I drank all I could hold, but after forty-five days, milk was stacked everywhere. Nothing else would fit in the refrigerator. I didn't know enough Portuguese to cancel the milk delivery, but I wasn't about to admit my ignorance to my neighbors Glenn and Marlene. So the sunrise milk delivery kept arriving, morning after morning.

This milk abundance turned out to be symbolic of God's provision since my childhood. The milk analogy perfectly describes my forty-plus-year journey of mission work. At the greatest times of thirst, the doors in God's kitchen opened and packages of refreshing milk fell at my feet.

When the Campbell family returned to Brazil, I moved into the maid's quarters in the home of Preston and Laura Massey. When Howard Norton made his Abilene recruiting trip in 1969, Preston was working on a master's degree at Abilene Christian. Within a week of Howard's invitation, Preston and Laura received full support and set their arrival in Sao Paulo for February 1970.

The Masseys lived in a simple triplex with an outside entry to the maid's room. A maid's room was included in all houses in the cities of Brazil. To have a housekeeper's help with the laundry, heavy house cleaning, and meal preparation without the convenience of frozen or canned foods was equivalent to those of us in the States hiring grass mowers.

Since the Masseys couldn't afford a maid, the room and a bathroom at the back of the small lot were available for rent. With its private entrance, it was an ideal setup for me. Arriving in Brazil just prior to the rainy season, it was in that room that I began to think mission work was hanging out in the bathroom and listening to a Noah-like rain.

In the New Mexico desert, the word *rain* was more like a euphemism for a "shower falling from the sky a few times each year." We called that "raining cats and dogs." The Brazilians had a better description. The tropical rain came down so hard it was "raining pocketknives." The rain felt like a powerful showerhead cutting into your skin. I easily understood the pocketknife analogy.

It was on one such occasion that I had my thirty-seventh bout with "Montezuma's revenge." It lasted two or three days at a time, often when the city decided it would be fine to cut off our water so that other areas might get their share. Why anyone should lack water with the sky falling was beyond my comprehension. After two twenty-four-hour days, all toilet paper was gone.

It was time for another language lesson. Once again, my grade-school Spanish came in handy. I knew the word for "paper" was *papel*. Surely, that would work in Portuguese. Armed with the word, I walked to the corner shop and asked for *papel*. It was not what I had in mind, but my mission was partly accomplished. I returned home with a half-dozen sheets of beautiful wrapping paper under my arm.

Becoming a Team Member

The first year, cultural acquisition and language study were my top priorities. That meant daily Portuguese language classes and astute observation of culture.

My church assignment was to attend a startup church in the Campo Grande area of the city. There, I learned the basics of leading songs and directing elementary prayer in Portuguese. I have never been among a people who prayed more fervently. They prayed expecting an answer. Veteran coworker Don Vinzant often kidded me about the night I was leading singing at the midweek prayer meeting during the 1970 World Cup Soccer games in Mexico. As the song came to a close, firecrackers erupted across the city. Instinctively, I closed out the song with a thumbs-up in honor of Brazil's goal.

I first met Don in Brazil in January 1970. I had been a missionary for sixty days. Don, Carol, and their four children were moving back to Sao Paulo. Their immediate task was to find a house to lease. The house of the furloughing missionary family was the interim stop. So while house hunting, they moved in to help me housesit for a few days. Thus began a friendship that spanned forty years.

In Sao Paulo, we were colleagues with John and Catherine Pennisi on the Campo Grande church plant. We worked together on the steering committee, the recruiting committee, and on the Sao Paulo Training School.

Don taught me to love used bookstores, shop for old furniture, and discover blue-collar Brazilian lunch cuisine on hidden streets.

Great Cities Missions has always been a work in progress. Don loved the Brazil mission team. From his earliest days in Brazil, he was a champion of recruiting new mission teams. Prior to the organization of Great Cities as a 501(c)3 nonprofit organization, Don served on a task force of the 1980s, helping to forge many of today's operational standards.

As the ministry continued to mature under the direction of the Central Church of Christ in Amarillo, Don served on the board of trustees for seventeen years prior to his death. He led as chairman of the trustees from May 2005 through April 2008. From his hospital room, as a trustee and as a friend, he was still providing me encouragement.

Don Eugene Vinzant passed from this life in Edmond, Oklahoma, on March 10, 2011. He was born in Fort Worth, Texas, on June 21, 1936. From the Brazilian culture, he learned well his trademark warm Brazilian hug. His generous spirit, kind and peaceful manner, his infectious smile, and enthusiastic—often uncontrollable—laugh, his keen intellect, his love of truth, his genuine love for all people, his servant heart, his vision, his love for God, Jesus, and for every member of his family, all left the stamp of Jesus as portrayed by Don Vinzant on our lives and on the direction of Great Cities Missions.

Carol—Don's wife, soul mate, and partner of a half-century—overflows with giftedness. While a young college student, she was at the front of the line signing onto the Abilene Christian mission team. Carol had a special interest in Brazil as a destination for the Sao Paulo group. Her great-grandmother was born in Brazil in 1853 and returned to Germany in 1861 prior to moving to the United States in 1870.

A gifted teacher, speaker, and writer, Carol has countless friends and is a superb conversationalist. She is a wonderful mentor to her children, their spouses, her grandchildren, and great grandchildren. Like the other men and women of the Sao Paulo group, her lifelong commitment to Jesus stands witness as her greatest priority.

In addition to working with team members on the local church level, I was also drawn into team business meetings. By the time I reached Brazil, the Sao Paulo team evolved from the mandatory weekly business meetings to monthly meetings. Since the team's earliest days, the meeting guide of choice was *Robert's Rules of Order*. Its guidelines ensured everyone a voice while limiting domination by strong, verbal personalities.

As a new arrival, I had to comply with policy and just observe business meetings for six months without voting or expressing opinions at formal meetings. The missionary team was rightly cautious to limit zealous opinions of neophyte workers. Prudence called for restraint until a new arrival could reach a partial understanding of the new and unfamiliar culture and was able to begin to connect the dots.

Because business meetings were important, the agenda was carefully prepared prior to the meeting. Highly crafted motions were in place before entering the room. Leaders always have an opinion and feel the impulse to express why their idea is the right idea. I marveled at the vigorous discussion and intense debates, and I never ceased to be amazed at how such intensity stayed at the meeting site. Team members who vigorously opposed each other on an issue later went together as friends to enjoy a united lunch.

Slowly, through business meetings, team retreats, team celebrations, lunches, office conversation, joint movies, recreation, travel, increased responsibility, and the execution of mutual assignments, I became a member of the team I admired.

Love and World Cup Soccer

The first evening of my arrival in Brazil on November 19, 1969, Pelé, the world's most famous soccer player—whom I had not heard of—scored his one-thousandth professional goal on a penalty kick. Cheering for the popular Santos team against Vasco de Gama, the eighty thousand fanatical fans at the Rio de Janeiro Maracana Stadium went wild. Every Brazilian watching a television or listening to a radio went into instant celebration. Culture lesson number one—soccer is king.

Pelé's goal set the stage for the importance of the World Cup Soccer Tournament. In 1970, after my sixth month in Brazil, the nation of Mexico hosted the World Cup, and from May 31 through June 21, all of Brazil went nuts.

Young people from the Nove de Julho church united around the television every time Brazil played, and I received an invitation to the soccer television parties. It didn't take long before a beautiful medical student caught my eye. A soccer fanatic, her favorite team was Santos. Pelé starred on the Santos team and was a selected starter for the third time on Brazil's World Cup national team. In Mexico City, Pelé won his third World Cup. By the time Brazil was crowned champion on June 21 with a four-to-one victory over Italy, I, too, was an avid soccer fan and, as they say, head-over-heels in love with a soccer-crazed, twenty-two-year-old Brazilian medical student.

The day came to ask her dad's permission for her hand in marriage. Somehow, I strung enough Portuguese words together to make my request. I suspect his daughter had already briefed him as to my reason for coming that evening. It's also possible he didn't understand a thing I said. But no doubt about it, I understood his affirmative response.

Supporting Churches

My move to a new country as a bachelor required limited financial support. Fellow missionary Don Vinzant often reminded me that "two could live as economically as one—but for only half as long." My single status had not lasted as long as I'd anticipated. And getting married would require more money.

After a year in Brazil, I returned to the States to raise support so I could marry my newly discovered love. I began to understand just how hard fundraising could be. At the absolute last minute, just as I had given up hope of ever getting back to Brazil, God opened a door for full support from an Alabama church.

Our marriage took place at my home church in New Mexico. Sao Paulo team member Glenn Owen—who had taught and baptized my bride-to-be while in Brazil—officiated our entire wedding in Portuguese. The audience had no idea what Glenn said, but when the time came to kiss the bride, those attending were satisfied Glenn had indeed conducted a marriage ceremony. After a short honeymoon, we worked four months with the Alabama church before returning to Brazil.

Once back in Brazil, I resumed learning Portuguese, adapting to the culture, increasing team responsibilities, and adjusting to married life. Life was good. I was where I was supposed to be.

Two years later, it was time for our first furlough to the States—and our first traumatic experience in the missions enterprise.

An important ritual of the Brazilian church and the Sao Paulo mission team was the airport sendoff. Each time a missionary family left on furlough, Brazilian Christians and the missionary team converged on the airport to wish the travelers well, show love and appreciation, and make sure the furloughing family knew they were important to the Brazil family. Honoring a team tradition, the Brazilians and the American missionaries sang in Portuguese, *"Deus vos guarde com seu poder"*—"God be with you till we meet again."

In great tradition, our first furlough sendoff was spectacular. Highlights were quickly forgotten, however, when we arrived in Alabama to an ancient, dilapidated, white stucco, ten-room motel reserved for us by our church elder/banker. The five-dollar-per-night rate should have been a tipoff. The motel came complete with a massive infestation of two-inch-long cockroaches and raised windows for air conditioning. We lasted one night at Cockroach Motel—and our furlough would get worse.

What we did not know at the time was that two of the Alabama church leaders had been in a continuous struggle. It was a tug-of-war between a lawyer and a banker. The lawyer believed in missions to his very core. The banker believed the local church's primary goal should be to pay off the building note to his bank as fast as possible, and ahead of schedule.

Before our arrival on the Alabama battlefield in the summer of 1973, the lawyer moved from our rural supporting church to Birmingham as a newly appointed federal judge by President Nixon. The banker could now have his way. It was a long two months.

As we left Alabama to visit family in New Mexico and Texas, the bank owner asked for our telephone number so he could call us when we arrived in Texas. We knew what was coming and resolved not to stop for gasoline, lunch, or anything else until we crossed the state line into Mississippi. We wanted nothing more to do with the state of Alabama. In my mind, there were now only forty-nine states.

Hardly had we walked in the door of our Texas family when the phone rang. It was Mr. Alabama Banker—we were fired.

Sao Paulo team member Ellis Long quickly wrote a four-page, seven-thousand-word letter in small type that filled the margins. An excerpt from the letter not only was meaningful at the time, but through the years it served as an important compass:

> I awoke at 6 a.m. thinking of you two and fighting mad—as Martin Luther said, "I always preach better when I am a bit mad." As you both know, the Brazil work, while it looks impressive on the surface of our publications, is a struggle behind the scenes, just like government, universities, and even our happy homes.
>
> Having just been through exactly what you are now experiencing, I thought I would roll out of the sack and put these thoughts down quickly. . . . We will be working for you.

Life in a Great City

Remember the group in Sao Paulo loves you guys. You probably don't know how much you are respected, no fooling, by everyone—Brazilians and Americans—in Sao Paulo. We simply must have you stay. . . . Always be thankful for Alabama and positive about getting on with the future.

Don't allow one grouch to get you down. He can if you let him. Remember, we work for Jesus and not brother "grouch" in Alabama or Florida. . . . Be positive even when it hurts on the inside. You are going through a period that will temper you, and that you will someday be grateful for, and that will actually help the preacher students in Brazil as they learn that we, too, have to struggle to make it.

"Never will I leave you; never will I forsake you," says the Lord in Hebrews. We will all be praying and pulling for you during your difficult period . . . and, we believe that you will come out of it in flying colors . . . it is not a permanent state but something you can see through, work through, and come through.

The Lord was merciful. Nine days later, Ernest Clevenger, the evangelist of the West End Church of Christ in Birmingham, Alabama, called. We met the Clevenger family a few weeks earlier when they hosted us in their home for several days while my wife was recuperating from major surgery. Ernest informed me that the West End church, where the new federal judge was attending, had full support awaiting us. After visiting with family, I began to eat my "never return to Alabama" words, and we were on our way to Birmingham.

Arriving at the West End church for the Christmas season, we attended a month of Christmas parties and scheduled church services. The major piece of the get-acquainted blueprint was breakfast, lunch, and dinner in the homes of the majority of West End families. Practically everyone's name in the four-hundred-member church was committed to memory. Judge J.

Foy Guin and Dr. Ernest Clevenger, along with their wives, Dorace and Glenda, are now lifelong special friends of our family.

We returned to Brazil feeling loved and supported by the great people of Alabama's West End church, and Alabama was once again in good standing among the fifty states.

Two Tracks

Mission team members in Sao Paulo worked on two parallel tracks. Each person was responsible for a team assignment and for a church assignment.

I like to see the challenge of the big picture. Serving at the team level, we looked out for the overall good of the city, the state, and the nation. It was on the team track that missionaries operated the radio, the airplane, the correspondence course, the training school, publications, the Christian camp, public relations, nationwide outreach, and missionary recruiting. Planning and executing projects with fellow missionaries on the team track was a good fit.

The second track was church planting and development. Missionaries planted churches. As Brazilians found Jesus through church plants, each congregation took on a life of its own. National members slowly and methodically learned to move the work of their congregation forward.

Novice Brazilian members became excited about their new relationship with Jesus. Being evangelistic, new Christians invited their families and neighbors, all the while learning to take responsibility for their own church.

Many lessons learned at Brazilian churches made great impressions on me and have stayed with me through life. I will never forget the morning sitting in a poverty-stricken church in Tres Pontas in the state of Minas Gerais. Among the small group in attendance was a leper who had found Jesus. Sebastian, stricken with leprosy, his face disfigured and stubs where fingers had once been, prayed fervently, "God, take care of us who do not know how to read." For those of us who grew up with books and reading the Bible, the simple plea of a fellow disciple of Jesus caused me to stop at once and thank God for a blessing I had always taken for granted. I have never forgotten the lesson of that afternoon in the town of Tres Pontas.

Planting a Church

After two years working at the Campo Grande congregation in Sao Paulo, this young Baby Boomer was ready to plant a church. Even though evangelism is not my strongest gift, I was determined to give church planting a try.

Baby Boomers are children of parents who experienced both the Great Depression and World War II. Somewhat like our parents, we lived by the duct tape principle prior to its invention. Life took on a certain creativeness. Should something break, the proper response was to discover why it was broken and fix it. To get a new replacement was not a concept within our reality.

With the genes from the Great Depression in my DNA, while tenaciously learning day by day and event by event to trust God, the idea of starting a church generated more thrill than fear.

When veteran missionary colleague Ted Stewart encouraged me to put together a church planting team, I could hardly wait to get started. Ted and Dot Stewart brought their giftedness to the large Sao Paulo group of missionaries. Arguably, Ted was the most brilliant person on the team. What made him unique was that his humility exceeded his brilliance. Ted knew the Bible and the Author. Ted knew the Scriptures so thoroughly that if the Bible were to be wiped from the face of the earth, he could have replaced it with a close paraphrase, and for many sections, word for word.

Through the years, health was not Ted's close friend. Near the end of his life, Ted's daughter described a bittersweet picture of Ted in the grip of Alzheimer's disease. Daily, with his Bible clutched to his chest, he paced the floor or sat in his recliner, unaware of his surroundings and the people who love him. To his final breath, Ted loved God and His holy Word.

Ted's imprint was on every aspect of the Sao Paulo team's work. He was a writer, a teacher, a preacher, an evangelist, a fundraising master, a par excellence administrator, and an untiring problem solver.

After we returned to the United States, I called on him one day to find copies of ancient manuscripts spread across the floor of his living room. He was in the beginning stages of a twenty-four-year project, resulting in the book *Solving the Exodus Mystery, Vol. 1: Discovery of the True Pharaohs of Joseph, Moses, and the Exodus.*

Ted researched the ancient documents of Babylon and Egypt plus the astronomical and carbon-14 dates of their kings and pharaohs. His research led to identifying the biblical pharaohs of Joseph, Moses, and the Exodus, all in the twelfth dynasty of Egypt. He defended the thesis that through carbon-14 dating and new astronomical dating, the twelfth dynasty should be dated three hundred years later. By so doing, the dates align accurately with the events described in the Bible.

His wife, Dot, a gifted teacher, editor, writer, and speaker, was the perfect match for Ted. In Brazil, with four children, she was a master at scheduling time for her many duties. Through five decades of ministry, their influence spread around the globe.

With Ted's encouragement, three factors converged in God's timing for the Metro Sul church plant. First, Oswaldo and Neldi Lalli, a middle-class Brazilian couple from the Nove de Julho congregation, wanted to start a church in their section of the city.

Second, the city of Sao Paulo was deep into a futuristic subway transportation project. The first line, soon to be open, would traverse Sao Paulo from north to south, ending near the door of the Lalli home. That first north-south line was the beginning of a modern subway system moving people across every sector of today's multimillion-population city. Church planting along the new subway line was a strategic move.

Life in a Great City

Third, three other young missionary families: Teston and Jo Gilpatrick, Ken and Liz Lewis, and Larry and Loretta Williams, excitedly joined the venture.

On June 17, 1973, we held the inaugural worship in a rented facility two blocks from the Santa Cruz subway station. Two months later, on August 28, another key step unfolded: the motion to invite Brazilian evangelist Walter Lapa and his family to join our team of church planters passed unanimously. The project was now ready to make progress.

Seekers found Jesus. Stateside supporting churches of the four missionary couples joined the project. We found land two blocks from the Jabaquara subway station. On April 22, 1979, the building was complete with a three-hundred-seat sanctuary, classrooms, offices, and fellowship space.

Today the Metro Sul congregation is a Brazilian church led by Brazilian elders, deacons, teachers, and an evangelist. For many years, God has continued to bless the efforts of the team families and their partnering U.S. churches. Brazilian Christians are leading the church into the future.

The Big Picture

I received the most personal satisfaction from working with fellow missionaries on the team track. I have always liked to see the challenge of the full picture as opposed to a specific piece of a puzzle.

The local church provides the arena for Christians to live together in community and to interface with people of the city who need Jesus. There should not be a more important role than leading in the area of the planting and establishment of a local church. Thankfully, there are people whose strongest set of God-given gifts fills that important role. That is not my principal gift set.

There is another important kingdom skill set—the God-wired gift of being able to see the needs of an entire geographical area of churches. Meeting such demands goes beyond the gifts and resources of any one local church. It is in this area where I feel God has blessed me with my greatest spiritual gift.

A School

From the first day, Brazilian leadership of the churches was an important value of the Sao Paulo mission team. By the close of 1968, after six years of training, only one Brazilian man had completed the full curriculum. The demands of employment, the rigors of living in a megacity, and the drain and time consumption of using public transportation undermined success. There was no more room to insert comprehensive and intensive training into the life of the city dweller.

The need for a change in approach seemed obvious to the mission team and to the Brazilians. The missionary group reached the decision to begin a two-year, scholarship-based Leadership Training School. To make it possible for students to leave their employment, American churches provided scholarships equal to the current income of each student. The lawyer and the blue-collar worker, the single student and the married family man would all have the same opportunity to study.

On March 2, 1970, the school opened with sixteen enrolled students. The mission team appointed Ted Stewart as the director and Don Vinzant as the associate director. Students performed at such an advanced level that we soon added a third year of study, knowing that the group would play a key role in the transition of the church from American to Brazilian leadership.

In the 1972 team assignments, I committed to the Leadership Training School as my major team responsibility. Ted Stewart continued as director; Don Vinzant continued as associate director. Thus began my five-year tenure as director of finance while working on the training school team.

By mid-1972, I found myself in the missionary plane making trips to recruit for the next class of the Sao Paulo Leadership Training School. The truth is, I was not a fan of flying in the six-seat missionary plane. Some of my dislike of that plane has its origin in my first weeks in Brazil. Carl Henderson was also new in Sao Paulo at the time. As an original member of the Belo Horizonte mission team, he transferred to Sao Paulo to pilot the missionary plane.

Shortly after my arrival in Brazil, Carl asked me if I would like to go flying with him on Sunday afternoon. In the process of upgrading his pilot's license to qualify for flying the new six-passenger red-and-white Cessna, he needed some weight in the backseat. *Sure,* I thought. I loved to fly and, blessed with plenty of weight, I signed on.

What Carl cleverly hid from me was the preplanned engine-stall practice. Time after time, as the plane made a steady climb, the flight instructor would stall the engine just to catch Carl by surprise. As the plane dropped at breakneck speed, Carl reacted to get us out of the free fall, and I found my stomach somewhere between my ears and my eyeballs.

So hesitantly, I asked Carl to take me to the city of Curitiba in the state of Parana, about a two-hour flight away, to interview prospective students Aramis, Carlos, Celso, and Ilton.

About thirty minutes into the flight, a torrential jungle rainstorm hit. After flying an hour seeing nothing beyond the windshield, Carl finally gave up and retraced our flight back to Sao Paulo. The feel of solid, red Brazilian ground under my feet was never more beautiful.

By the end of the recruiting season, twenty-two men were ready to enter the school on February 11, 1973. During the next two years, three significant advancements took place: a two-year study program was set up for the scholarship students' wives. In addition to the full-time school, we reinitiated classes in a night school format for the greater Brazilian church. And, taking advantage of the new Camp Mount of Olives, the school started a series of intensive training workshops covering special topics pertinent to a growing church.

Leadership training work, exhilarating and a fit for my creativity gene, had great potential for setting a positive future for a growing church in a dynamic nation. In 1977, my future seemed bright as the newly appointed director of the school.

A Christian Camp

Christian camping matched perfectly with a nation that is now home to 203 million people in the concrete jungles called cities. Despite having over 500 years of history, Brazil is a young nation, with 60 percent of the population under twenty-nine years of age. The vision of Lynn and Phyllis Huff to carve a camp out of 126 acres of nearby second-growth jungle was a courageous act by any standard. That act alone demonstrates tenacious trust in a providing God.

A Greek language major with a minor in Bible is not exactly the preparation one would expect of a jungle builder, but Lynn Huff is a leader sold out to Jesus. Being extroverted and outgoing likewise are not exactly Greek geek traits, but with unbelievable ease, Lynn and Phyllis attracted large circles of friends. Their outstanding Portuguese, wisdom, and love for people allowed them to make a great contribution to the lives of Brazilian families.

When I arrived on the scene in 1969, Camp Mount of Olives was still primitive, to say the least. Primitive was a highly advanced state compared to the way Lynn found the property in 1967. Located about an hour south of Sao Paulo, the land's boundary lines first had to be cleared, a task reminiscent of the biblical description of dividing the land for the children of Israel.

The purpose of a prospective owner clearing the boundaries was to verify that the land was actually complete and located where the deed claimed. The deed's perimeter described following rocks, gullies, streams, and mountain ridges. It read in part: "Start at the dip beside the road on the north side of the land of Jose Pinto, and follow the ridge until you get to the amarisco stick. Turn north and follow the trail down to the water."

Life in a Great City

With an assortment of primitive tools known well to Brazil's rural farmers, Lynn and other team members enlisted the aid of Brazilian Christians to clear the overgrown boundary lines. The land was all there, and in 1967 the purchase was complete.

The camp opened for the January 1971 month of camping. Due in part to a huge downpour of rain on the first day, only six campers arrived. The second week picked up considerably, with forty-three people, including campers and staff. In March 1974, electricity arrived on the camp property. The following year, on March 11, I, too, arrived on the camp property as the new director of Camp Mount of Olives.

It was hard to see Lynn and Phyllis Huff return to the States. On a personal level, I felt somewhat overwhelmed to see my responsibilities increase as a member of the mission team. I was still trying to figure out how much load I could carry while remaining sane and remembering I was now married.

The camp had fifteen brick structures and capacity for eighty young people per week. Even with increased use, it was amazing how long it took the jungle mud to dry after clearing the land. Truckloads of rock purchased annually allowed cars and buses to pass over the fresh-cut roads. Torrential rains and hot sun energized vegetation growth that constantly threatened to reclaim the land.

Newly arrived missionaries Teston Gilpatrick and John Curtis joined me on the camp project. Together we would plan sessions, recruit staff and campers, rent buses, oversee employees, purchase groceries, pay bills, and address the mud challenge. Untold times we helped dig out stuck vehicles. Like stunt drivers, we'd often take high-speed multiple attempts at getting up the slick road on the hill that led to the camp.

I doubt anything influenced more profoundly our little corner of the kingdom in Brazil than *Acampamento Monte das Oliveiras* (Camp Mount of Olives). What a great tool. Through its gates, untold numbers of young people have found both Jesus and a Christian mate. Thousands have grown in their relationship with the Lord and in their skills to minister to others. I will forever be grateful to God for allowing me to play a small role in trusting Him for the future of Brazil's youth through a tool He continues to provide.

New Missionaries

From the beginning, Ellis Long, one of the three men who recruited me for Brazil during my senior year at Abilene Christian College, was an encourager and a friend. Finally, in 1973, it was my good fortune to work closely with Ellis on an assignment. That year, the group organization selected Ellis as the chair of the team steering committee. John Pennisi and I were committee members.

As the name indicates, the responsibility of the steering committee was to guide the group in a coordinated direction to maximize the team effort. Its responsibility was to look out for the well-being of the entire team and the overall work. At the start of 1973, after eleven years on the field, seven of the original thirteen families had returned to the States, and two other families were to leave Brazil within the year.

The 1973 steering committee took on the responsibility of recruiting New Men for a Growing Nation. We advertised recruiting in the U.S. through the team publication, *Inside Brazil*, and through team members' contacts.

John Pennisi and Ellis Long were remarkable coworkers. For me, the eight years spent working with the men and women of the Sao Paulo team were equivalent to another college education. It would be difficult to imagine a greater group of mentors.

John and Catherine Pennisi have given their lives to the Brazilian people. Catherine, raised in Denton, Texas, attended Abilene Christian College and graduated from North Texas State University. As a talented artist, musician, and Bible teacher, she, too, left her mark on Brazil.

Life in a Great City

John had unique training for being a church planter. His father, Louis Pennisi, an Italian immigrant, moved to Florida and built a lifelong business selling delicious hamburgers, finally retiring at ninety-nine years of age, and lived to the age of 105.

John Pennisi completed his bachelor of science degree from the University of Florida prior to entering the navy, where he excelled as a lieutenant (junior grade). After his navy days, he graduated from Abilene Christian with a degree in Bible and completed a bachelor of divinity from Southwestern Baptist Theological Seminary in Fort Worth, Texas.

John and Catherine have played key roles in numerous church plants. Through the years, John served at one time or other in most areas of service on the mission team. He was known across Brazil in the 1970s for his talent as a Bible teacher on the *Open Your Bible* radio program.

By 1971, Ellis had received his PhD in communication from Florida State and returned with his family to Sao Paulo. It was my privilege to work with Ellis on a daily basis for fifteen years.

The New Testament letter to the Galatian Christians lists the fruit of the Spirit in chapter five: love, joy, peace, patience, kindness, goodness, faithfulness, gentleness, and self-control. There could not be a better summation of the qualities of Doris Long, Ellis's wife. Whether she is teaching a class or working quietly behind the scenes, Doris has always carried out a super load of kingdom work.

To work with Ellis was to witness a meticulous, goal-oriented, single-minded, visionary man. Never does a week go by that I do not use something Ellis taught me.

The 1973 steering committee assignment of New Men for a Growing Nation started a recruiting project that lasted for three years. The work resulted in seven families casting their lot with the Sao Paulo mission team.

Two important results came from the efforts to recruit additional missionaries. The ongoing recruiting mode from within the 1961 Sao Paulo mission team resulted in having missionary personnel on the ground in a consistent manner for enough years to allow the Brazilian church to mature and accept responsibility for its own future.

Indicative of the Brazilian church maturation was a special meeting called by young Brazilian leaders in July 1975 to be held at Camp Mount of Olives. The Brazilians invited Howard Norton and me to attend as observers rather than participants. The gist of the meeting was a weekend conversation among the Brazilians challenging each other to take on the responsibility as leaders of their church. From a small start, the annual meeting of Brazilian church leaders has evolved into a dynamic three days at Camp Mount of Olives with over four hundred Brazilian leaders in attendance.

A second result of the New Men for a Growing Nation campaign was the spark for Ellis Long to put recruiting at the top of his agenda.

The Breakthrough Brazil plan announced in Sao Paulo in November 1968 had shown little results. Concerned missionaries met in Belo Horizonte, Brazil, in 1973 to narrow the focus from fifteen cities to seven in hopes of jump-starting recruiting. Breakthrough Brazil would be just another good idea unless infused with passionate and sacrificial leadership.

Ellis and Doris Long were ready to meet the challenge and signed on to provide crucial leadership. Their decision to focus on recruiting resulted in their family's return in June 1976 to open a U.S. recruiting office.

With the full backing of the Sao Paulo missionary team, Dr. Ellis Long, Doris, and their children, Beth, Kent, and Roy Southern departed Brazil on June 26. Their next mission: to open a stateside office for recruiting, training, and caring for South American missionary teams.

5

LEAVING BRAZIL

With the beginning of 1977, I was in my groove. It was a climactic year packed with transition. Five couples (Jarrell and Nancy Edwards, Jack and Nancy Hill, Robert and Jackie Humphries, David and Carolyn Mickey, and Leon and Marion Tester) of the original sixteen had already returned to the States before my arrival in Sao Paulo. Jerry and Barbara Campbell left in June 1971, so our time together in Brazil was short.

Prior to my move to Brazil, the Walter Kriedels relocated from Sao Paulo to Curitiba, Brazil. The Allen Duttons moved to Porto Alegre in the most distant southern state of the nation. Not to be able to work with these eight families while in Brazil was my loss.

By 1977, the Huffs, Longs, Owens, Stewarts, and Vinzants were all living in the States. The Looper, Pennisi, and Norton families from the 1961 group were still in Sao Paulo. The Nortons announced their plans to return to Oklahoma at midyear.

On the good news side of the ledger, due to team recruiting efforts, the team started 1977 with fifteen families. Sixteen years of teamwork in Sao Paulo was now history. It was encouraging to witness capable Brazilians accepting responsibility for the church in their own nation.

In my own life, two huge adjustments were playing out. The first was an overload on my daily work-related responsibilities, and the second was a growing family. The work overload was my own doing. It came partly from my own youthful, optimistic tendency to believe I could balance great amounts of work. Tied closely to that misguided belief, I agreed to chair both the Leadership Training School and Camp Mount of Olives. I was the first person on the Sao Paulo team to break the rule of limiting each person's role to chair one major committee. In addition, my responsibility with the Metro Sul church continued. While the workload grew, life was moving forward in the Sorrells household.

Blessings and Crisis

Here I need to back up two years to 1975. She was beautiful. Her full head of black hair spiked at the top gave the word *cute* a new and wonderful meaning. Peering through the hospital nursery window was our new baby girl, Regina. Well, maybe it was the ones outside the window doing the peering. From one day to the next, life became an all-night marathon of newborn colic. I do not know when that phase ended, but eternity seemed like an appropriate description.

Like all new dads, I couldn't keep every responsibility straight. One night as we were leaving church and I was making my way to the car, my wife explained in great distress that I had forgotten Regina on the back row of our little church. A great quality of newborns is their inability to hold grudges against dads who are clumsy learners.

One of my missionary colleagues pointed out that little boys are super, but there is a special bond between fathers and daughters. Was he ever prophetic!

When May 1977 arrived, there were twin boys, Jay and Michael, on the other side of the nursery glass. Two days later, we took the twins home. We gladly accepted the help of many volunteers to get us through the nights of the initial ninety days.

Then something went terribly wrong. We noticed the eyes of one of the twins were not following our movements across the room. Immediately, we made an appointment with a neuro pediatrician. Two such specialists were in Sao Paulo. After our return to the United States that summer, we discovered the practice of neuro pediatrics to be rare. In Texas, there was only one doctor with that level of training, and he was practicing in Houston.

The very day we were able to see Sao Paulo's neuro pediatrician, Dr. José Salomâo Schwartzman, baby Jay started to seize. Upon examination, the doctor sent us directly to the hospital. Immediately, he placed a shunt in Jay's skull to drain fluid from his brain. It was a nightmare, and the doctor was candid with us as to the poor prognosis.

We spent the following four weeks in the hospital with all three children. The other two kids transferred in and out intermittently with dehydration and intestinal disorders. The four weeks in the hospital and our move the following week were a traumatic blur.

The highly skilled Brazilian doctors came from outstanding medical schools around the world, their training was second to none. What was lacking was medical infrastructure. To our dismay, we learned there were only two CT scanners in South America. One was in Buenos Aires, Argentina, and the other was in Sao Paulo, but it had been broken for some time. We also discovered that Brazil lacked the equipment to adjust seizure medicines through blood levels.

Within a week, we sold all of our belongings, flew to Brasilia to prepare documents for an emergency departure, and worshipped with our Brazilian friends at the Metro Sul church for the last time. At the close of the worship service, the congregation surrounded us and sang, "Be not dismayed, God will take care of you." We left Brazil with a sorrow I had never before experienced.

6

Open for Business

Since the genesis of the Brazil group experiment of 1957, which began on the campus of Abilene Christian College, it seemed fitting, with ACC's new university status, to launch the full-time mission team recruiting effort from the same place.

A full-time ministry to recruit missionary teams for the great cities of South America was in many ways a greater vision and a more ambitious goal than the one spawned in 1957. The dream had grown from sixteen families moving to Sao Paulo to a vision of hundreds of families moving in teams to the great cities of the Latin world. It was a grand goal focused on people who needed to know about the gift of Jesus.

Ellis and Doris Long were God's people for God's timing. With their experience in Brazil, their skills in administration, and their trust in Jesus, the Longs were ready for an ardent adventure. Commissioned by the Sao Paulo mission team, Ellis set a meeting with Abilene Christian University's president, John Stevens, seeking his good will and endorsement for opening a recruiting office for South America.

The academic discipline of missiology was then in its infant stages. This new academic area sought to create a multidisciplinary area of study, embracing the theological, anthropological, and practical applications for spreading the Christian faith. Fuller Theological Seminary of Pasadena, California, was in the forefront of missiology. One of the spokespersons was senior professor and former missionary to India, Donald McGavran, the father of the church growth movement.

In 1968, a formal missions study at Abilene Christian got its breakthrough when Dr. George Gurganus, former missionary to Japan, arrived on campus with his Summer Seminar in Missions.

Dr. George offered the missions seminar at Harding Graduate School of Religion in Memphis, Tennessee, during the summers of 1963 and 1964 and then moved it to the Harding campus in Searcy, Arkansas, for the summers of 1965, 1966, and 1967. Wendell Broom, who had worked in Nigeria, was Dr. George's coteacher.

Prior to the 1968 Summer Seminar in Missions, Wendell Broom completed a master's degree in missions at Fuller Theological Seminary. Drs. Gurganus and Broom opened the Center for Mission Education on the campus of Abilene Christian University.

At the invitation of Dr. John Stevens and Dr. George Gurganus, Dr. Ellis Long accepted the offer to office at Abilene Christian. He and Doris initiated the new missionary team recruiting thrust at the Center for Mission Education in September 1976.

Sponsorship of Two Churches

Simultaneous to the decision to relocate was the need to seek financial backing and program oversight. In Churches of Christ, foreign mission work is not administered by a mission board. Each missionary family is responsible to a supporting church. Upon graduation from Abilene Christian in 1957, Ellis and Doris began their Brazilian adventure sponsored by the Sao Jose Church of Christ in Jacksonville, Florida. In the latter years of their work, the Golf Course Road Church of Christ in Midland, Texas, sponsored the Long family.

Open for Business

The Golf Course Road church entered the Sao Paulo work with great enthusiasm. Being located in the middle of the West Texas oilfields, they were a well-resourced church from the standpoint of finances and executive leadership. Ellis proposed they continue his salary and be a cosponsor with the Central Church of Christ in Amarillo, Texas, which would provide administrative funding. Golf Course gladly accepted and stood by the work for another fifteen years.

Central Church of Christ

The story of the Central Church of Christ in Amarillo, Texas, deserves special attention. I'm unaware of another church with a history of sustaining fifty-plus years of partnership with a specific ministry.

My earliest relationship with the Central church began in 1972, when I began to work on the Sao Paulo Leadership Training School's finances. During the two decades between 1990 and 2010, it was my good fortune to have a close working relationship with this special group of people. Through classes, small groups, travel, worship services, retreats, and work groups, I know well over a hundred of their leadership members. It would be difficult to find a more loving and gifted church.

Their involvement with the Sao Paulo team began with Ted Stewart, a young boy who grew up in their congregation. Ted, a native of Amarillo, was baptized in 1950 at age sixteen. Ted left Amarillo on a full navy scholarship in engineering for the University of Colorado. But God wanted Ted to preach.

Ted transferred to Abilene Christian, where he met class favorite, Dot, and married her in 1957. Ted graduated with both a bachelor's and a master's degree in Bible. Prior to their Brazil departure, Ted taught Greek at Fort Worth Christian College, while serving with the Rosen Heights Church of Christ in Fort Worth.

Make Your Vision Go Viral

Sponsorship of Team Families

Central agreed to the financial support and oversight of the Stewart family. A story less well-known is the way its church elders backed the entire team. They assured other congregations of their commitment to the Brazil group and encouraged other churches to join them. As churches came on board, Central passed the sponsorship of each family to the congregation agreeing to accept the supporting responsibility.

The Brazilian Evangelist

From the beginning, Central in Amarillo was the "go-to" church. In 1965, Central took on the responsibility of publishing the *Brazilian Evangelist,* the newsletter sent to the U.S. supporting constituency of the work. The monthly, four-page publication served to keep a fellowship of churches aware of progress in Brazil. An added result of the publication is the historical record left for later generations to read and to be inspired.

Fundraising for Land and Building

The mission team's first major request of Amarillo's Central church was huge. In February 1962, after seven months in Brazil, the group received the first of two impactful visits. Otis Gatewood, missionary to Germany, encouraged the men and women to follow the principle of concentration. They should resist the pull of new converts to draw individual missionaries to new cities.

Because of his pioneering work in Germany at the close of World War II, throughout Churches of Christ people knew Otis Gatewood. He encouraged young families to work together to leave a visible church in Sao Paulo. Gatewood advocated the construction of a large church building so space would be available to grow the congregation. This is the principle of a building as a place to grow the church as opposed to merely a place to house the church—a subtle but critical nuance.

Open for Business

Reuel Lemmons visited the Brazil missionaries in December of the same year. Lemmons took the polar opposite opinion of Gatewood. Reuel Lemmons edited *The Firm Foundation* magazine, read weekly by thousands. *The Firm Foundation*, an influential publication, was begun in 1884 by Austin McGary and edited by Lemmons from 1955 to 1983. In addition, Lemmons was a gifted orator. Thousands heard him speak. Both men were household names in Churches of Christ. Both men were highly influential.

While visiting the missionary team in Sao Paulo, Lemmons proclaimed the most productive approach to church planting to be the spreading of the seed. He advocated covering Brazil with Bible correspondence courses. The team should spread out and start "brush fire" churches throughout the nation.

The result of the visits had an impact on the Sao Paulo team. It created a healthy tension within the team that lasted for the next two decades. Some were committed to concentrating together within Sao Paulo. Others were committed to scattering seed from border to border. The radio program, the correspondence course, and the airplane all played key roles in the seed-scattering philosophy.

In retrospect, both men were right. Some on the team planted churches in the city of Sao Paulo. Other team members planted seed in the smaller, interior cities. To critics, the sparse seed planted across Brazil and infrequent water made it seem as if it had zero chance of bearing fruit. Yet the seed germinated and grew, and churches stand today as witness to God's blessing.

The missionaries arrived in Brazil having read the books *Indigenous Church* by Melvin Hodges and *The Planting and Development of Missionary Churches* by John Nevius. From reading these agrarian models, the intent of the team was to plant churches without outside aid. In the early years, it became apparent to some of the Sao Paulo group that the indigenous theory described in the two books, as developed through colonial rural missions, did not fit the challenges of a megacity. In the words of Howard Norton:

> The philosophy we adopted in the beginning was the indigenous approach (self-governing, self-propagating, and self-supporting). We were not going to give money to Brazilians. We were not going to pay for anything that the Brazilians could pay for. In late 1963 or early 1964 we questioned these principles, and we decided to compromise those principles enough to rent a building with American money [and to] build a church building.

By 1964, the Sao Paulo team, encouraged by Brazilian Christians, made the decision to build a large church building on a visible avenue in South America's largest and most influential city. The plan was to merge three small churches that were meeting in a storefront, a house, and an apartment into one permanent location.

The team worked together. Assignments were completed. An action plan was readied to execute a $250,000 campaign to purchase land and build a building. This was in 1964, when $250,000 was a staggering amount of money to a group of West Texas kids.

With plan in hand, missionaries Ted Stewart and Howard Norton boarded the plane for Abilene, Texas, to launch the campaign on October 3, 1964. Since the roots of the team were in Abilene, it was appropriate to return to that place of origin for the announcement of the quarter-million-dollar plan. Leaders from the Amarillo congregation were present and took the lead. An article in the *Christian Chronicle*, dated October 23, 1964, described the kickoff: "About 90 elders and representatives from 27 congregations and 14 cities lunched together at the Starlight Restaurant in Abilene to discuss a $250,000 building program for the church in Sao Paulo, Brazil."

Open for Business

The Church of Christ in Amarillo was both the obvious church and the right church to oversee the funding and building campaign. It was not a small request to ask a stateside congregation to fulfill the daily banking responsibilities, handle the correspondence, and be accountable to all contributors for a large expenditure on another continent. Central's evangelist, Joe Barnett, described the request:

> When missionaries Howard Norton and Ted Stewart approached elders of Amarillo's Central congregation with an appeal for them to sponsor a quarter of a million dollar building program, the load they were already carrying seemed to magnify. The reluctant acceptance of the task emerged out of a sense of obligation more than desire.

Barnett quickly added:

> But today, nine months later, these elders are the first to admit that involvement in the endeavor has delivered some of the greatest blessings in the congregation's fifty-seven-year history.

Inaugurated in November 1968, the beautiful Nove de Julho church building was host to 1,200 people. Daily, the building reminds hundreds of thousands who travel along Nove de Julho Avenue of God's presence in the city. It continues to serve Sao Paulo and the nation, having planted thirty-plus churches.

The Amarillo Central elders set in order a plan to turn the Nove de Julho church property over to the Brazilian church. From the beginning, the American elders wanted the Brazilian church to accept complete ownership and responsibility of the new building. The Central church made plans to place the Nove de Julho church building in the name of the Brazilians when they met two conditions: (1) the church was to appoint national elders and deacons, and (2) the congregation had to demonstrate a three-year period of living in peace while carrying out the ministry of the church.

Make Your Vision Go Viral

As special envoys of the Amarillo Central church in July 1974, Paul and Neva Cook, with Dub and Nell Henderson, presented ownership of the property to the Nove de Julho congregation.

Those of us who worked on the Sao Paulo team will always be grateful for the forward thinking of a group of people in Amarillo, Texas. We will forever remember the trust they placed in God and in a young mission team.

Leadership Training School Sponsorship

Leadership training followed the same evolutionary change regarding the use of American funds for church buildings. After seven years of night school training, only one Brazilian had completed the course of study.

Two realities faced the missionary team. First, with the attrition of seven team families, the Americans were aware of the ticking clock. Something needed to change to ensure the Brazilian church had capable, trained leaders. Second, while consulting with the Brazilian church, it became obvious that lack of time and the physical drain of living in a megacity were the culprits to conquer if training was to progress.

In November 1969, team members Jerry Campbell and Johnny Pennisi departed with their families for the States to raise scholarships for seventeen students. Once again, the Central congregation in Amarillo stepped forward and agreed to sponsor the school and oversee the scholarship money raised from churches and individuals.

Inside Brazil

The *Brazilian Evangelist* covered the preparation of the team while in the States and continued to report on the team's work since their arrival in Sao Paulo. It was time for a new publication.

By 1972, a new era was beginning. The work was touching cities outside Sao Paulo. Many on the 1961 team had left Brazil. New missionary families were leading exciting projects built on the foundation laid by the original team. Perhaps the most exciting development on the horizon was the methodic move to Brazilian leadership. New converts of the first wave of missionaries were becoming the colleagues of the second wave.

From a marketing standpoint, it was time for a new look and a new expanded publication to communicate progress and expansion. As in times past, Amarillo Central accepted additional responsibility. This time they agreed to pay the monthly cost of production and mailing for the new communication piece. With the church's financial backing and logistical expertise, *Inside Brazil* became a premier missions publication among the churches in the '70s.

Leadership Visits

The Amarillo church sent their first two elders to Sao Paulo to see the work in 1966. In today's world with packed airports and crowded airlines, it is difficult to envision the limitations surrounding air travel during the 1960s and '70s. Costs were high, salaries were low, flights were infrequent, and direct routes were nonexistent. In Churches of Christ, it was not a common practice for the missionary family to receive on-field visits from supporting churches. With the newly acquired oversight of the church building project, Amarillo began to participate in encouragement and oversight visits.

Since that first visit by elders Paul Cook and E. R. Carver in 1966, key leaders from Central have made multiple oversight trips. Through the years, more than fifty people from their elders and leadership groups, plus scores of youth, have visited their work in Brazil and in other great cities of South America. Truly, Central's direct, on-field involvement for the past forty-five years is exemplary.

Dream Catchers

In early 1976, Ellis Long and the Sao Paulo team asked Central to be a cosponsor of the full-time recruiting effort. The leadership of the congregation caught the dream of seeing quality missionary teams placed in the great capital cities of South America. No one had to sell them anything. They were onboard. Great Cities Missions owes a huge debt of appreciation for their adaptability in leading the ministry from its inception.

It was cutting-edge willingness on the part of the Amarillo Central church to organize Great Cities Missions in January 1993 as a 501(c)3 entity with a national board of trustees. Their foresight in overseeing the Great Cities ministry through a board of trustees has allowed the ministry to grow beyond the resources of the Amarillo church. Since that time, the Great Cities board has maintained a strong representation of elders and other Central members.

Frazier Foundation

Walter Frazier made his fortune mining uranium in southwest Colorado. In the late 1970s, Frazier started the philanthropic process of determining how his wealth might bless others in the future. It was my understanding that at first he decided to work through five churches. The Central Church of Christ in Amarillo was one of the churches on that list. Walter sent $60,000 directly to Amarillo Central at the end of 1978. After further deliberation, the Frazier Foundation became the preferred instrument to carry out the wishes of Walter Frazier.

On January 9, 1979, the Frazier Foundation awarded a five-year grant totaling $300,000 to Central in Amarillo. The gift was to enhance the Brazil work and to launch the missionary team-recruiting project. Bill Johnson, an elder at Central, took the lead with the Frazier Foundation. The combined 1978 and 1979 gifts, totaling $360,000, fell under the responsibility of the Amarillo church.

Reuel Lemmons wanted everyone in the world to know Jesus. At the time of his death in 1989, he had preached on every continent and in seventy-nine countries. It was consistent with his vision for the world to begin the Pan American Lectureship in 1963. With Guatemala City selected as the first site, the Pan American Lectureship sought to bring together church leaders from the United States with missionaries from Latin America. Lemmons felt these encounters would expose U.S. church leaders to the needs of the Latin world.

I first met Walter and Sylvia Frazier at the Pan American Lectureship in Belo Horizonte, Brazil, in November 1974. On that occasion, I learned an important lesson. A wealthy man is not obvious in a lineup. People blessed with wealth are often quite ordinary. Dressed in his cowboy vest, bolo, and wide-brim felt hat, it did seem a good bet he was from the West, but I would never have guessed he had money.

In October 1976, the Fraziers visited Sao Paulo. By now, through previous gifts, we were aware of their generosity. We didn't want them to leave Sao Paulo without giving an update on projects blessed by their earlier grants. Zealous workers that we were, I am sure we injected an extreme dose of information overload.

As we often did with visitors, we set a schedule with the purpose of shuttling our guests from committee meeting to committee meeting. It never dawned on us that cowboys might not enjoy hour after hour of sitting in closed rooms for missionary enlightenment. We found that Walter Frazier could take only so much. In midpresentation, he would walk out of the room to find sunlight and fresh air while leaving his wife, Sylvia, to be enlightened.

Walter was not a man of pretense. On two other occasions, I was inspired by the humility of this servant of God. One day as the mail arrived in Sao Paulo, I opened an envelope and there was a check to help purchase the property of the Metro Sul congregation. What impressed me was his short, handwritten, jagged-edge note, torn from the bottom of a napkin: "I hope this can be of some help."

Another time, I stopped by to visit my uncle in Carlsbad, New Mexico. Sitting at the kitchen table was Walter Frazier. He had flown a young man from Durango, Colorado, to Carlsbad in his plane to help him settle into a Christian assisted-living home. It was just another normal act of kindness in the day of Walter Frazier.

Faithful through Economic Downturns

No one likes economic downturns. As unpleasant as these downturns can be, they have the upside of helping us focus on what we value most and reevaluating what is important.

In the early 1980s, Central received the keys to a beautiful new worship area. By any standard, it was an aggressive building program. The Amarillo economy was strong. Many in leadership were growing their personal wealth through oil, real estate, and the stock market. Central organized a bond program to finance the new construction. Members not only gave and pledged with sacrificial hearts, but they also purchased high-interest bonds of the day to back the construction project.

Good financial times were not to last. A severe recession hit the global economy from July 1981 through November 1982. Due to overdependence on high-interest bonds for financing the multimillion-dollar building program, the effects of the recession practically strangled the Amarillo church for two decades.

At the lowest point, most of each Sunday's congregational offering went to meeting the bank note. The church compensated as best it could, under the circumstances. Staff who left through attrition were not replaced. Eventually, they were down to a youth worker and two veteran staff members—one doing the preaching and the other aiding in pastoral care for a church of twelve hundred.

In the face of extreme financial difficulty, the leaders stood behind the Brazil work. After two decades of sacrificial giving and renegotiating the interest rate on church bonds, the congregation had met every financial obligation and emerged debt free. What a glorious day it was to attend the note-burning ceremony.

Times like that show the fiber of this unique church. It is admirable how they have maintained their support and involvement with the work in South America for over fifty years. Their leadership exhibits a tenacious trust that God has called Central to work on behalf of people whose heart language is Portuguese and Spanish.

Leadership Style

Trusting the Lord to be in control, the Central elders' strength is rooted in a deep commitment to prayer. I often reflect on what has made the Amarillo Central relationship with Latin missions work so well. My conclusions are simple, yet hopefully not simplistic. At the heart of the answer is trust. Those of us who have worked with Central through the years have a profound trust in their leadership. They, in turn, exhibit a deep trust in those who carry out the day-to-day work. As leaders, they practice a management style characterized by reaching agreement on basic goals and by rapid decision making. I have never worked *for* Amarillo Central—they always made me feel I was working *with* them.

Like any relationship, there must be nurturing for it to grow. Various individuals at Central took it on themselves to feed the relationship. They accepted personal responsibility to do their part to make our rapport with Central succeed. The idea of relationship implies a two-sided contract. Those who only receive do not build bonds. Receivers must reciprocate. I've always believed I must do my part in helping the relationship grow and mature. And it's with great satisfaction I count many members of Central as dear friends.

Make Your Vision Go Viral

Great Cities Missions

Beginning with the 1968 organizational meeting of Breakthrough Brazil, great Hispanic capital cities were included in the vision. When the recruiting effort started in Abilene, Ellis Long chose to highlight six cities and two regions, all within the borders of Brazil. He printed a color brochure with the title "Brazil Breakthrough." Focusing on Brazil, the list included Rio de Janeiro, Brasilia, Recife, Salvador, Fortaleza, Vitoria, Trans-Amazon, and the Western Frontier.

Dan Coker, missionary to Central America, arrived at the ACU Center for Missions Education shortly after Ellis opened the missionary team recruiting office. Dan and his wife, Elise, had lived in Guatemala, Honduras, and Mexico. He holds BA and MA degrees in Biblical Studies from Abilene Christian University and a PhD in Intercultural Studies from the University of Florida. As outstanding Spanish speakers, Dan and Elise have devoted their lives to evangelizing Latin America.

Ellis was experienced in the Portuguese language, Brazil, and recruiting. Dan's experience was among Hispanics in Central America. He had also traveled extensively in South America.

In 1979, the Amarillo Central congregation, a Frazier Foundation grant, and the Southern Hills Church of Christ in Abilene made it possible for Dan to join the recruiting effort. The expanding emphasis was to be on the great Hispanic cities of the South American continent. A new brochure, "Continent of Great Cities," appropriately described the scope of the joint thrust. Dan would take the lead with Hispanic South America's great Spanish-speaking capital cities, while Ellis was to continue to lead out recruiting teams for the great cities of Portuguese-speaking Brazil.

The new 1979 brochure, "Continent of Great Cities: New Mission Teams for South America's Major Cities," continued the push for teams to the Brazilian cities of Rio de Janeiro, Brasilia, Recife, Salvador, Fortaleza, and Vitoria. Added to the Brazilian city list were Manaus, Campo Grande, and Cuiaba. Great Hispanic cities became visible on the radar: Buenos Aires, Argentina; Bogota, Colombia; Santiago, Chile; Asuncion, Paraguay; La Paz, Bolivia; Guayaquil, Ecuador; Lima, Peru; Caracas, Venezuela; and Montevideo, Uruguay.

It was a great vision for Brazil and Hispanic America. But, as with all grand visions, the difficulties of fruition were impossible to imagine.

7

Recruiting Begins

When Ellis Long started full-time recruiting, he encountered young people in church schools and universities contemplating the idea of moving to Brazil. Two decades of news coverage from the Brazil group, coupled with the new popularity of travel among students, had Brazil on the radar.

Hispanic South American cities did not have the same backlog of publicity enjoyed by Brazil. There were, however, scattered pockets of students beginning to look at Argentina, Bolivia, Colombia, Chile, Paraguay, Peru, and Uruguay.

After Dan Coker joined Ellis Long at Great Cities Missions, both men became aware of an uphill challenge. Young people were not standing in line looking for advice. As teams formed, Ellis and Dan had to lobby students to be able to share experience and guidance.

Current culture rather than genuine need and opportunity often determine our attitudes and actions. The students of the late 1970s were no different. They were living the history of their time.

The capture of Saigon by the North Vietnamese army in April 1975 marked the end of the Vietnam War. Students witnessed presidents, cabinet members, and generals engaging in truth coverup. After deception by two U.S. presidents—Nixon, who lied to the nation; and Johnson, who misrepresented the on-ground reality of the Vietnam War and even the validity of the war itself—young people were in no mood to trust authority figures. They could make it on their own, thank you. Students were not looking for others to make their own dreams a reality.

The story of the Brazilian visa crisis told later in this chapter made it easier for Ellis to work with prospective Brazil teams. Dan did not have equal advantage in helping those going to Hispanic South America.

World Missions Context

With his sermon "Expect Great Things from God, Attempt Great Things for God," preached at Nottingham, England, on May 30, 1792, William Carey became the father of the modern-day mission movement. For the following two hundred years, missions was seen more as seeking lost souls in rural and tribal areas than in reaching out to lost people in the great cities of the world.

To be fair, churches hadn't totally ignored cities. Protestant missionaries have worked in Brazilian cities since the Methodists entered Rio de Janeiro in 1835. But with the study of missiology and anthropology at schools and universities in the 1970s, the city missed the curriculum.

New mission teams would need to become aware of urban realities and the implications resulting from a world rapidly moving to the city. In 1976, South America was a continent of great cities. In 2012, 83 percent of the South American population lives in cities.

Invitation

Ellis and Dan, inviting teams to cities as modern as any cities in the world, they strove to avoid the pith-helmeted, machete-carrying stereotype of the suffering missionary. They sought young, professional families prepared to identify with the modern middle-class leadership families of South America's great cities.

Recruiting Begins

Success would mean departure from mission methodology used in tribal Africa, rural Central America, and the approaches that left small storefront and house churches in Europe. Neither Ellis nor Dan could have possibility predicted the difficulties they would encounter from other missionaries of the day. Many had served faithfully and successfully in rural and tribal missions. To these respected missionary soldiers, urban mission work was a new and foreign concept.

African tribal missions, in particular, had enjoyed a period of success. Veteran missionaries from tribal and rural settings who staffed seminaries, schools, and universities saluted the indigenous principles of the new missiology.

In the summer of 1981, in preparation for Abilene Christian's summer missions seminar, Dr. Ellis Long compiled the first bibliography on urban missions and offered the first university-level class taught on the subject. At that time, neither Fuller Theological Seminary in California nor Trinity Evangelical Divinity School in Chicago offered a course on urban missions.

From his experience in Brazil and from his doctoral training at Florida State University, principle by principle Ellis shared a strategy to reach the urban world with the message of Jesus. True, the strategy would adjust through the years, but it gave new missionary teams a solid place to start in planting an urban church. From the start, he introduced missionary candidates to the main goal: to establish a church with national leaders on a main avenue of the city.

Establish, Not Plant

Although *church planting* is the buzzword used by missionaries, a key principle in urban church planting is to establish, not plant. I remember a conversation with Brazilian elder and attorney, the late Wilson Castellan. The context of the conversation was having witnessed the close of a church plant after six months of operation. Dr. Castellan's conclusion was, "Sr.

Gary, anyone can plant a church; few know how to be used by God to establish one."

The idea was to establish a church that would shine as a light in a city for decades into the future. It would be a church free from outside dependence on monetary and leadership intervention. It would be a church capable of meeting the city's needs and opportunities. Much like a public library, not everyone uses it every day. But when the need arises for a book, those in the city know where to look first. Ellis often declared his missionary strategy as one with an address. Anyone who wanted to see its results could go to 4805 Nove de Julho Avenue in Sao Paulo. There you would find an established church.

National Leadership

The New Testament describes both healthy churches and diseased churches. Obviously, the desire was to build a healthy church. The apostle Paul described leaders that would be needed to lead a healthy church.

> So Christ himself gave *the apostles, the prophets, the evangelists, the pastors and teachers*, to equip his people for works of service, so that the body of Christ may be built up until we all reach unity in the faith and in the knowledge of the Son of God and become mature, attaining to the whole measure of the fullness of Christ.
>
> Then we will no longer be infants, tossed back and forth by the waves, and blown here and there by every wind of teaching and by the cunning and craftiness of people in their deceitful scheming. Instead, speaking the truth in love, we will grow to become in every respect the mature body of him who is the head, that is, Christ. From him the whole body, joined and held together by every supporting ligament, grows and builds itself up in love, as each part does its work. (Ephesians 4:11–16; emphasis mine)

Recruiting Begins

Let me make two quick exegetical points.

First, the New Testament office of apostles and prophets seems to be limited to historical roles; both serve as the foundation of Christ's church. Their faithfulness and influence is in the foundation of churches planted today. In New Testament terms, with the death of first-century prophets and apostles, their assignment on earth was complete. Apostles were those called specifically by Jesus. With Jesus as the fulfillment of the prophetic voice, the New Testament does not indicate the continuance of prophets after the first century.

A second exegetical point: the common usage of the word *pastor* in churches today is not the way the New Testament used the word. *Pastor* was synonymous with the words in our Bibles for *shepherd, elder, overseer,* or *presbyter.* In the Acts of the Apostles and in the Epistles the pastor, shepherd, elder, overseer, and presbyter were one in the same and an appointed office with specific qualifications.

That takes on importance in the Ephesians 4 roles sought for a healthy church. Portions of Paul's letters found in Titus 1 and 1 Timothy 3 set out guidelines for those appointed as church pastors. In Pauline terms, a healthy church needs pastors, evangelists, and teachers.

A healthy church also has deacons. Paul the apostle described this role in his first letter to Timothy:

> In the same way, deacons are to be worthy of respect, sincere, not indulging in much wine, and not pursuing dishonest gain. They must keep hold of the deep truths of the faith with a clear conscience. They must first be tested; and then if there is nothing against them, let them serve as deacons.
>
> In the same way, the women are to be worthy of respect, not malicious talkers but temperate and trustworthy in everything.
>
> A deacon must be faithful to his wife and must manage his children

and his household well. Those who have served well gain an excellent standing and great assurance in their faith in Christ Jesus. (1 Timothy 3:8–13)

With the Great Cities Missions recruiting office open for business, Ellis Long and Dan Coker sought missionaries who would do more than just do good. The desire was to recruit and train teams who would be willing to trust God while putting in the time and the work it would take to leave in place a church led by its own people.

Main Avenue Church

Be not deceived. To build a church on a main avenue of a megacity is not easy church planting. I think of my own experience traveling in the cities of South America looking for specific churches. Often, with address in hand and a veteran taxi driver, it might take three or four hours to track down a church on the backside of nowhere. Someone had planted a church, but no one could locate it. Once, I handed a church address to the cab driver and his response was, "I have been driving a taxi in Rio de Janeiro since the end of World War II, and I have never heard of this street." After two hours, stopping multiple times to ask for directions, we located a dead-end street only one block long. How a visitor could have found the church was beyond my wildest imagination.

Establishing a church on a city's principal avenue is expensive and time consuming. It takes reams of government paperwork. It takes an untold amount of time building the necessary networks with government officials. Raising funds and following through on the process of construction is not for the timid soul.

But for those willing to commit to the task and to trust God to provide, there is unbelievable satisfaction in leaving a great city with a main street church. That's especially true when the possibility exists of a congregation of God's people being readily available to minister to the needs of the city for a hundred years or more.

What a challenging invitation it was to young, optimistic missionary teams—asking them to establish a church with its own national leadership on a main avenue of a great city that would make a difference in eternity for hundreds if not thousands of people. They could be part of building a church that would not only serve while they were on the field but would continue to provide light many years after they returned to their home country.

Those in the Brazilian pipeline responded first. Young people claimed Recife, Campo Grande, Manaus, Fortaleza, and Brasilia. Then, totally unforeseen, before anyone's departure, the Brazilian government closed down all missionary visas.

Visa Crisis in Brazil

From 1964 until November 1989, there were no votes cast by the Brazilian people for Brazil's presidency. Led by a military dictatorship from 1964 to 1985, as in all political systems, Brazil faced abuses of power. At the same time, it was a period of great advancement for the nation.

The last military president was General Joao Figueiredo. Appointed president of Brazil by the previous president, Ernesto Geisel, President Figueiredo served from March 15, 1979, through March 15, 1985. Though President Figueiredo was not in favor of popular elections, it was during his term that Brazil began its move toward democracy. The democracy seeds that President Geisel planted were just breaking through the Brazilian soil.

President Figueiredo's appointment came on the brink of severe economic times for the nation. Difficult economic times do not make popular presidents. By 1983, the people in the street were beginning to demonstrate, seeking open presidential elections.

Make Your Vision Go Viral

As President Figueiredo began his presidency, James Earl Carter was in his second year as the president of the United States. Early in his term, President Jimmy Carter established as the centerpiece of his foreign policy an international campaign for human rights. He criticized many countries, including Brazil, for violating human rights.

Brazil reacted by closing the issuance of all missionary visas from the United States in 1977. The timing could not have been worse. Ellis had teams in the pipeline for the Brazilian cities of Brasilia, Campo Grande, Fortaleza, Manaus, and Recife: five teams with no place to go. Ellis and Doris could close the recruiting office, declaring the door to Brazil shut tight, or they could place their trust in God and begin to look for ways to join Him in opening locked doors. Trust was the only option that made sense.

It seemed impossible for the visa situation to get worse. But on November 18, 1978, it did. The Jonestown, Guyana, mass murder of 914 people, orchestrated by the deranged cult leader Jim Jones, was front-page news in Brazil. It gave the Brazilian government—rightly so—one more reason to be cautious about issuing missionary visas.

God's answer to closed doors came in the form of two missionary families. God placed Allen and Maria Dutton to open a door with the head of the Brazilian Secret Service. Simultaneously, God placed Alaor and Miriam Leite to open a door with the vice president of Brazil.

Allen and Maria Dutton and their children Cynthia, Allen Jr., and Priscilla, were living in Porto Alegre, Brazil, since their move from Sao Paulo in 1967. There they met Nelson Veiga, a Brazilian Army sergeant and director of the Military Officers School. The Dutton and Veiga families became friends, visiting often, eating together, and enjoying discussions about the Bible.

Sergeant Nelson Veiga received a promotion and transferred to the nation's capital. The Duttons also moved back to the Sao Paulo family

Recruiting Begins

land of Maria in the community of Cabreuva. Allen and Maria would continue to fly to Brasilia to visit with the Veigas and, in turn, the Veiga family would visit in the Dutton home in Sao Paulo. When the Veigas' daughter married, Allen and Maria flew to Brasilia for the wedding.

Promotion in rank continued. This time his promotion was to the rank of colonel, with the assignment to head the office of the Brazilian Secret Service. Seeking a solution for opening the closed visa door, Allen flew to Brasilia to visit with Colonel Veiga in May 1978. While visiting the colonel's office, in typical Brazilian fashion of receptivity to a friend's need, Colonel Veiga picked up the phone and set an appointment for Allen with Brazil's secretary of state for eight o'clock the following morning.

Allen left Colonel Veiga's office and flew twelve hundred miles north to the city of Manaus to meet with Ellis Long. Ellis was in Manaus to research information for a team considering Manaus. When Allen arrived, the topic became how to take advantage of this unusually large open door with Brazil's secretary of state. With agreement upon a strategy, both men boarded a late plane and flew all night to reach Brasilia in time for the eight o'clock meeting.

After shaving and changing into suits and ties in the airport, they met Colonel Veiga's driver waiting for them outside of Brasilia's President Juscelino Kubitschek International Airport. They were on their way to meet with the Honorable Jose Whitaker Sallas, the secretary of state of Brazil.

The office was bulging with people—the line, eternal. Everyone held a number. It would be a long wait. While Ellis and Allen were assessing the situation, the door opened and Mr. Sallas came to talk with his secretary. In Allen Dutton fashion, he promptly got up, introduced himself, and said, "This is Dr. Ellis Long. He came all the way from Texas just to talk with you." Immediately, the secretary of state invited them into his office and doors began to open for missionary visas to Brazil. It was a huge first step.

Brazilian editor and church leader Alaor Leite worked with Allen Dutton and Ellis Long to solve the visa challenge. Alaor and Miriam Leite have given a lifetime of expertise and hard work to advancing the cause of Jesus. I know of no couple with a greater dedication to Jesus and His Word than the Leites. Alaor grew up in the town of Tres Pontas, Brazil, in the state of Minas Gerais. Miriam, the daughter of North American missionaries, also grew up in the state of Minas Gerais.

It would be difficult to overstate what Jesus has accomplished through this couple over the past four decades. Their contribution to the success of Great Cities Missions and the Brazilian church is a story that merits telling at a future time in all of its deserving detail.

Alaor's hometown of Tres Pontas was the birthplace of Aureliano Chaves, whose father was a fishing friend of Alaor's father. As a youngster, Alaor had also been a student of Professor Chaves, the father.

Aureliano Chaves followed the road of public service, serving as governor of Minas Gerais from 1975 to 1978. In 1979, as the first nonmilitary office holder, Antonio Aureliano Chaves de Mendonça, elected by the Brazilian Congress, became Brazil's vice president under President Joao B. Oliveira Figueiredo. Vice President Chaves served as president for two months in 1981 and one month in 1983 while President Figueiredo dealt with heart issues.

Meanwhile, it was the fourth meeting with Nelson Veiga. In the comfort of Brazil's Secret Service office was the director, Colonel Veiga, his assistant, Allen Dutton, and Dr. Ellis Long. In discussing the visa stalemate, Colonel Veiga suddenly proclaimed, "I think Dr. Ellis should meet with the president." That was an indication the visa situation was even more serious than imagined—no one would say yes until the president himself gave the green light.

At the initiative of Colonel Veiga, the meeting was set for Monday, December 10, at 5:00 p.m. Dr. Ellis Long, Dr. Alaor Leite, and Allen Dutton prepared to meet with Brazil's president. It was quite a day. The three looked back with great humor as they imagined what the hotel people must have thought. Standing by the hotel desk, the three checked signals on the meetings for the day. "At 11:00 a.m. is our meeting with the head of Brazil's Secret Service. At 2:00, we meet with the vice president. Then, at 5:00 we will be received by President Joao Figueiredo." What an extraordinary day was December 10, 1979.

With the backing of the president, the process of meetings continued. From December 1979 through September 1982, the vice president graciously granted five different meetings with Alaor Leite and select personnel of Great Cities Missions. It was my privilege to be in one of those meetings in March 1981 with Alaor Leite, Ellis Long, Amarillo Central church representatives, and Frazier Foundation representatives.

In addition to the combined ten meetings with Vice President Aureliano Chaves and with Colonel Nelson Veiga, Alaor set meetings with the Brazilian Ministry of Foreign Relations; five meetings with a top military official, Helio Cunha da Rocha; the Maritime Police; the Department of Indian Relations; and other senators, government ministries, and federal representatives. God's orchestration of Allen Dutton, Alaor Leite, Ellis Long, and Brazil's top officials culminated in 1980 with Brazilian government officials granting Churches of Christ missionary visas.

In 1981, another visa barrier arose. Ellis had a team ready for the state capital city of Manaus at the heart of the Amazon jungle. At the time various groups were exploiting the Brazilian Indians. Profiteers invaded Indian territories and compromised the heritage and customs of Indian tribes. Since Manaus was in the region of many Indian tribes, missionary visas for northern Brazil remained closed.

In addition, and more important to the government, the Brazilian Army located troops in Amazon border regions to prevent Communist infiltration from Cuba. The Brazilian government didn't want the Cubans reading missionaries' reports and picking up pieces of information as to the army's location. Ellis agreed with officials that our missionaries would stay out of sensitive areas by confining their work to Manaus and agreeing not to have contact with any Indian—period. Officials agreed.

One day a secretary in Brasilia called Alaor and said that our Manaus team's request was on his desk and he was going to deny the receipt of their visas. In customary fashion, Alaor Leite and Allen Dutton made their way to the Guarulhos Airport in Sao Paulo, destination Brasilia. Alaor had with him the name of Senator Tancredo Neves from Alaor's home state of Minas Gerais. The senator would possibly be able to help.

When Alaor and Allen arrived in the senator's office, they learned the senator would not be in his office that morning. As they were moving toward the door, the secretary turned to Alaor and said, "He is cutting his hair on the first floor."

Quick-thinking Alaor at once turned to Allen and said, "Wait here in the office. I just remembered I am in need of a haircut." Upon arriving on the first floor, he saw a vacant chair next to the only customer in the barber shop. Alaor claimed the empty chair and a second barber went to work.

Barbers are skilled in two areas: cutting hair and conversation. If barbers were serving in elected office, they would solve the world's problems in short fashion. Skillfully, throughout the day, haircutters weave their conventional wisdom on world affairs.

Alaor's opening salvo, in listening range of the other barber chair, was, "I came all the way from Sao Paulo this morning just to meet with Senator Tancredo Neves to talk with him about the missionary visa situation for the Amazon region. Unfortunately, I can't stay any longer than this morning, and now I learn he will not be in the office."

At once, the senator responded from the neighboring chair. "I am Senator Tancredo Neves. When you finish cutting your hair, come up to the office and we can visit for a while."

Recruiting Begins

The result of that visit was missionary visas for the Manaus team.

Tancredo Neves was born in the city of Sao Joao del Rei. During a short experiment with parliamentary governance from 1961 to 1963, Tancredo—as known in Brazil—served eight months in the administration of President Joao Goulart. In 1964, a military coup overthrew the Goulart government. From that point forward, Tancredo was against governance by the military.

Tancredo was elected in 1978 as a senator for the state of Minas Gerais and then as governor from 1983 to 1984. As an opponent of the military regime, he became a leader in the Brazilian Democratic Movement party (MDB). In 1984, he became the leader of the popular democratic movement known as *Diretas Ja*, or "Direct Elections Now." In 1984, President Joao Figueiredo led the Congress in defeating the popular vote amendment. The Electoral College elected Tancredo Neves president of the Republic on January 15, 1985. One day prior to taking the oath as the president of Brazil on March 14, 1985, he became ill and died on April 21, 1985, after seven surgeries attempting to save his life.

The work of Alaor Leite, Ellis Long, and Allen Dutton with top officials of the Brazilian government made it possible to reach agreement on new guidelines for reinstating missionary visas. As government leaders in Brasilia came to know Alaor Leite, Ellis Long, and Allen Dutton, the question became how to establish a system that allowed legitimate missionary personnel into the nation. Systematically, Ellis and Alaor negotiated guidelines with government officials to reinstate missionary visas.

To enter Brazil on a religious visa, prospective North American church workers would need a college transcript documenting their preparation in biblical studies. They would be required to have studied a year of university-level Portuguese and completed a college-level course on the history and culture of Brazil. Religious workers could come to Brazil only if granted an invitation by an official religious entity previously recognized by the Brazilian government.

These guidelines found their way into the new Brazilian Constitution ratified on October 5, 1988, just prior to the election of Brazil's president, Fernando Collar, by a direct democratic vote of the Brazilian people. Brazil was now a democracy in every sense of the word, and Great Cities Missions opened the way for Brazil to restore the issuance of missionary visas.

The Brazilian visa crisis turned out to be a huge blessing for missionary team recruiting and for Brazil. Young mission teams could no longer form and go to Brazil without proper preparation. Ellis no longer had to lobby prospective teams attempting to convince members they must study Portuguese. For young people to go on mission teams to Brazil, the Brazilian government demanded they be prepared.

In part because of the demands of the Brazilian government, Brazil has received some of God's most capable servants. In many ways it is unfortunate that the Spanish-speaking nations of South America did not present a visa challenge. Dan Coker still struggled with the independence of '70s and '80s students. He did not have the advantage of Hispanic nations demanding authentication of missionary personnel. The sad result was that many teams going to South American nations during that period self-destructed on the field. If they left anything at all, results were minimal at best.

Fortunately, through the years, as young people moved away from their independent stance of the 1970s and 1980s, Great Cities teams are doing successful work in Hispanic capital cities.

8

Reentry

We reentered the United States before we knew what reentry was. In 1977, reentry was real, but neither named nor understood. We went through all of its stages with no label to paste on our emotions.

Our reentry journey started with arrival in the States. We reached Birmingham, Alabama, on Saturday, August 27, 1977. The following morning I took our daughter to worship service. Jay's condition was so fragile we could not find anyone willing to stay with him during the service. Therefore, Claudia stayed with the four-month-old twins at the home of our hosts.

On Monday, we flew directly to Midland, Texas, to pick up a car en route to Scott and White Medical Center in Temple, Texas. While still in Sao Paulo, we had contacted Dr. David Morehead, a Christian doctor heading the Scott and White Neonatal Unit.

David and Marcia were gracious hosts, inviting us to stay in their home for the following two weeks. All three children received medical attention to clear up normal childhood infections, and in the case of twin Michael, to discover a case of lactose intolerance. The prognosis for twin Jay was not encouraging. He continued to have seizures.

Next on our list was to find a place to stay. In God's providence, my childhood church in Carlsbad, New Mexico, had hired a preacher who was unable to move immediately. Thus, the house the church held for the new family was available. The church invited us to use the house and fill the pulpit on Sundays while looking for employment. I was trying to figure out what had just happened, so on Sunday mornings the book of Job and sermons on trusting God received a generous airing. I was preaching to the pulpit, not to the pew.

The job search was not encouraging. I was young and inexperienced in Stateside churches. I was also trying to find a job within commuting distance of Scott and White Clinic.

Our Stateside adjustment was not going well. We had just left a city of 8 million that never closed, and now we were in a little town in eastern New Mexico where we had to remember to buy milk and baby formula before the town closed at sundown. For the past eight years, we spoke Portuguese most of the day at work and every night in our home. English did not come as readily as one might think.

The unidentified fog of reentry was messing with me in ways I did not understand. A part of me was excited to be home. But that part of me was constantly under siege by the remorse of leaving Brazil. In Sao Paulo, I knew I was doing something significant that only a few people in the entire world could and would do. Now, in the United States, all I could see ahead of me was a job, assuming I could find someone to hire me. Significance no longer seemed a part of my reality.

Toward year's end, I brokered a deal with Lubbock Christian University and Lubbock's Vandelia Village Church of Christ to serve as a missionary in residence on the LCU campus. The job would include teaching Bible and Missions and coordinating summer evangelistic campaigns for the students.

Lubbock, Texas

On a cold January 10, we moved from Carlsbad to Lubbock, Texas. One constant throughout forty years of marriage is our uncanny ability to schedule each move in extremely cold weather.

Reentry

Working with the Bible faculty at Lubbock Christian was a highlight at a time when life was dark. Daily class preparation was a new challenge. I enjoyed both the faculty and the students, who were not afraid to express their concerns and opinions. I still remember a student reminding me I could not go two or three minutes past the bell or he would be late for lunch.

In Lubbock, we continued to face medical challenges with the twins. We recognized Jay would not develop beyond the stage of infant care. And Michael's temperament was puzzling, to say the least. Being new to Lubbock, we quickly discovered that only beginning doctors were taking new patients. After our fingers did the walking through the yellow pages, we located Dr. John Iacuone, who had graduated four years earlier from Indiana Medical School.

To us, it was a God thing. Immediately this young "kid of a doctor" fresh from medical school saw a small, ash-leaf white skin lesion on one of the boys. Most likely, for the first time since medical training, where he learned about rare diseases, he uttered the words: tuberous sclerosis.

Tuberous sclerosis complex (TSC) causes tumors to form in many different organs, primarily in the brain, heart, kidney, liver, pancreas, skin, and lungs. The disease affects some people severely. Others are mildly affected, thus it often goes undiagnosed. Some people with TSC experience developmental delay, mental retardation, and autism. Yet there are people with TSC living healthy lives who enjoy what society would refer to as white-collar professions.

Over thirty-three years, we learned volumes about this dread disease. It is extremely rare. In terms of the entire world population, only two babies are born each day with TSC. That means in a world of 7 billion people, only a million have tuberous sclerosis complex. Of the million, only 50,000 live in the United States.

In that one visit, like the rising and the setting of the sun, tuberous sclerosis complex became an everyday reality for the remainder of our lives. It was in Lubbock that we began to understand more deeply that developing a tenacious trust in God and moving forward one day at a time were our only options for surviving life.

While working with the Leadership Training School in Sao Paulo it was my joy to coordinate a monthlong intensive study visit for Adelino Silva of Oporto, Portugal. We quickly became friends and colleagues in ministry. Adelino readily agreed to host a group of students from Lubbock Christian for a summer trip to Portugal.

After adding Dwight Robarts from Freed-Hardeman University in Henderson, Tennessee, as a cosponsor, we were on our way to Barcelona, Spain, and Oporto, Portugal, for a month of summer campaign work. What a trip it was!

I learned a great lesson on that trip about the art of making your point in a labor dispute. The train from Barcelona to Oporto was an overnight train that traversed seven hundred miles, taking the better part of twenty-four hours. We boarded the train in Spain early in the afternoon. About noon of the following day, the train stopped in open country. After some time passed, I discovered that the engineer disconnected the engine from the train and left us all sitting on the track. There was no engine in sight. The workers had gone on strike.

A short walk was sufficient to find a telephone. Our Christian contacts in Oporto came to the rescue. It was the beginning of a marvelous two weeks. What a joy it was to know the wonderful people who made up the little Oporto church. The Portuguese culture was rich in every way. Its architecture, fabulous food, history, vibrant city, and engaging people all made for an unforgettable two weeks. One of my valued possessions to this day is a wonderful poem written by a teenage Portuguese Christian in honor of our student group. It translates into English as follows:

Reentry

To you our esteemed brothers who have been with us and given examples of Christians.

I want to dedicate to you, as proof of my affection, these verses, which I write from my heart.

It has been marvelous to spend these days working and living with you. Oh! Days to be remembered when we were united in praise to the One in whom we believe.

Thank you for the love you have shown us. You are worthy of honor for all that you have done for us.

Your love is great, your friendliness yet greater, your work greater still. And, in your understanding you have reached great heights.

When I think of your leaving, my eyes become misty, and my heart becomes sad, as these days in my life have been the best yet. They have been days that I will not forget. They are forever engraved on our hearts.

We have engraved in our hearts proof of your love. You are about to leave for another nation. But, in our hearts, your names will remain. Selma, Patrick, Wendy, Peter, Lana, Melody, Regina, Becky, and Gary, we will never forget you.

May God be your companion, and keep you in His power. May He give you each day the courage to be victorious.

Courage to overcome all of life's thorns and one day, if God wills, we will all be reunited in the "promised land," with a happiness beyond description, and we will again embrace, sharing our love, and together, hand in hand we will sing, praising the Lord.

Oporto, Portugal
June 20, 1979
Jose Do Egito

To this day, I regret not having the financial resources to place missionary teams in Portugal and Spain. I should have trusted God more.

In 1979, I hosted a recruiting dinner and invited Ellis Long to the Lubbock Christian campus. Our target city was Vitoria, Brazil. I began to realize that students, like their more mature adult counterparts, had the same ability to make strong commitments and then renege as it dawned upon them that commitments came with a cost.

Over the next few days after the recruiting dinner, a team emerged but quickly fell apart. The good news was, three couples eventually joined with other teams. Two of the couples demonstrated admirable records of accomplishment over multiple decades dedicated in the Brazilian cities of Belo Horizonte and Salvador.

In 1980, the Jimmy Carter presidency was unraveling. Record-high inflation and the fifty-three Americans held for 444 days in Iran was not exactly creating a bull stock market in the United States. Lubbock Christian, like any new school, struggled to survive the first thirty years. Jobs were on the line, and their dynamic resident missionary was on the list to receive a notice of dismissal. As I carried my boxes to the car, passing the new tennis court construction, it crossed the mind of this idealistic missionary that we humans do not always opt for expenditures that effect eternal destinies.

Employment feelers went out. For medical and family reasons we were still trying to remain in Texas. Nothing opened. Too many of the church want ads read:

Wanted, young man with perfect family and no dog, 30 years' experience, who wears blue tights, and a flowing cape with a bright red S outlined in yellow. House and utilities provided. Bring your own salary.

Abilene, Texas

The job search continued to go nowhere. Looking back, I have to believe God was closing doors as He moved me toward the one He would open.

Reentry

After five months, Ellis Long called. He invited me to join him and Dan Coker at Great Cities Missions. Ellis assured me we could work together to raise the necessary funds.

In early November 1980, I took my first official trip related to the new work. The occasion was the Pan American Lectureship in Caracas, Venezuela. The trip was significant and my first working trip with Ellis Long. Over the next decade I would log thousands of miles and countless trips with Ellis. It was in Caracas that I began to learn from Ellis many of the skills and additional insights on urban church planting that I would need as tools for the years ahead.

Caracas was my first visit to a Hispanic megamillion-population capital city in South America. Right off, it was easy to see Caracas as a city that would be receptive to the saving love of Jesus. It was also easy to see that Caracas, like great Brazilian cities, would present a similar challenge to overcome for successful church planting. With its hoards of city dwellers, difficulty in obtaining adequate urban space would be a barrier. Unfortunately, to date, that problem remains unsolved, not only in the nation of Venezuela, but also in most great cities of the Latin world.

In Lubbock on a bitter-cold Thanksgiving Day in 1980, we loaded the U-Haul trailer containing our earthly belongings and a struggling trust in God to care for the future. We departed on the 160-mile trip to Abilene for what would turn out to be a twenty-six-year stay in a city we will always call home.

The Center for Missions Education at Abilene Christian University was the former home of the late Don Morris, a beloved president of Abilene Christian from 1940 until his death in 1969. The former Morris home was an old two-story, brick veneer structure moved adjacent to the ACU campus on Campus Court to serve as the Missions Center.

By the time I arrived, there were no bedrooms left for office space. Knowing it's easier to get forgiveness than permission, I claimed a closet and built a makeshift partition with a door. I had an office. I was ready to go to work.

Working with Ellis Long and Dan Coker came as naturally as riding a bicycle after years of the old bike being in storage. As former missionaries, we knew how to work together. Admittedly, not all missionary situations are ideal. But when missionaries are able to work as colleagues focused on a goal greater than building one's own ego, it would be hard to imagine a more satisfying assignment.

Shortly after our Abilene arrival, my major assignment in 1981 was twofold: I was to find family financial support. And I was to research and identify the initial target group of capital cities for missionary team placement. I concentrated on Brazil. My list of cities finally evolved into a big eight: Aracaju, Curitiba, Florianopolis, Goiania, Maceio, Natal, Ribeirao Preto, and Santos.

In March, I took what was to be the first of many research and on-field support trips to five cities on the list: Aracaju, Curitiba, Florianopolis, Goiania, and Natal. Recruiting was underway. Funding and successful reentry back into unfamiliar U.S. culture were yet to be realized.

Fundraising

Money is not life's highest goal. Nor is money unimportant.

I agree with the apostle Paul that the love of money causes all sorts of evil. It does not take a very astute observer to see from the daily news the flourish of evil that exudes from the love of money.

Money does have its holy side. It is a gift of God. In the Industrial and the Information Age, money is still quite useful in providing food, shelter, transportation, clothing, and a toy or two, not to mention important in providing for the poor and for spreading Jesus' message across the face of the earth.

Perhaps its key value is its use by God to gauge our trust in His provisions. He wants to know how much of the money in my possession I have the guts to give back to Him. The answer to that question directly relates to the amount of trust I am willing to place in God's hands. Since He chooses to work through human vessels, God is somewhat limited to the good He can do when His creatures hoard the money for their own comfort and security.

My challenge was to redirect a portion of God's money floating around the kingdom toward recruiting missionary teams. I'm not a talented fundraiser, but I began to learn more about tenacious trust. The truth is, money is not a high priority in my life, yet I recognize and enjoy the many good things money provides.

My family of origin did not have money, nor was money a lofty value. Dad was a building contractor when that was not a lucrative business in southeast New Mexico. He'd bid on jobs and scrape out a living, but there was hardly discretionary money available. We were the definition of frugal but did not make a big deal about it. Dad made repairs for friends and family and for our local church because there was a need. There was no pay involved.

At the time of Dad's eightieth birthday, I happened to see a congratulatory card from a family friend thanking him for overseeing the construction of a new building on the church property at no cost to the congregation—just because there was a need. I guess some of that ended up in my DNA. I have heard it said that missionary types gravitate toward unfunded employment—just because kingdom things need accomplishing.

The years of 1980 through 1983 were more than hard. It was a period of survival on a dollar at a time. It didn't seem like daily manna was lying on the ground each time we looked at the landscape. The Golf Course Road church in Midland, Texas, gave as they could, Amarillo Central church added funds from time to time, a few individuals helped as they could, and used goods and hand-me-downs became all too familiar. We somehow hung on. The truth is, God did provide, even though we felt like we were bobbing up and down in deep seas.

On January 1, 1984, we became an official line item in the annual budget of the Golf Course Road church. We were elated and relieved. After six years, for the first time since our return from Brazil, we would actually have a real salary coming in every month. We did not know at the time that our reprieve from raising funds for our salary and working funds would last only seven and a half years, but what a glorious reprieve it was. Our reentry was nearing completion.

Reentry Accomplished

In today's world, were we to speak of reentry into one's own culture taking six years, it might seem overstated. In the early 1980s, cross-cultural reentry knowledge was anecdotal. The Vietnam War was bringing reentry issues to the neighborhoods of North America. Researchers were trying to understand the reality of reentry as it related to military families, international corporate assignments, and missionary personnel. Research hidden in file cabinets, journal articles, and deep in libraries was limited. This was all happening during the precomputer, pre-Internet age.

I reentered the States, but what was lacking was the words to describe the difficulties experienced in my adaptation. Dr. Clyde Austin, a colleague at Abilene Christian, provided me with the vocabulary on which I needed to hang my reentry experience.

I first met Dr. Austin and his family in May 1970. It was four o'clock in the morning at the Viracopos International Airport near Sao Paulo. Howard Norton invited me to accompany him that morning to meet Clyde and his wife, Sheila, at the airport. They were to stop over in Sao Paulo for a short visit with the Abilene missionaries before proceeding to Argentina. Clyde and Sheila Austin and their four children would spend eighteen months in Buenos Aires, where Dr. Austin would be working with an international school.

Reentry

Upon my arrival at Abilene Christian University, again my path crossed with Dr. Austin, a highly qualified psychologist with a broad-based interest in the complete cycle of the international experience. Because of a common interest and due to his interest in missionary candidate assessment, we quickly became friends and colleagues in a common purpose.

Dr. Austin was deep into his passion of learning all he could about reentry. His wiring does not allow him to leave a stone unturned. He attended professional conferences and pertinent workshops and traveled throughout the States to interview every person he could locate who researched and wrote about reentry.

Along with his wife, Sheila, a research assistant, and a secretary, they reviewed hundreds of journals, dissertations, theses, and other publications. Dr. Austin's research led to the publication of *Cross-cultural Reentry: An Annotated Bibliography* (1983) and *Cross-cultural Reentry: A Book of Readings* (1986). For the first time, pre-Internet, multiple reentry materials were made available within the pages of two books.

Through constant contact with Clyde and gleaning from his prepublication research, I began to discover the missing vocabulary. I was learning words and concepts to describe the change, frustration, and out-of-step feelings provoked by my reentry into my own homeland—which felt so foreign. I could now declare reentry accomplished.

Finally, I was ready to focus totally and completely on the task every experience of my life had prepared me for—to proclaim Jesus by establishing churches in the great cities of the Latin world. To do this with success, I would have to learn the many intricacies needed to recruit, train, and care for missionary teams. And I would have to learn to trust God for the results.

Part 2

THE FIVE STEPS

9

STEP ONE: TRUST GOD

Two stories weave their way throughout the pages of this book. The first story is the more obvious: thirty-one college kids launching the vision for Great Cities Missions—to recruit, train, and care for missionary teams building Christ-honoring churches in great cities of Brazil and the Hispanic world.

The second story runs parallel. It is my story as an adopted member of their group. It is the story of a lifelong journey, learning to live by faith in the unseen and learning to trust God to provide. The emphasis is on *learning*. I do not consider myself to have arrived. Both stories intertwine. They play out in the context of Brazil and a growing love and respect for the people of the Latin world.

Just as it is a maturation process for youth to learn wisdom, it is also a maturation process to learn to trust God. When I came up from the waters of baptism, my trust factor was sincere, but I was naïve and unaware of how deep that trust would need to become. More fortunate than many, my birth into a trusting environment enhanced my trust journey. There was never a moment when I saw my parents as untrustworthy. I never had an occasion to distrust them. Consistently, they demonstrated integrity and trustworthiness.

With the trust I experienced in my family background, it was not a difficult leap to trust God. The very fact of being a child limited my knowledge of God. Listening to Bible stories during my formative years, I knew He could be trusted to provide manna for the Israelites. I learned He stood by His prophets. Time after time, I saw God could be trusted to move obstacles beyond the comprehension of those facing impossible odds.

When I departed for Brazil at age twenty-two, I had no idea how difficult life could be. It never dawned on me that life would bring challenges I could not have imagined. Through the process of living life, while recruiting, training, and caring for missionaries who planted churches, I have many times encountered an unmovable wall.

Often, the obstacle was impossible to climb over, dig under, or go around. On my own steam, I was dead in the water. Sometimes, I encountered a dim light in the distance, revealing a long and encumbered trail. It was not a sure route but was the best hope I had at that moment. The one thing I learned early on was just how little control I had.

In sharing the need of a lost world and inviting a person to become a missionary, the response is always within the control of the invitee. A recipient of my time-tested advice may decide to ignore my counsel. I can spend months and years encouraging team members to focus on the goal, yet they still have within their power the decision to abandon ship at any time during the mission. I have no control over others' decisions.

I may ask for a financial gift to sustain the work, but the issuance of the check is only at the will of its owner. It is always discouraging when vast amounts of time and effort are spent on missionary candidates and churches who quit when the road turns from paved interstate to a rub-board dusty obstacle.

I have learned to trust Jesus increasingly with each passing year. It is His mission. As hard as it is at times for me to believe, He wants His mission to succeed more than I do.

Step One: Trust God

I take great encouragement from Paul the apostle. Jesus miraculously selected him for a lifelong mission. Jesus even spoke audibly to him and provided him with unmistakable visions at key junctures in his life. To top everything, Paul said he knew a man who received a guided tour of heaven (2 Corinthians 12:2).

Then I see the apostle signing up to go on mission trips for Jesus. Remember, Paul was the same apostle handpicked by Jesus. On three different occasions, he found himself bobbing up and down on a piece of broken board after a shipwreck in open seas. He trusted Jesus and landed in prison. He served in Jesus' name and eight times was beaten with whips and rods. While on missions, he faced bandits, suffered from cold, hunger, thirst, and a lack of sleep. How could Paul stand up to such difficulty?

His life bears witness to the fact that he placed his trust in the One who called him. He was tenacious; he did not give up. He trusted the One who set the example by trusting His Father one night in a garden. Jesus prayed, pleading not to go through a torturous and humiliating death to carry the sins of humankind. Then he concluded, "My Father, if it is possible, may this cup be taken from me. Yet not as I will, but as you will" (Matthew 26:39).

Paul understood he had signed up for the mission of his Master, Jesus, who was nothing less than the Son of God, the Creator. For Paul, in light of this reality, no sacrifice was too great.

It would be difficult to find a greater example of dedication to following Jesus than Paul. My little trials fade when placed against his courageous life. Often my stomach ached when I had no idea how to meet payroll. From day one, through the entire forty years, money was hard to come by. Through the years, as the Great Cities ministry grew, we met every payroll. Seldom were our bills more than thirty days behind.

In my more faithful moments, I recognized that God honors the manna system. He always provides enough for the day. In my weaker times, I would feel a great kinship to the Israelites and think, *God, sure You came through before, but can You do it again?* I have come to believe that God knows and cares about my daily struggles. In monetary trials or myriad other roadblocks, I trust Him to be faithful.

From childhood, one of my favorite stories is from the book of Daniel—Shadrach, Meshach, and Abednego and the fiery furnace. I love their response:

> King Nebuchadnezzar, we do not need to defend ourselves before you in this matter. If we are thrown into the blazing furnace, the God we serve is able to deliver us from it, and he will rescue us from Your Majesty's hand. *But even if he does not,* we want you to know, Your Majesty, that we will not serve your gods or worship the image of gold you have set up. (3:16–18; emphasis mine)

I want to learn to trust God even if, in my limitations, I do not see His provisions each time I ask.

Sometimes friends apply certain adjectives to me, both in jest and in candid seriousness—tenacious, focused, bulldog, stubborn, intense—all words I accept as a compliment. It has taken a lifetime to learn these traits, though stubbornness is an unlearned trait that comes naturally. Some might dare to describe these words as synonyms of *faith* and *trust in a powerful and providing God.*

On a day-to-day, more personal level, life has not been easy. Through the course of forty years of ministry, I've dealt with some difficult times. I learned of the death of my grandfather by way of telegram. He was my very own fishing buddy. In those days, it was impossible to return to the United States for his funeral. Also by telegram, I learned of the brutal auto accident of a cousin who'd lived next door and had grown up with me through childhood. I have buried two sons and both my father and mother. Hospitals, surgeries, and extremely rare diseases are all too familiar to our home.

Step One: Trust God

In the midst of loss, God's light continues to appear. This past year as I moved my Dallas office to a much smaller home office space, I found myself purging through forty years of files. I read with love, delight, warmness of soul, and severe guilt file after file of family cards for Father's Day, birthday, Valentine's, Easter, Christmas, anniversary, and other expressions of love and connectedness. The guilt came from reading a lifetime of cards from my daughter. This young woman is the richest of blessings to Claudia and me. A consistent theme expressed in her cards year after year was her feeling of loss due to my absence in ministry travel. I didn't see it at the time. It finally hit me as I read the cumulative stacks of cards that expressed the high cost to her due to her daddy's work.

I feel an acute guilt for my lack of sensitivity to my daughter. God is good, and my daughter continues to be as forgiving as the night I forgot her in her baby basket on the back row of the church. Regina's marriage to Darrell, a quality Christian mate, is just one more way God has honored our trust in Him. They are the love and light of our lives.

It is these experiences and the stories told throughout this book that have brought me to the point of being grateful for the formative experiences of life and being able to begin to declare a tenacious trust in the Creator God, His Spirit, and in His Son, Jesus.

To trust God is the first and most important step in church establishment. In fact, to trust God is the cornerstone on which to build anything of eternal value. It is only from the posture of trust in God that missionary recruiting can begin.

10

STEP TWO: RECRUIT THE BEST

As the SS *Del Norte* pulled from the Port of Houston on June 1, 1961, Ellis Long declared, "Look! We are missionaries." Indeed they were. Sent by God, the Abilene Christian young people were on their way to share the message of God's saving grace through His Son Jesus.

Recruiting for God's mission is as ancient as the written word. When God has a message to communicate, He looks for messengers. God recruited Jonah by means of a great fish, Noah with a colossal flood, Abraham through a direct call, Moses through a burning bush, and Paul the apostle through a blinding light and an audible voice on the road to Damascus.

Recruiting is more of a God thing than a human thing. It has the God component of the Creator at work in the lives of his children and seeing assignments where His people can meet human need with His provisions. It has the human component of presentation of the opportunity and the ultimate acceptance or rejection of the one asked to go on a mission for God.

Due to the evolving nature of culture, learning to be a recruiter for God's mission is an ongoing process. Since culture is not static, yesterday's presentation will not meet today's need. Recruiting is an art rather than a science.

Recruiting is primarily a spiritual endeavor that includes the execution of on-the-ground logistics. Most importantly, missionary recruiting depends on the Holy Spirit to urge and nudge. Success in recruiting the right person is, first and foremost, tied to identifying capable people. Those capable individuals need to be introspective, reflective, and prayerful in distinguishing between God's call and a mistaken human response that could be their own unstable and wrongly motivated desires.

For two thousand years, Paul the apostle has served as a model for missionaries. Fourteen of the twenty-seven books and letters of the New Testament trace the call and mission of this man. He was smart, well trained, stubbornly tenacious, totally committed to Jesus, highly energetic, adaptable, unselfish, and visionary. His greatest desire was that others would come to receive the same gift of grace that he received from Jesus. He wanted every person on the face of the earth to know Jesus. His target audience was the great cities of his generation. He heard the call loud and clear from God's Son.

The Sao Paulo team was highly trained in Scripture and well acquainted with the apostle Paul. Two basic recruiting principles of Great Cities Missions are rooted in the DNA of the Abilene Sao Paulo group. With the assumption that their recruits would come from among those who had already accepted the lordship of Jesus, the top two objectives were to recruit for talent and recruit for cities.

Recruiting for Talent

When Ellis Long opened the recruiting office, his Sao Paulo teammate, Ted Stewart, was teaching at the Sunset International Bible Institute in Lubbock, Texas. Ted invited Ellis to speak on campus to recruit a team for the city of Recife, Brazil.

Recife, known as the "Brazilian Venice," is a thriving industrial, business, and educational center of four million located on the coast of northeast Brazil between the Beberibe River and the Capibaribe River, which flow through the city as they make their final descent into the Atlantic

Step Two: Recruit the Best

Ocean. To build a church in Recife would require talented people who would be willing to embrace a great city.

Ellis spoke at the Sunset chapel service and invited those with interest to bring their brown-bag lunch and meet him in room 200 for more information. Cline Paden, director of the school and former missionary to Italy, called Ellis to his office after chapel. Cline, never shy, told Ellis he was wrong in his approach. The students who would meet him in room 200 would be the same students who met speakers in room 200 week after week but were not going anywhere.

Cline Paden offered to shoulder-tap a number of the school's most capable students. And handpicked, talented students assembled to consider the challenge at hand. Never again did we depend on an open invitation to an audience as the primary means of recruiting. For over three decades, we have invited the most talented students to steak dinners in nice restaurants rather than to room 200. The joke among current missionaries working in the great cities of the Latin world is "How many steak dinners did it take for you to sign on?"

Recruiting for Cities

It takes a certain amount of sophistication and education to be credible to city dwellers. From the first days in Sao Paulo, we were intentional about fitting in with city dwellers. Only a few short years before my arrival in Sao Paulo, a man could not ride a streetcar without a coat and a tie. Proper attire was required for lunch or dinner at all restaurants.

Due to our educational status as North American college graduates and as members of the international community living in Sao Paulo, the higher classes accepted us. The expectation was to go to work daily with coat and tie just as our Brazilian counterparts did. Through the years, dress codes have become more relaxed, but the cultural adaptation principle remains the same. As urban missionaries, we want to fit in and be credible in the urban world.

As recruiters for the urban world, we have intentionally attempted to be professional in our approach to prospective recruits. It is our desire to help young people love the city, fit in with city dwellers, and build credibility that will allow others to see Jesus alive and inviting.

Research

Recruiting starts with grunt work on the part of the Great Cities staff. Specificity is an elementary step in preparing the recruiting appeal. That means the Great Cities staff must do its homework through prayerful research and planning. The need is so great and so widespread that we could not go wrong in city selection. But we want to be as sure as possible to select the optimum city for each recruiting project. Sitting around the table, a priority list emerges. Pros and cons surface around the circle. Prayer for wisdom rises from the table to the heavens. After multiple sessions, often over a period of weeks, we reach consensus and choose a city.

Before recruiting begins, it is important to do on-the-ground empirical research in the target city. In May 1982, I made a strategic recruiting mistake. Ellis and I were working together to recruit teams for the Brazilian cities of Belo Horizonte and Salvador. I agreed to take candidates for the two cities on a survey trip to Brazil. I was somewhat familiar with Belo Horizonte; however, Salvador was foreign to my experience.

While at Lubbock Christian, Tim and Janet Brumfield were candidates for what eventually turned into the disbanded Vitoria, Brazil, team. It was my first attempt to help Ellis recruit a team from a Christian college campus. The failed attempt was somewhat the result of my lack of experience. After this failed attempt at a team for Vitoria, I was an accomplice in directing Tim and Janet Brumfield to the Salvador team.

The Vision Begins

Sao Paulo, Brazil, 1961

The 1980s

Brasilia, Brazil, 1980

Recife, Brazil, 1980

Campo Grande, Brazil, 1981

Fortaleza, Brazil, 1981

Manaus Brazil, 1981

Belo Horizonte, Brazil, 1982

Rio de Janeiro, Brazil, 1982

Salvador, Brazil, 1982

Curitiba, Brazil, 1986

Florianopolis, Brazil, 1987

The Vision Grows - 1990s

Buenos Aires, Argentina 1990

Vitoria, Brazil, 1992

Montevideo, Uruguay, 1993

Natal, Brazil, 1995

Rio de Janeiro, Brazil, 1998

Santiago, Chile, 1999

2000S

Buenos Aires, Argentina, 2001

Porto Alegre, Brazil, 2002

Asuncion, Paraguay, 2003

Bogota, Colombia, 2003

Salvador, Brazil, 2005

Santiago, Dominican Republic, 2006

Baranquilla, Colombia, 2006

Cartagena, Colombia, 2008

Carlon Puente Studio, 51 Photography (817) 682-2210

Hispanic Fort Worth, TX 2008

Niteroi, Brazil, 2008

Brasilia, Brazil, 2009

Cusco, Peru, 2009

Mexico City, Mexico, 2009

Step Two: Recruit the Best

The official name of Salvador is "The City of the Holy Savior of the Bay of All Saints." I can see why city fathers would opt for the shortened version, Salvador. With its population near four million, it is the largest city in the northeast of Brazil and the capital of the state of Bahia.

I knew nothing about Salvador except its map location. Vital to the recruiting experience is helping a candidate couple experience their chosen city in a positive manner. Having made a good decision helps them grow confident and begin to envision success in the mission. A good experience in getting to know the city aids in the anticipation of becoming new residents. With regard to Salvador, I failed in every possible way to meet this expectation.

The cities of South America offer many wonderful amenities, but the nature of cities is that each one overflows with human need and incomprehensible challenges. My experience on the Salvador survey trip caused me to see the need to present future cities in their most positive light. From that vantage point, missionaries can begin to assimilate the dark side of the city without being overwhelmed.

From guidebooks, maps, and the scantest of information, I planned our stay in Salvador. Having never visited the city, the hotel I picked was less than ideal. It was located in the oldest section of this 450-year-old city.

The first morning started terribly wrong. At the hotel desk, I asked for a city map. The clerk didn't have a map, so he gave me the supposed address of a tourist agency, and we set out on foot. From the beginning the instructions seemed to be a mistake. Located in the old part of the city, the street could not have been more than six feet wide, most likely dating back to the 1500s. Houses with open doors and open windows lined each side of the descending street.

Dogs and drunks cluttered the neighborhood, and even sober passersby looked shady. Needless to say, I was more than a little concerned for the safety of my small group. Brazilians often refer to American tourists as "filet mignon." And I was sure we were about to be had for lunch.

Reaching the bottom of the narrow street that snaked down the side of the mountain, no tourist bureau was in sight. I was not surprised. Reality at once came into focus. The only way back to the hotel was to climb back up the same street.

The afternoon outing was no better. As the old slave-trade capital of Brazil, Salvador, in many ways, is more akin to darkest Africa than to progressive Brazil. The driver we hired thought we must see one of the largest squatter cities in Brazil. The shantytown, built on stilts above the water, allowed open sewage to fall into the water below. Poverty was everywhere, and as far as the eye could see was society's displaced people.

That night as we gathered to debrief, Janet Brumfield cried her eyes out. In an attempt to console, I offered the observation that Brazil had other cities. Perhaps they should reconsider their choice. I will always remember Janet's response: "I don't understand why, but God has called me to Salvador. I will answer His call."

The Brumfields spent twelve years building a great church in Salvador, changing the eternal destiny of hundreds. They would tell you many of their most precious friends in life are residents of Salvador. Their tenacious trust placed in Jesus, in the face of the unknown, stands as one of the many monumental examples of God's missionary servants throughout history.

My portrayal of Salvador is unjust, which is the point I want to make. Had I visited Salvador prior to the survey trip, I would have learned of a great city, unrivaled in culture, history, beautiful beaches, inspiring architecture, and warm, wonderful people. It is our responsibility as advocates for the great cities of the Latin world to do our homework and represent each city and her people in a fair but attractive light.

Step Two: Recruit the Best

Marketing

With research complete, marketing begins. Unlike the high-profile cities of Europe or the Holy Land, Latin American capital cities, less publicized, are hidden jewels. Hiring a highly trained marketing firm is a costly yet important step. In human terms, we are launching a multimillion-dollar project. The merits of the city must come through in stunning high-quality print pieces, video clips, news releases, and public presentations. The vision is significant, so we want our prayer-bathed marketing plan to be created and executed in a manner that will affect the chosen city until Jesus comes again.

Recruiting Events

The greatest of care goes into planning the details of each recruiting meeting—a life-changing event for the bright, talented people who will consider moving to a foreign nation. Should they answer the call, they will be challenged in ways not seen before. They will spend a lifetime learning a new culture and a new language. They must be willing for their children to be born, raised, and educated in another country. It's a serious request with huge implications.

In a nice dining room with delicious cuisine, we share the plea on behalf of a great city. With great and hopefully exciting detail, we present the steps of how to get from the dinner to the city. Then we encourage everyone to pray about it.

It is the job of the recruiter to present the opportunity in its most accurate light. It is the work of the Holy Spirit to move a heart.

Introductory Retreat

A cultural change from my baby boomer generation to the current climate is the decision-making process. Today's youth deliberate big decisions over an extended time period. They are less likely to receive an invitation, talk it over with God during the night, and be ready to move forward the following day.

For a generation needing more decision-making time, an introductory retreat is helpful. A weekend is set aside for those who want to continue to explore the mission team idea. The weekend focuses on worship, prayer, and additional information. The opportunity for questions and answers in an informal setting aids in the decision making. Those who accept the challenge are then ready to enter the assessment track.

The Game Board

Together with Ellis Long and Dan Coker, we identified steps in the recruitment process. In the late 1980s, Bob Waldron, with missionary experience in Guatemala, joined us in the recruiting effort. Bob helped us envision the entire process, from recruitment to the final reentry of the missionary family into their home culture, as a Monopoly game board.

It was a wonderful vision piece for missionary candidates and their potential supporters. People could see the expectations of where to enter the project and how to get from here to there.

Application

Each candidate walks through an assessment process. As the missionary candidate considers the possibility of serving God in another nation, the first important step is to complete the Missionary Biographical Information form (MBIF), which serves as the application form.

While working at Abilene Christian with Dr. Clyde Austin, I was introduced to the MBIF as a vital tool still moving toward its final form. In the 1980s, Dr. Austin began to work with us to assess missionary teams. The thirty-two-page document has undergone many revisions and adaptations through the past thirty years. Seeking to draw out background information, the MBIF looks at a candidate's personal history, family history, spiri-

Step Two: Recruit the Best

tual history, marital history, educational history, work history, volunteer service history, financial and support history, and health history, as well as references. The final section of the MBIF asks the candidate to write his or her spiritual autobiography.

In recognition of the missionary assignment encompassing the entire family, there is also a questionnaire for each child. Children are vital to the success of a missionary team. The doors they open for Jesus from diaper days through their adolescent years are astonishing. We missionary types can only wish to have a fraction of their influence.

Psychological Assessment

The MBIF identifies red flags and potential trouble spots. Depending on the degree of difficulties encountered through the pages, a candidate will receive a green light to continue, a caution light—also allowing continuation but with supervised remedial intervention—or a red light, bringing the application process to a halt. Should the latter occur, candidates are encouraged to consider alternate ways to better align their life with current reality.

The MBIF confirms that each of us owns more of the fallen traits of creation than we would like to admit. It offers a good preliminary overview of the potential a missionary team candidate brings to the table. But knowing the future demands to be placed on a missionary team living and working in a foreign culture, there is the need to take a deeper look.

A staff PhD-trained psychologist uses four additional instruments. The Minnesota Multiphasic Personality Inventory-2 (MMPI-2) and the Millon Clinical Multiaxial Inventory-III (MCMI-III), both empirically validated and reliable instruments, assist in the diagnosis of mental disorders. It is useful to utilize two instruments when evaluating individuals for pathology, because it is possible to compare results of assessment feedback.

Due to the twenty-first-century, sex-charged, and violent U.S. culture, it is prudent to explore the possibility of past trauma in a candidate's life resulting from aggressive sexual encounters or violence. The Sexual History Questionnaire (SHQ) and the Trauma History Questionnaire (THQ) identify a missionary candidate's need for healing from sex or violence exploitation.

At the close of the four written assessments, a clinical interview—three interviews if married—is scheduled to examine areas of concern discovered from the instruments. The staff PhD interviews the husband, the wife, and finally the joint couple to work toward a better understanding of each individual. The clinical interview is also an opportune time to probe for additional events that could have a significant impact on the individual and the team when placed in long-term cultural transition and adjustment situations.

Psychological assessment of missionary candidates was a hard sell. When I first began working with missionary team recruiting, I was unaware of its existence. Later I discovered that the International Mission Board of the Southern Baptists began using the tool in 1937. We in Churches of Christ are not exactly at the forefront in our willingness to learn from others. The first teams going through Great Cities Missions went without assessment.

In the mid-1980s Dr. Clyde Austin of Abilene Christian University brought the assessment need to the three of us on the Great Cities staff after teams departed for Brazilian capitals Recife, Brasilia, Campo Grande, Manaus, and Fortaleza, and Hispanic capitals Asuncion, La Paz, Lima, and Santiago. Team members and the churches they were attempting to establish paid a high price, in part due to our ignorance of assessment and in part due to the independent nature of team members wanting to do everything on their own. We faced four challenges in making missionary assessment a nonnegotiable step at Great Cities.

First, missionary colleagues accused us of playing God by the very act of our questioning a candidate's "call from God." I liked the response of Link

Step Two: Recruit the Best

Care founder, Dr. Stanley Lindquist. Dr. Lindquist, a pioneer in advocating missionary wholeness, makes this observation:

> Sending people to the field because they have a "call," without adequate evaluation and preparation, would seem to be a failure to discharge this stewardship. . . . God has called me to my vocation, too. Right now, this call is to help you determine what your gifts are, to maximize in your preparation, or to discover if there are areas of concern about your present personal adjustment. Your call is for preparation for the task, as well as for the task itself. Therefore, this information will help you to fulfill God's call. My call is to serve God by serving you. That's why I am here and that's why you are here.[1]

Dr. Lindquist would say, "I have been called by God to test your call."

Money was a second challenge. Assessment tools, a licensed psychologist's time, secretarial support for drafting reports, and travel between missionary candidates and their supporters all came with a price—a significant amount for aspiring students already struggling with the cost of school. It was easy to withhold cooperation as soon as they compared the assessment cost to that of their family's much-needed new washer and dryer. As the ministry grew, we reached the point of loaning the money for the assessments with the assurance of repayment when the missionary family raised funds for the field.

A third lesson in the establishment of missionary assessment was timing. In the early years, it was convenient to do the assessment of a team during the annual Summer Mission Seminar at Abilene Christian. Often the seminar's mission curriculum courses—some of which were required to meet visa requirements of the Brazilian government—were offered as the last stop before the team's scheduled departure to South America. The required courses were a draw to the summer seminar.

Each team arrived with its membership in place. They were on their way to their chosen mission field. In retrospect, the assessment was taking place en route to the airport. Unbelievable trauma arose when it was determined one or more team families should not go. Families may have been involved in the project for two or three years, emotionally committed to the team and to South America, and out of the job market. With airfare in hand and disaster predicted, the dilemma was incredible.

It was obvious a change was needed. The change came with the recognition that team membership couldn't be confirmed until the completion of the entire assessment process. Furthermore, no training would begin until the entire team's recruitment was complete.

The fourth obstacle dealt with communication and confidentiality. In the beginning, we were recruiting on the campuses of various schools. In keeping with the principle of "shoulder tapping," a faculty recruiting partner helped place talented prospects on our radar. We soon found the campus recruiting partner's knowledge of a star student to be limited.

As the assessment process ran its course, occasionally we discovered the brilliantly recommended student had, in addition to a mission interest, a hidden interest in ungodly extracurricular activity or addictions. The problem came after giving a red light to a missionary candidate and, with confidentiality restraints, we were unable to tell the faculty member why the outstanding candidate received a thumbs-down. The solution was to make sure students signed a release-of-confidentiality form before beginning the assessment, which would allow the faculty member to follow the assessment process.

The Abilene Christian Sao Paulo team was far from perfect. They did not go through a formal assessment process. Like family, because we lived and worked so closely for so many years, we knew each other's flaws as clearly as we knew each other's strengths. However, as the Abilene Sao Paulo team members departed for Brazil, they had a lot in their favor. Due

Step Two: Recruit the Best

in part to their exceptional leadership ability, their background of growing up in Christian families, and a huge serving of God's grace, the team was not plagued with overly difficult emotional baggage. Though not perfect, they had the insight and commitment to deal with any arising difficulties. Historically, that's not been the case with all missionary families.

Being in the South American missionary family for forty years and highly involved in world missions, I am privy to a greater worldwide missionary community and am aware of much of the hurt present in missionary families.

Some years after the time when we were taking enormous criticism for our strong stance in initiating psychological assessment, I sat down and compiled two lists.

On one I listed thirty-nine missionary families who served over a period of thirty years in different cities in South America. These families had experienced tragic family breakups, a suicide attempt, serious marital difficulties, sexual molestation, incest, marital infidelity, alcoholic fathers, complete psychiatric breakdowns, alcoholism, and incompetent job performance. They did not have the advantage of self-introspection and constructive intervention through a quality assessment prior to going to the mission field.

The second list included missionary candidates directed away from service in South America after going through an assessment process. That list included those who had not adjusted to damaging divorce, had not dealt with sexual addictions or family sexual abuse, and rape victims still battling with trauma. There was the wife abuser, those with criminal records, and those in chronic pain. The list also included a couple whose children from the wife's previous marriage were taken from her through the court system. She had no idea where the four children lived. The list included sufferers of hallucination, bulimia, and anorexia. There were former drug dealers and current drug users. The second list was short—only twenty-five families—but more than enough. Due to our intervention, we spared them from working through these difficulties under the added pressure of living in a foreign nation.

I determined never to participate in any missionary entity not taking seriously a complete assessment process in their missionary candidate evaluations.

Through the MBIF and the use of instruments for psychological assessment, we made great strides in enrolling whole people in the mission enterprise. The current missionary personnel working on Great Cities teams are the best. That is not to say Satan cannot still wreak havoc, but churches and supporters can have a justifiable level of confidence in the current missionaries serving on the field.

The Quest Event

I feel we must always be alert for new ideas to enhance the effectiveness of missionary teams. Team effectiveness reaches beyond selecting missionaries with a healthy emotional system. At times people successfully negotiate the assessment process but can't seem to fit on the team. Teams of seemingly healthy people have gone out through the Great Cities ministry yet failed because they couldn't work effectively together.

Events leading up to 2010 caused us to add an additional step to the assessment process. Some years before, we encountered a church planting group called Stadia. In their own words, "Stadia is an international ministry dedicated to planting independent Christian Churches by supporting church planting networks all across North America."

Stadia's affiliation with the Independent Christian Church gave us common heritage dating back to the Stone-Campbell movement. We opened a dialogue with the Stadia leadership. They were experiencing success in the North American context, but attempts at church planting within the North American Hispanic culture were not working. We were experiencing

Step Two: Recruit the Best

success in the South American Latin culture but had a desire to see if the same principles could work among North American Hispanics. We were curious about how they first identified a team leader and then worked with the team leader to train the team that the leader selected. This was in contrast to our model built on the foundation of a democratic team of equals.

One component Stadia brought to light was discovering how to identify specific people who possessed the gift for planting churches. To better identify potential team leaders, they wanted to know what could be learned when mature people with life experience observed, one-on-one, the new candidates with their spouses and with an improvised team. The Stadia component also wanted to explore how peers would assess potential team colleagues and how new candidates would assess themselves. This process took place over a long weekend under the watchful eyes of five nonpartisan couples and a lead assessment coordinator.

Ron Freitas, Bryan Gibbs, and Ken Lewis of the Great Cities staff contacted Philip Claycomb, at the time a member of the Stadia staff. Together they participated in a Stadia assessment weekend. In October 2004, we invited Philip to speak to our board of trustees meeting at a retreat center in Glorieta, New Mexico.

On the inside, the conversation continued around our table through staff meetings and retreats. In the meantime, newly formed nonprofits were beginning to explore the Stadia approach. In 2004, Dr. Gailyn Van Rheenen, formerly of the Abilene Christian University Department of Missions, founded Mission Alive in Dallas as a church planting nonprofit. The Mission Alive group adopted the Stadia Discover Lab as part of their selection process.

Missions Resource Network of Fort Worth, Texas, is a 501(c)(3) nonprofit entity providing resources for churches and foreign mission points. They received permission from Mission Alive to modify evaluation questions used in their Discovery Lab. The questions were redesigned to reflect cultural concerns encountered when expatriates work in other nations. It was with Missions Resource Network that the first designated weekend of this laboratory, aided by a five-couple assessment team, received the nomenclature "Quest."

Dr. Dottie Schultz and Dr. Becky Holton were faculty colleagues at York College in Nebraska. Dr. Schultz and her late husband, Tom, after working as missionaries in Amsterdam for fifteen years, returned to the States with a heart ready to help missionary families. Both completed advanced degrees in missionary reentry. Dr. Dottie Shultz now serves as Director for Missionary Care for Missions Resource Network. She caught the vision of the usefulness of the Quest and became an advocate.

Dr. Becky Holton became Director of Missionary Care for Great Cities Missions in 2009. For her first assignment, I requested a comprehensive evaluation of the Great Cities missionary assessment process. I was concerned that we were experiencing missionaries randomly "falling through the cracks" as they encountered on-field difficulties we had not anticipated.

In addition to the reexamination of the current psychometric instruments we were using, I wanted her to meet with Dr. Dottie Schultz and design a pilot run with the Quest for team candidates in the Great Cities pipeline. We had a solid foundation, but this could be a valuable supplemental tool.

In the Quest weekend, three crucial instruments complement the MBIF and the other four metrics used in the Great Cities' assessment process. Prior to the Quest workshop, candidates complete the Prepare/Enrich 2000 Inventory for married couples and the Taylor-Johnson Temperament Analysis (T-JTA), designed for individuals. The two instruments draw out valuable relationship information. The third instrument to prepare before arrival is the Leading from Your Strengths Profile. The candidate will receive a twenty-eight-page report of personality strengths, values, and communication strategies.

STEP TWO: RECRUIT THE BEST

Five areas of inquiry, assigned to five assessor couples, will glean information to aid in seeing a missionary candidate in a more complete light. The candidate will pass as an individual and as a married couple from assessor couple to assessor couple, circulating through each of the five assessor couple teams.

The assessor couples will look for resilience to life's setbacks, failures, and losses and for flexibility and adaptability. How do the candidates react to change? Do they have the humility to abandon their brilliant idea to embrace a better idea presented by a colleague?

The assessor couples look at the candidates' skill in building relationships and accepting others. Can the candidate couple promote a secure, comfortable environment for deepening relationships? Is the candidate couple doing well in learning skills to set appropriate boundaries on relationships? The relationship of the candidate mission couple is important. Do they model a wholesome family life before their team, the church, and the community? Does the couple share the ministry vision?

Another assessor couple examines the commitment to planting a church built on the lordship of Jesus. Do the candidates place a high value on seeing lives transformed? How do they understand walking by faith? Are they willing participants on God's mission, or on a solo mission? Do candidates see the difference between the will of God and their own personal preferences?

Do the candidates believe in God's capacity to do great things through their work? Do they have a vision for the future? Are they able to cast a vision and attract others to help bring the vision into reality? Do they view challenges as opportunities or obstacles? How do candidates cope with the nonvisionary—with opposition, with walls, or with limits?

Are candidates growing in the ability to discern spiritual gifts and the giftedness of others? How well do they avoid personal overload by delegating effectively and recognizing the giftedness of others? What are the candidates' plans for being able to equip and release others to do ministry work according to their spiritual gifts?

What about their personal motivation? Do candidates have a driving desire to do well? Is there a commitment to excellence in serving an excellent God? Do they have a track record of persistence, or of losing interest when the task becomes too difficult? Are they willing to work long and hard without running over others? Are candidates self-starters and willing to build from nothing? Do they have high energy and good physical stamina?

Finally, an assessor couple looks at candidates' daily work and professional relationships. Do the candidates support leaders and others in authority? finish tasks well? have realistic standards for measuring success? Have the candidates developed an effective communication style? established good ministerial ethics?

After a long, intense weekend under the scrutiny of ten assessors and a trained psychologist coordinator, newly discovered information and transparency increase the understanding of the information previously obtained.

Final Review

If applicants have been red-flagged in any of the assessment steps, a final review of all materials and assessment results is prayerfully considered by a minimum of three Great Cities staff members. Within two weeks of the Quest seminar, a recommendation is reached. From the time an applicant submits the MBIF until the final review and recommendation steps are given, the assessment process takes ninety days. It is only at this point that a candidate is approved to participate as a full-fledged member of a Great Cities missionary team.

Team Integration Seminar

When team chemistry is right, working with a team of colleagues is pure magic. Even the hardest work is fun when everyone wholeheartedly signs

STEP TWO: RECRUIT THE BEST

on. To the contrary, when a team member is the proverbial fly in the ointment, the perfume of teamwork can take on a foul smell.

It is important to get team chemistry right. The final step of the recruiting process is a team integration seminar. The seminar is a multiday event led by the director of team care who has led the team through the entire team assessment process. Prior to this session, team members sign off to allow disclosure of personal assessment results with the whole team. The primary purpose is to explore the strengths and weaknesses of the team as a whole. The big question for consideration is, "As a team, is the integration of our individual strengths sufficient to complete the task before us?"

A second question is of equal importance: "Is my own personal wiring such that I can be a harmonious member of this team?" Much like in marriage and family, this is a question of being able to disagree at times while maintaining respect for all team members that allows relationships to grow and be fruitful for the kingdom of God. Like marital divorce, team divorces radiate hurt.

The assessment's uncovering of any team member's deep personal insecurities should give pause to the entire team. The team's goal is to plant a church, not to focus time and effort on keeping a team member happy.

At the end of the team integration seminar, after time spent in deep and prayerful consideration of personal commitment, it's decision-making time. "Can I allow God to use me as a harmonious member of this work group, with my highest purpose being to plant a church by sharing Jesus with lost people, while growing with my team in the image of Jesus?" Those who can answer yes, are ready to make a formal commitment to God and to each team member.

Together, the new team pens a declaration of trust. With the document in an adjacent room, one by one, each team member enters the room alone. After soul-searching and prayer, each individual signs before God and team membership is sealed.

Looking Forward

Some may question the value of such an extensive missionary assessment process. With each passing year, my conviction increases that talent matters. God gifts people with talent and uses them as high-impact leaders for His purpose. The stakes of church planting are too high not to be concerned with the wiring and ability of those sent on the mission.

From a financial standpoint, over the life of a successful church plant, the cost reaches millions of dollars. God calls us to be good stewards of His gifts.

From a care standpoint, there should be no greater commitment than the care taken to send whole people, emotionally equipped to complete the assigned task, with the assurance of remaining whole through the project's completion.

From a significance standpoint, a church plant deals with the destiny of peoples' eternal souls. It is important in the initial church plant to introduce the first generation of lost people to the saving Jesus, but the ultimate goal is not limited to salvation for the first generation. A greater goal is for leaders to influence a church plant for generations to come. The planted church must serve as a lighthouse to a lost world for decades into the future.

Why should we be content with sending less than our best to work toward God's great eternal task? Why should we be content to send those limited to reaching only a handful of people? Why are we not looking for God-given entrepreneurial talent that God can bless with a harvest of thousands of changed lives?

Let us commit to helping high-potential leaders follow God's path. To recruit the best is an important step in visionary church planting.

11

STEP THREE: DO THE HOMEWORK

Astronauts train. Teachers train. Doctors train. Lawyers train. Engineers and architects train. Why is it unreasonable to expect missionaries to train for one of the most challenging tasks imaginable?

During our stay in Sao Paulo, I followed from a distance the plight of a North American family who moved to Salvador, Brazil, to work as missionaries. Their lack of preparation was no different from that of the majority of missionaries working in South America. Due to the lack of a support network and no coworkers to provide the blessing of working on a missionary team, their difficulties became major obstacles. The events that placed them in that circumstance were all too common to the missionary story.

Their missionary journey began with the best of motives. In their U.S. hometown they met an exchange student from Brazil who captured their hearts. In general, the zest for life and the warm hearts of the Brazilian people are an irresistible draw for building friendship. With the vision of a friendly people in need of hearing God's story, the couple and their children soon committed to move to Salvador. With the purest of motives, there was no time to waste in taking the good news of Jesus to the Brazilian people.

Foreign exchange students are wonderful people, but their youth, marked by a lack of wisdom and experience, do not make dependable counselors for an international move. The unprepared and unsuspecting missionary family boarded the plane for the move to Salvador without sufficient financial backing. Completely bankrupt of tools or strategy for integrating into their new culture, they arrived in their host city. The missionary family had not studied Portuguese. They knew nothing of Brazilian culture, not to mention the intricacies of the African culture of Salvador. They could not have been more unprepared for culture shock and the difficulties of adapting to their new home.

One year after their arrival, the dad, mom, and children all returned to the States in complete defeat, with no visible sign of their work remaining.

Their story is neither unique nor uncommon in the annals of missionary history. One might expect years of mission work in the receptive cities of South America to have produced large, dynamic churches, but the opposite occurred. Missionary efforts of Churches of Christ began in South America's Spanish-speaking capital cities in 1952 and in Brazilian cities in 1927. Yet with the rare exception, prior to the work of the Great Cities, the average church had less than forty members.

Why have we seen such poor results? Missionaries sent to affect their cities lacked sufficient personnel and finances. Missionaries took with them their rural backgrounds and rural methodologies, proving largely ineffective in urban settings. The cities scarcely realized the missionaries were there. As a result, missionaries, discouraged by years of working undermanned, underfunded, and undertrained, returned home. Other cities waited for the same mistake to repeat itself once again by the next arrivals.

One-half century after the U.S. census recognized the Church of Christ as a member of the North American religious scene, we started to struggle with how to meet the need of training missionary families. Not until the 1970s, did we become proactive with specific training for families who were

Step Three: Do the Homework

willing to make an international move for the sole purpose of offering the light of Jesus.

As discussed in chapter 7, it took the teeth of the Brazilian government's visa requirements to require training for missionary teams recruited through Great Cities Missions. I wish I could claim training was a great success from the start. I cannot. I can claim that from the beginning training started to make progress. Ellis Long launched training on a solid foundation and in an accurate direction. The goal of the mission would drive the training.

Main Goal

Train with expectation. Being a missionary with Great Cities is more than an expectation of doing physical good for others. Helping others is at the heart of Jesus' teachings and should always flow from the heart of His followers. That is a great expectation.

But to be a missionary with Great Cities, there is also the expectation of participating in building a church of eternal significance. I want young people to build in a manner that will touch people's lives from now through eternity. Based on his Sao Paulo experience, Ellis envisioned a clear goal for missionary team recruiting and for what a new missionary in training can expect to see accomplished with God's blessing:

> To establish in each selected capital city a church as described in Ephesians 4:11–16. Each congregation will be built around a nucleus of middle class families; have an attendance of at least 300; select its own elders, deacons, and teachers; and fully support its own staff. A key to attaining this goal is the acquisition of a permanent and adequate building, attractive to all classes of people, at an accessible, centralized address.

From this established base, national Christians and career missionaries will continue, in time, to evangelize and to establish other churches in the rest of the city, state, and nation. This goal drives training at Great Cities.

Make Your Vision Go Viral

Seven Building Blocks of Preparation

Before sending a missionary to a foreign city, seven solid blocks must be in place.

1. *Financing the mission.* A cornerstone to success is money. Without the acquired skill of resourcing the mission, the commitment to the missionary task will die a stillbirth. From training to going to executing to returning fundraising will be in the equation. A solid block of training is learning how to finance the mission. The mission task of the twenty-first century will follow twenty-first-century realities. Airline tickets are more expensive than donkeys, foot travel, and the wooden sailing vessels of the apostle Paul. Skyscraper megacities require more expense than rural or jungle living.

2. *Mastering the language.* New missionaries need to speak Portuguese or Spanish fluently. Understanding the new culture is only possible through language acquisition. The communication of every truth links to a form, and language links to culture. The communication of any message demands both language and culture.

3. *Understanding the culture and history.* To make friends and to win the confidence of city dwellers, each missionary must integrate into the culture and the history of the chosen country. Missionaries who are illiterate of history and culture will have difficulty demonstrating competence; there will be no bridge to cross to teach others of God's culture and about the historic Jesus.

4. *Building a team.* The work will succeed or fail based on the ability of the team to work together. Team success will rest, to a great degree, on learning to focus the varied array of God-given individual giftedness and uniqueness on the church plant. It is vital to implement individual giftedness toward kingdom building in an atmosphere of harmony.

5. *Creating a church-planting strategy.* Doing good may distract from leaving the lighthouse shining at the end of the mission. Jesus modeled life

Step Three: Do the Homework

by doing good, but He also modeled the courage to follow through with the mission: His death on a cross.

History bears out the struggle of the past two hundred years to integrate eternal salvation with the current suffering and reality of today's world. A strategy is important to a holistic church plant that sees eternal needs as incorporating the physical needs of the here and now.

6. *Growing in Christ.* To grow in one's walk with Jesus and to survive while planting a three-hundred-member church in a new country, one must learn to be a self-feeder. Through Bible study, prayer, meditation, and nurturing relationships, life is not only survivable but becomes a growth experience.

7. *Researching the city.* The research trip is a systematic approach to data collection. On the research trip, the new mission team will encounter fundraising, be immersed in the language, encounter history and culture firsthand, have a three-week around-the-clock team experience, see the principles of church planting strategy in various stages of progress, and begin to obtain a greater appreciation for the need to trust God for sustenance.

These seven building blocks are the training curriculum. Let us look at them in more detail.

Building Block 1: Financing the Mission

Other than selling Girl Scout cookies or Boy Scout popcorn, it is a fair assumption that new missionaries lack experience in fundraising. For most missionary types, the word *daunting* is a superunderstatement of the task before them. For some, money may seem to fall from the sky, but for the vast majority it is an exercise in tenaciously trusting the Creator of heaven and earth. It is living out an ardent demonstration of faith, working as if He did not exist, while knowing that His existence is the only hope for adequate sustenance.

It takes money to raise money. There is a need for money to live during preparation for the move to a great city, to scout out the land, for visa acquisition and documentation. There is a need for money to move to a new country, to establish a home in an unfamiliar land, to study the language, and to plant a group of Christ followers. The task for the new missionary family becomes identifying sources for over a half million dollars to cover the preparation period and the first five years on the mission field.

As the missionary team reaches its sixth or seventh year on the field, growth will progress to collaboration with the new national church to solve the problem of accessible and adequate urban space for a growing congregation. The new church will give sacrificially. However, the new brethren will rarely be able to finance the lighthouse church property and building from which continual church planting will take place in a megacity. The mission team will have to do its part to raise supplemental funds.

To place the fundraising challenge facing each missionary family in perspective, Bryan Gibbs, a ten-year veteran of the Great Cities Rio de Janeiro mission team and a second-decade member of the Great Cities staff, addresses the need with a multiple-day seminar titled "Funding the Vision." Based on practical experience, Scripture, and the classic 1993 book by William Dillon, *People Raising: A Practical Guide to Raising Support*, Bryan helps the new missionary see the task as doable.

Building Block 2: Mastering the Language

I arrived in Brazil unable to speak a word of Portuguese—big mistake. In the first years of my life in Sao Paulo, I could go through an entire year without encountering an English speaker outside of team members. After marrying a Brazilian, I spent the first seven years of our marriage speaking only Portuguese.

Partially from a lack of a predeparture language foundation in the States, and partially from being an introvert with limited natural wiring

Step Three: Do the Homework

for language acquisition, I was never a flawless Portuguese speaker. Still, I do not recommend that anyone purposely set out to live in another culture without learning to be conversant in the host language.

Each team member must study and pass first-year Portuguese or Spanish at a university or professional language school. Charles A. Weitz and Elmer S. Miller, in *Introduction to Anthropology*, state what should be obvious to any serious student of cross-cultural learning:

> Most contemporary anthropologists no longer accept the view that culture and language are completely separate phenomena. They do not believe that either culture or language can be studied in isolation. Anthropological linguists have come to see that language tells us a great deal about culture itself.[1]

As guidelines are set for the training process to ensure the establishment of the Ephesians 4 church, language learning emerges close to the top of the list. A team of missionaries speaking their adopted language at a grade-school level will not be able to establish a growing church. In addition to the one-year language study requirement in the United States, the primary job of a team during its first year on the field is to work on language acquisition.

Through Great Cities, missionaries prepare linguistically to the point of being able to converse intelligently with all residents.

Building Block 3: Understanding the Culture and History

Attaining the goal of an established church will require missionaries who understand the history and culture of their chosen nation. Understanding the nation and its people is important if the team is to reach the national leaders who can one day fill the roles of elder, deacon, teacher, or evangelist in an urban church.

An important building block in training is to provide a university-level course on the history and culture of the target nation. Team members will need to know the names of political leaders, celebrities, prominent educational institutions, influential philosophers, teams and sports heroes, and how the culture's family unit functions.

A vivid memory of my first year in Brazil is of being around the dinner table of a family with three daughters. I loved the family interaction—the jokes, laughter, and animated conversation—and enjoyed their delicious, home-cooked meal. What a marvelous family—in need of the gift provided freely by the grace of a loving God. But until I could relate to them through their own culture, history, and language, there would be no available bridge to cross over into the core of their lives.

Building Block 4: Building A Team

Since graduation from Abilene Christian, my life's work has evolved in the context of teamwork. I find great satisfaction working with capable colleagues toward grand goals and objectives impossible to accomplish by working alone.

In the early 1980s, prior to the recognition of the value of teams in the business world, I designed one of the first college-level courses on Team Missions. Books on teamwork were not available. Today it is possible to build a whole library with books on team building.

Great Cities uses a team approach to implement the goal of church establishment in Latin America. A team is three to seven families going together with a commitment to remain together for a minimum of five years with the one team, the one city, and the goal of one church.

Team missions brings the advantages of numerical strength, increased resources, a greater chance for continuity, better decision making through the group mind, increased vision, multiple talents, and mutual edification.

Step Three: Do the Homework

To maximize these advantages, the group of individuals must learn to work together and remain together.

It is important to train as a team. By way of the team assessment process, we have a team free from excess emotional baggage, but that does not mean we have perfect people. It means we have solid people who must learn to enjoy, trust, and honor each team member. To build trusting relationships, a first step is to train as a team. It is imperative for everyone to start the training together, remain together, and finish together.

We have learned this lesson the hard way through multiple failures before getting it right. In the early years, we made major mistakes before understanding the importance of team training and arriving on the field together. Team training does not end when the team arrives in its chosen city. During the first year on the field, the team works together in language training and in preparation for the launch of the church plant. We learned a hard lesson in the 1980s when the first team sent to Rio de Janeiro staggered team members' arrival over eight separate dates during six years. The team succumbed to the convenience of individual members' schedules instead of training as a team from recruitment to team arrival on the field.

Even today, with a better grasp of its importance, team missions continues to be a difficult principle to follow. In the early years, we attempted to address the foundational training blocks by scheduling around the needs of team members still in college. Courses were limited to weekends and college breaks. We made the fundamental mistake of scheduling around members' needs rather than making sure a training schedule met the demands required for eventual success.

This approach to training lacked the ability to draw team members into building intense relationships. It also lacked consistency. Not all team members could or would be present for every course. Too often, we found ourselves caught by people who joined the team after their teammates finished a preparation block. And often the late member was unable to complete a piece of the training.

In June 2001, with the newly recruited team for Buenos Aires, Bryan Gibbs took the lead to implement a six-month, full-time training internship. It was a step in the right direction, but it did not solve the problem of late additions to the team and of conflicts in schedules, as some team members were completing university degrees while in the Great Cities internship.

We still found ourselves under the control of others' priorities. It took moving the ministry to Dallas in 2007 to get away from the distractions of nearby colleges and to implement a policy restricting candidates from joining teams while still completing degree programs.

That all works fine until an unmarried missionary in preparation falls in love and brings a future spouse into the process. There is always a challenge to overcome and an exception to the rule to train as a team, but the closer a team adheres to the "train as a team" principle, the greater the odds of the team working in harmony toward team objectives.

A difficult area related to team missions is interpersonal relationships. It is hard to imagine a situation, other than in the nuclear family, where individuals live and work more closely than do members of a missionary team. Teams that fail in the early stages to develop skills for dealing with conflict will experience great difficulty in remaining together.

In the Great Cities ministry, a forty-hour Interpersonal Relationship Workshop is held close to the beginning of the preparation track. Trained professional communicators work with the team to provide each member tools for problem solving and conflict resolution. Generally, it takes forty classroom hours to create the necessary atmosphere to teach the needed skills to the team.

The objectives of the session are to heighten awareness of individual differences among group members; to review, critique, and strengthen the

Step Three: Do the Homework

group process; to enhance team members' communication skills; and to study stress and its management.

In teamwork, having the right skill sets on the team is vital. The key to ultimate success is the ability of the group to self-orchestrate harmonious process and harmonious progress. This is an acquired skill obtained by training together in an intense format with huge doses of prayer and Christian grace.

Building Block 5: Creating a Church-Planting Strategy

A well-thought-out strategy is important to reaching the goal of an established church. To depart for the field without a strategy or to adopt the strategy fad of the day will result in failure.

Strategy is never a substitute for ardent prayer. It is never a substitute for being in tune with the Holy Spirit dwelling in the believer. Ardent prayer and walking in tune with the Spirit will confirm strategy and allow adjustments as needed.

Not every strategy is the right strategy for the city. In the 1960s, the twentieth-century interpretation of a New Testament house church was taught as the pattern for church expansion. This oversimplified view did not address the fact that, living twenty centuries removed from the first-century church, we cannot know how first-century community worked. We should have the humility to admit a lack of knowledge of the intricacies of the first-century sociological dynamic.

Alone, the house church model in a large South American city could never match the description of the Ephesians 4 church. Separated from a corporate church identity and group assemblies, even if thousands of disconnected house churches were to exist, how could elders, deacons, teachers, and evangelists emerge? It is interesting to see the house-church advocates reemerge a half-century later with the same lack of answers as their twentieth-century counterparts.

Make Your Vision Go Viral

To reach the goal of an Ephesians 4:11–16 church in a capital city, built around a nucleus of middle-class families, reaching an attendance of at least three hundred, with its own elders, deacons, and teachers, fully supporting its own staff requires a specific strategy. At Great Cities Missions we teach the following eight-step church planting strategy.

1. Follow a Clear Goal

Defining a clear goal is an important element of the strategy. The Great Cities mission follows a measurable objective. Teams do not go into the great cities of the Latin world for such nebulous tasks as "doing good works," "sharing your faith," "working in campus ministry," or "witnessing for Jesus." These are very noble tasks, but it is possible to accomplish them all and not establish a strong church.

When the overarching goal is to establish the Ephesians 4 church, the noble tasks cited above can in fact play an important role. But we must always keep in the forefront of our minds the objective of leaving first-generation churches at the heart of urban centers.

2. Locate on a Primary Avenue

An important aspect of strategy for the established church is to locate it on a well-known street. It is possible to make a case for this aspect of the strategy based upon the commonality of cities. There are characteristics of cities that justify locating the work on a main avenue. The following list of characteristics, although not exhaustive, includes features common to urban settings that influence the decision to locate the church building on a highly visible street. The wise church planter will consider the following urban universals.

Urban transportation systems. Every urban center has a system of transportation that includes public and private buses, trains, and automobiles, an increasing number of many megacities providing a growing subway system.

Step Three: Do the Homework

Traffic flows via networks of freeways, boulevards, avenues, streets, and sidewalks. To affect the city, the church must be accessible to all who live in the city proper and in outlying areas. A principal avenue location takes advantage of the urban transportation systems in reaching out to the city.

Urban population distribution. Population density is a factor in all urban centers. People live in clusters of houses, apartments, and shantytowns, divided among the wealthy, the middle class, and the poor. By locating on a main avenue, the church is accessible to all segments of the population.

Urban communication. Urbanites communicate by radio, television, newspapers, magazines, advertising, the postal service, social networking, telephone, and word of mouth. City residents participate in the communication process through friendship and commercial networks established through social, educational, and business communities.

These communication networks include parent-teachers associations, neighborhood groups, unions, and family recreation clubs. By locating on a main avenue, the church can more readily become a part of the network. On a familiar street, the church is easily available to residents of the city by use of these communication systems.

Urban educational systems. Education is organized into public and private schools and universities. Specialty schools teach a variety of skills, from driving to sewing. A recognizable address provides the church with the opportunity to function within a familiar framework by offering classes to the community in a culturally appropriate location.

Urban religious systems. The community has certain cultural expectations of religion. These expectations are derived from what is perceived as legitimate. Such expectations surface in many areas of society. As human beings, we create perception based on experience. A church is perceived to be valid because of the image we have created in our minds. It is possible to argue that a main-avenue church is valid in the eyes of the city because "that is where churches are supposed to be located."

Another important perception is legitimacy. The church is not exempt from these factors as they relate to building design and location. In Latin America, churches have been located on a well-known city street for centuries. Location is an important factor of perceived legitimacy for the church in the eyes of the city. Architecture should also not be overlooked. It is an opportunity to contribute to city aesthetics.

Urban commercial systems. The web of commerce weaves its way from commercial streets to high-rise office space to large industrial zones. An important concept in South American urban centers is expressed by the Brazilian concept of *ponto*, literally meaning "point," referring to the all-important location or place of business. A highly visible and accessible *ponto* is expensive. In determining an urban strategy for the establishment of first-generation churches, the wise strategist will want to locate the church on a main avenue *ponto*.

3. Grow a Three-Hundred-Member Church

An Ephesians 4 church must aim for about three hundred members. To establish a church that will grow and develop, it is necessary to reach critical mass. If leadership is to emerge in the form of the roles described in Ephesians 4, there will have to be a group statistically large enough for that to happen. For a church to become financially self-sustaining in an urban center, it will need to have a membership of sufficient numbers to support the work. Through observation, experience, reading, and research, first generation churches need to be close to three hundred people for the church to generate financial support and the various roles of leadership necessary for a self-sustaining church.

It takes a hundred people for a potential elder to emerge. To be able to see three elders mature through the years within the Christian community, the church will need to reach an attendance of three hundred. From this number, new Christians will evolve into teachers, deacons, and an evangelist to grow and sustain a healthy church.

The number three hundred is a minimum for creating the critical mass of continuity. Obviously, three hundred is the floor and not the ceiling: the church must reach three hundred members before it can grow to three thousand.

4. Aim for the Middle Class

At the heart of the objective of the ministry is a one-time planting of a church in a South American capital city based on the model of Ephesians 4:11–16. The church must begin on a solid footing in such a firm manner that it can play a key role in the future evangelization of the city, the nation, and the world. For this to happen in an urban context, the socioeconomic middle class must play a role. Found in the middle class are both adequate financial support and the leadership for ongoing church growth.

This is a key point. Jesus was prophetic when He told His disciples in Mark 14:7, "The poor you will always have with you." I have never attended a church in South America without a generous representation of the downtrodden, the poor. Urbanites from the middle class can reach both the lower and upper classes, while those from the lower class face an almost impossible task of crossing cultural barriers to influence those of the middle and upper classes.

"Middle class" in South America is a designation describing those with a high school or college education. Normally, they are able to maintain a small house or apartment, own a car, and purchase food and clothing. In Latin America, the luxuries for the middle class are few but continue to increase.

The middle class is as lost as both the poor and the rich, so to focus on the middle class is not a question of being discriminatory. To target the middle class is not to be exclusive. In the process of converting the middle class, the church will reach out to the poor and take advantage of every opportunity to teach and save those who are rich in this world.

Another of the miracles of the kingdom is the disappearance of the classes within the fellowship of the church. Equality evolves as Latin people grow in their relationship with Jesus. It is a beautiful scene to sit among members of a church composed of all socioeconomic classes as they pray, worship, and fellowship together. It is heartwarming to see the church members embrace and care for the needs of their fellowman regardless of class.

5. A Permanent Church Building Attractive to All Classes

In the Sermon on the Mount, Jesus compared His followers to both salt and light and declared both useless unless dispersed among people (Matthew 5:13–14). Our goal is to establish a church at the heart of the city so that it can more readily disperse salt and light to the people.

The message of Jesus cannot be easily accessible to the city's residents, even from a main street location, if the church is hidden on a tenth-floor apartment building or a fourth-floor school. The church needs to have an easily recognizable identity in a permanent building that is attractive to all classes of people.

Permanence is a major consideration in the task of church establishment. The goal is to establish a permanent point of light where God's redeeming quality illuminates the metropolitan area as long as the city exists. The consideration of permanence strongly influences the approach of Great Cities Missions. Any strategy for church planting that sees the job as less than a permanent ministry to the city is inadequate.

A permanent church building not only fulfills the cultural expectation of the people but offers an atmosphere of stability in which the work can grow and develop. The lack of a permanent building has too often hindered the work of church establishment in South America. A cursory reading of missionary newsletters of past decades from urban centers throughout the world

STEP THREE: DO THE HOMEWORK

paints a common portrait of churches failing to grow beyond forty or fifty members. Multiple moves, provoked by rising lease costs, terminated rent contracts, inadequate space, and limited building access hinder the necessary stability for congregational growth and development. I listened in frustration as one member told me their church had moved so many times they were afraid Jesus would be unable to locate them upon His return.

As in the case of perceived legitimacy, the principle of cultural expectation also applies to a permanent church building. For more than five hundred years, South Americans have gone to the church building to worship, to show repentance, and to plead forgiveness for ungodly living. It is the culturally legitimate place to communicate with God. Helping national Christians acquire a culturally relevant place of worship is not an innovation of the North American church. To the contrary, it is being sensitive to the culture of the Luso-American (Portuguese) and Latin American (Hispanic) city.

In foreign church establishment among Churches of Christ, the question of whether or not to build a church building has been a topic of discussion since 1953, when Melvin Hodges, a missionary with the Assemblies of God and an associate professor of missions at the Assemblies of God Graduate School in Springfield, Missouri, wrote *The Indigenous Church*. Works from missionary writers like Hodges and Harold Lindsell are representative of the mission literature written from a rural perspective, calling into question the practice of missionaries constructing church buildings in foreign countries with the aid of funds from the United States. While this may be a valid observation (referring to Hodge's thesis) for certain areas and certain conditions, it does not appear to be so for urban Luso-Latin American missions.

In his book *Keys to Urban Church Planting*, Roger Greenway, a pioneer in the field of urban missiology, recognizes this as one of the greatest problems in urban church establishment:

Most urban churches stay small for a long time, and the inadequate facilities in which they gather is one reason for their slow growth.... The secret of surmounting the building bottleneck must be found if we are to establish a more effective way of winning people to Christ in the city.[2]

I find it interesting in reading business books and articles that the discussion of proper facilities and location is absent. It is just assumed that every endeavor must work from an adequate location. We live and minister in the twenty-first-century urban world. The eternal, saving nature of the church makes it the most vital of all institutions. The effort to give the city church the same permanence as libraries, universities, and other institutions must not be overlooked.

The Sao Paulo, Brazil, team worked five years, 1961–1965, with the "indigenous model" before reaching the conclusion that it was not producing the desired results in terms of an established church for the city. Upon rethinking the objective, a plan of fraternal cooperation began to emerge in which the Brazilian brethren sacrificially participated with North Americans to construct a church building for all classes of people.

Beginning with the successful endeavor between the Nove de Julho Church of Christ in Sao Paulo and Stateside churches, Great Cities has come to see the importance of an adequate, attractive church building at the heart of great capital cities. The Churches of Christ have now experienced multiple decades of successful partnership with Latin American Christians in constructing permanent church meeting facilities.

Evangelism tool. The view of Great Cities Missions is that the permanent, attractive building is a tool with which to *build* the church, rather than a place to *house* the church. In addition to the personal experience of living over eight years in Sao Paulo, constantly I see the principle at work through multiple research trips taken to South America and through personal involvement working with teams of missionaries to obtain property and build church buildings on principal avenues.

Step Three: Do the Homework

In June 1988, I spent the day with Abramo Lucarelli, a gifted evangelist who served over twenty-five years as an elder at the Nove de Jueho Church of Christ in Sao Paulo. At the time, Mr. Lucarelli and his family lived in the Itaquera district of Sao Paulo. During the afternoon, we visited a new five-hundred-seat Baptist church, including an education facility, on a main avenue. It was interesting to observe that the only members were the newly appointed pastor and a few neighborhood residents. The builders recently left the property and the keys with the pastor. He received a tool for the task of building a five-hundred-member church.

Visible. If the church building is to be a tool for evangelism, it will need to be visible. People will need to know where it is, and it must have its own identity so that it can be easily advertised.

The visibility factor is important from another angle. The timing of receptivity to the Christian message cannot be foreseen. The Holy Spirit often moves people to feel their need for God at times of crisis. People may pass in front of the building for years without considering their need for God. But in time of crisis, due to the church's visibility and the caring community of believers serving from that location, the hurting person has the opportunity to find solace.

Because visibility is such an important element in urban church planting, it should always receive high consideration by the team of church planters as they consider a strategy to reach the city.

Adequate. Another consideration in using the church building as a tool for evangelism is to be sure to plan adequate space from the very beginning. It is difficult to develop a three-hundred-member church in a building with seating capacity for one hundred. It is hard to attract middle-class families if there is not sufficient fellowship and classroom space for their children. And it is a challenge to create a climate of nurture and care if there is no space to teach and host fellowship activities. It is not easy to provide counseling and to carry out the organizational roles necessary for home cell units without space for offices and organization.

Appeal to all classes. In the urban setting, it is important to make the building attractive to all classes of people. Middle-class Latin Americans shop in nice stores. They work in attractive office buildings and live in comfortable homes. On special occasions, people of the middle class are not strangers to fine restaurants. Their expectation of a church building is no less.

The church building in the urban setting needs to be built in such a manner that it will be inviting to the industrialist, the doctor, the university professor, and the lawyer. Far too many church planting efforts in South America project an image of poverty through their chosen meeting place. A professional would have to cross wide cultural barriers to attend.

On a research trip to Brazil in 1983, I was in the home of a man who was in charge of mail distribution for the entire nation. Although he was willing to study the Bible in his home, the chance of his attending the congregation that met in the basement of the local meat market was minimal. On the same trip, I visited with a family at their ranch resort property. I was also with a family of high achievers, their children recent university graduates, who loved world travel and eating at expensive restaurants. These people would have never entered the ragtag property owned by the majority of newly planted churches. These stories are not isolated cases. In all too many instances, the classes are unknowingly blocked from a ministering community because we fail to build the proper cultural bridge as we make decisions about the location of the church.

How does a church building that is attractive to all classes of people affect the poor? The poor also have cultural chasms to cross. In some ways, their cultural barriers relating to the classes are not as great as rich relating to poor. Even the poor enjoy the opportunity for social lift by attending a meeting place of the church that is often nicer than the place where they live. It provides contact with the classes that are normally unavailable to the

Step Three: Do the Homework

masses. For a lower-class person to tell his friends he attends church with a medical doctor or an architect provides greater social prestige than for a doctor to tell his friends he attends church with a bricklayer.

Although there is not extra spendable income in their lives, the poor frequent shopping centers and modern pharmacies and use modern buses and subway systems to traverse the city. The key is to build a church building that is attractive to all classes and to ensure that the ministry provided therein makes everyone feel welcome.

6. A Comprehensive Evangelistic Outreach

Great Cities Missions teaches a comprehensive, evangelistic strategy. A threefold approach includes the principles of concentration, impact, and intentionality. The wise mission team concentrates its resources on providing initial impact in the city. With focused intentionality the new church goes about sharing with the city the good news found in Jesus. The team is encouraged to multiply through study groups as a means to plant a fellowship of believers. As a part of the big picture for the entire city, a ministry of prayer, evangelism, nurture, fellowship, and meeting needs will grow along the lines of family and friends. These needs are met by creating small Bible study groups across the entire metro area. It is men and women of faith who can make Jesus credible to family and friends.

1. *Concentration.* The principle of concentration is crucial to the team objective of the established primary avenue church. For that goal to be reached, the evangelistic effort of the team must concentrate on the establishment of the one church.

The building—an evangelism tool—provides space for good public preaching and worship and offers a place for family-oriented activities. Because of the location, the church can concentrate on building a body of believers by offering the community helpful classes and services—always drawing the community in while reaching outward to focus on building the local church.

2. *Impact.* By itself, concentration is not sufficient. It is also necessary for the mission team to impact the city. Residents should become increasingly aware of what God is doing through His children. The larger the team, the greater the impact should be. Seven families can provide more energy, work hours, and channels of blessing than can three families.

Although the initial impact will depend on the team, as the church grows, this principle will remain important. To see the entire city as a whole is to remember the urban nature of the task of church establishment and the urban systems available to accomplish the goal. Therefore, the incorporation of social media and mass media becomes important in any plan to influence the city. Advertising through available means on bus, trains, radio, television, newspapers, billboards, and subway lines will also help impact the city.

Campaigns aimed at the masses, as well as smaller evangelistic meetings aimed at the classes need not be overlooked. The principle of impact is important if the city is to be made aware of what the mission team has to offer in the name of Jesus Christ.

3. *Study Groups.* Another principle in planning a comprehensive evangelistic outreach is the use of small Bible study groups. The church cannot be effective by limiting her energies to inviting people in and by influencing the city through mass media. The church also has the responsibility to act as leaven within the community. Churches of Christ have been latecomers in recognizing this principle.

The assembly of the entire church body is crucial, but just as important is what happens day to day in smaller meetings, across tables, and by social media. In order to build a church that is in touch with people's needs, it is vital to penetrate the city through home Bible studies and home friendship circles.

Step Three: Do the Homework

7. Train Elders, Deacons, Evangelists, and Teachers

To establish Ephesians 4 congregations, Great Cities works to train elders, deacons, evangelists, and teachers. When the congregation reaches a level of spiritual maturity that leads to the confirmation of believers gifted by God to serve in these roles, the goal of an established church is in sight.

On March 25, 1973, the team in Sao Paulo appointed national leaders. Ellis Long describes the event:

> Precisely six years and forty-six days after the present 225-active member congregation began at Avenue Ninth of July, two elders, one evangelist, and 10 deacons were ordained in a public service witnessed by 270 Christians from 5 congregations in Sao Paulo.

Always aspiring to the Sao Paulo team's goal of raising national leaders, Great Cities teaches new mission teams to practice a multilevel approach to obtain national leaders. New mission teams are to train national leaders at three levels:

First principles. The apostle Simon Peter tells his readers that after they have accepted God's cleansing power through the gift of Jesus, they must cultivate goodness and begin to grow in the knowledge of Jesus (2 Peter 1:5). The author of Hebrews speaks of the need to begin with elementary principles prior to receiving solid spiritual food (Hebrews 5:12–14). A new convert may need one to two years to work through elementary issues of Christian living and growth.

Mature teaching. After a new convert learns to live in the light of Jesus, a deeper level of teaching helps each Christian grow in spiritual knowledge and maturity. At this level, foundational biblical doctrines are studied. Entire books of the Bible are studied. Skills for sharing one's faith grow. Classes offered in multiple formats of a night school, during lunch hour, and other daytime slots can aid in spiritual growth. Intensive studies can be offered on selected weekends and holidays.

At this level, different types of church leaders emerge. Those gifted for teaching, serving, and leading begin to stand out. It becomes apparent who has the gifts of an evangelist. These developmental classes lead into the third level: training for specific tasks within the church.

Specific training. This area is vital to training national leaders. To stop short of specific training leaves the church without elders, deacons, evangelists, and teachers. Specific training modules can also be offered in multiple time formats. Depending on the situation, consideration can be given to a full-time study arrangement lasting from six months to three years. On-the-job training is an important concept at this level of training national leaders. Christians cannot train to become elders, deacons, teachers, and evangelists, but rather potential elders, deacons, teachers, and evangelists train acquiring skills to fulfill their roles.

8. Minister to the Poor

The eighth point of the strategy is to minister to the poor. God loves the poor, and poverty is an increasing condition in the big cities.

A cursory scanning of the word *poor* in a biblical concordance calls attention to God's concern for the poor. From His admonition to the children of Israel that "there need be no poor people among you" (Deuteronomy 15:4), to Paul's plea with the church in Galatia that they might "continue to remember the poor," (Galatians 2:10), God is touched with the plight of the destitute.

The parable Jesus told about the rich man and Lazarus (Luke 16:19–31) teaches the lesson of the obligation Christians have to care for the poor. A validation stamp of Christlike nature is the degree to which the church ministers to the poor.

Step Three: Do the Homework

Ministry to the poor is not the primary goal of the new mission team. Not even Jesus eradicated poverty as He pursued His primary mission on earth while purposefully moving toward the cross. It is conceivable that a mission team could go to a foreign country, minister to the poor, and fail to establish a church. The ultimate goal is to bring lost people into contact with the blood of Jesus and to unite the new believers together in an established church near the heart of the city.

Along the way to reaching this goal, the poor will be served. With each step toward the established church, the poor receive attention. As the church grows numerically and financially, it will increase in resources to provide loving concern for the poor. James, the brother of the Lord, sees ministry to the poor as validation of faith (James 2:14–17). Long after the missionary personnel leave an established church, the strong national Ephesians 4 congregation can continue ministry among the poor.

Building Block 6: Growing in Christ

It is good to remember that most missionary teams are composed of young people who have yet to walk with the Lord for multiple decades. They obeyed Jesus and now trust Him with the future. Their hearts and motives are pure. Committed to serving God in an unfamiliar culture with a different language, most are still learning to make their beds and be responsible for being on their own. After all, it has not been long since they left their bedroom in their parents' house in the care of a younger sibling.

Spiritual development does not magically appear upon emerging from baptismal waters. It is a process. A contemporary buzzword is the importance of becoming a "self-feeder." Because of the distance and the remoteness of the missionary task, sustenance is vital for the long and sometimes lonely haul in a foreign city.

This being an important training block, the Great Cities ministry emphasizes prayer and learning to trust God. Classes devoted to formation of the spiritual disciplines of prayer, fasting, reflecting, worship, solitude, and Scripture reading are at the heart of the training. Each missionary candidate teams up with a godly mentor for the duration of the internship. In addition to classroom instruction, there is structured time for participation and practice vital to creating daily spiritual discipline.

Building Block 7: Researching the City

In preparing for the research trip, the team in training receives orientation about the targeted nation and a daily schedule for the two-week trip. In today's world, resources are abundant on the Internet in both English and the host language.

Prior to the team trip, members of the Great Cities staff have visited the city. The preliminary visit by staff members allows for an initial familiarity with city resources vital to a successful team research trip. They familiarize themselves with hotels, schools, medical facilities, merchants, interesting aspects of the cities' culture and history, and the religious scene.

The staff investigative team is conscious of doing everything possible to make the team research trip the best it can be. We want the team to experience the twofold objective of falling in love with their prospective city and of researching pertinent information for the initial design of the team strategy document.

During the six-month team internship with Great Cities Missions, each new team designs and compiles a written strategy that will guide the work from beginning to end. It is the idea of planning with the end in mind. The strategy document is an attempt to envision the steps and resources needed to keep the team together, to do the best possible job of relating to the city, keep each family whole for the entire journey, leave an established church, and successfully reenter the home culture. The document serves more as a compass than a book of law. It is extremely useful in keeping the missionar-

Step Three: Do the Homework

ies and the supporting churches on the same page working toward a mutual goal. The research trip will influence the strategy document.

The team research trip keeps the goal of urban church establishment in focus. During the trip, each missionary candidate begins to conceptualize the different developmental stages through which the mission church must pass in order to reach the goal of the established church. Each research trip includes visits with Great Cities' teams who have arrived in previous years. These teams are at different phases on the continuum from arrival on the field to inauguration of the work to those obtaining permanent property to the established church operating within the model of Ephesians 4:11–16.

One week of the survey trip is on location in the chosen city. We guide the team through structured research to determine the cost and location of housing, office space, settlement, language schools, transportation systems, churches, healthcare, recreation, and schooling.

While in the target city, each team investigates six major categories.

Cost of living and prospective housing. To get a sense of realistic cost of living and prospective locations to initiate the team's work, the team sees housing in different sections of the city. The first step is to purchase a map and hire a driver to survey the city's middle-class neighborhoods. Real estate agents show the team examples of homes with cost estimates and appropriate legal expectations for assuming contracts. The team will want to know the availability and the expense of childcare and housekeeping assistance in the area.

Resources for daily living. Second, we investigate the resources for daily living. They will look into the availability and prices of schools, instructors, and resources for language learning. They visit shopping centers, supermarkets, furniture outlets, and variety stores. They determine the availability, cost, and documentation required to obtain telephone service. They consider the cost of different automobiles and the price of insurance.

Healthcare. In a world of expensive healthcare, the staff and team are interested in the cost and the availability of health insurance. We want the team to visit hospitals, clinics, and maternity wards. It's important to determine the availability of dentists, physicians, and mental health practitioners. It is also of interest to check the availability of expatriates in the city who might become a resource for emotional support while living abroad. Often it is nice to have a friend who is on the outside of the daily demands of teamwork to serve as a valve of emotional release.

Recreation. Next we check the availability of recreational opportunities at health and sports facilities. A part of staying whole as a missionary is to observe Sabbath rest by getting away from the daily routine and demands of the workload. Another outlet is to learn the availability of museums, theaters, orchestras, cinemas, and libraries. For some it is good to know the location and offerings of tourist sights, good restaurants, and major bookstores. The wise missionary will enjoy taking advantage of these.

Local religion. Information is always your friend. The staff and team will peruse the telephone book for the addresses of city churches and religious entities. By plotting their locations on a city map, they can devise a strategy for the city. I like to hire a driver and spend an entire day viewing churches and talking with as many people as possible regarding the city's current religious scene, taking special note of their locations and worship and educational facilities. Are there similarities and differences in how they relate to the culture? Often, those who administer Bible societies and religious bookstores are helpful.

Critical strategy factors. Next we observe and note critical factors for designing a church planting strategy. We observe the transportation system of the urban landscape—location of exchange terminals, bus routes, taxis, trains, subways, and major avenues. Find McDonalds. Determine the major areas of foot traffic. Identify newspapers, radio stations, and TV stations that target the city. How do they structure the prices for their ser-

Step Three: Do the Homework

vices? Study unique characteristics of the city that will need consideration in establishing the church. Determine the price and availability of office space. Collect as much information as possible about the city, including items that can be found in a phone book but not on the Internet.

Neither supporters nor team participants should ever think of the research trip in terms of a perk, a tour, a vacation, or anything less than a vital component in planting a church to influence the city for all eternity with God's saving grace.

The Bottom Line

Great Cities Missions has one main goal: working through the elders of the Central Church of Christ in Amarillo, Texas, to establish a biblically organized, functional church as described in Ephesians 4:11–16 in the world's largest Latin cities.

The Ephesians 4 objective can best be reached in the great Portuguese- and Spanish-speaking cities by going as a team with (1) a clear goal, (2) a primary avenue location, (3) an aim for at least a three-hundred-member church, (4) a plan to build around a nucleus of middle-class families, (5) the intent to secure a permanent church building attractive to all classes of people, (6) a plan of comprehensive evangelistic outreach, (7) intentional training of elders, deacons, evangelists, and teachers, and (8) a heart to minister to the poor.

To reach this objective, we must train expecting to plant churches of eternal significance. For the follower of Jesus called to plant a church in an unfamiliar culture, it becomes necessary to prepare in fundraising, language acquisition, culture and history, team missions, spiritual sustenance, targeted research, and strategy for leaving an established church when the mission is accomplished.

12

STEP FOUR: CARE WITH PASSION

Church planting falls into the category of high-stress assignments. Those who accept the assignment undergo rigorous preparation. While still Stateside, the decision to go has launched the family into unknown realms foreign to their reality. For two years prior to departure, with a growing dependence upon God, each family faces the stressful tasks of fundraising and training.

Then upon arrival in their foreign home, everything is new and different. They face years of stress as they conquer a new culture, a new language, and a new climate. Each new arrival confronts the stress of leaving extended family in their home country. New missionaries are under stress to meet communication expectations from other team members and financial supporters.

New stresses appear as new arrivals learn to communicate the message of Jesus across language and cultural barriers. Church establishment is an unfamiliar assignment. Most have no experience. Church planting doesn't always register success on the charts. Even a strategy document does not show barriers and detours in the road. The result is numerous unknowns and a lot of wear and tear over the life of a foreign mission.

At the end of the assignment, be it five years or thirty-five years, reentry into the home culture creates high stress when the family returns to a dramatically changed and unfamiliar homeland.

I love those who have the guts and the faith to take on the impossible. The difficulty of the assignment cannot be overstated. Our entire staff at Great Cities cares passionately for every father, mother, and child who serves on a team. We are committed to providing care at every stage of the missionary cycle, from Stateside recruitment, through fundraising, training, and on-field settlement, through the entire church establishment process, and to reentry into the home culture. As a staff, we commit to passionate growth in our capacity to provide quality missionary family care.

Stateside

Care begins Stateside with attention to relationship. Foundational to a successful ministry of care is to be present and approachable. From recruitment, through the attainment of funds, training, and departure, we commit to be present to teach, encourage, and dispel doubt.

Great Cities is building an aggressive ministry of missionary care as we form a partnership with the entire mission team, the supporting churches, the families who send out their loved ones, and the national church to be established.

Prayer

Prayer plays a role in the selection of each city to receive a church planting team. Missionary care begins, continues, and ends with prayer. It is vital during recruitment and formation. During the Dallas internship, each team member meets to pray with staff and team members. Prayer partners and prayer guides encourage others to pray for the missionaries. And the staff meets weekly to pray for all of the missionaries, the teams, and their unique needs.

Step Four: Care with Passion

Team-Specific Workshops

A series of workshops focuses on family, friends, and supporting churches. The first workshop is the Friends and Family Workshop, led by an experienced missionary couple and members of the Great Cities staff. They share insights into the team's strategy, its chosen city, and the culture in which it will be living. This care step helps prepare parents, friends, and family. The goal is to communicate our passionate commitment to supporting and caring for their loved ones.

A second workshop is an annual Team and Sponsoring Church Workshop to bring together representatives from sponsoring churches and mission teams. This workshop takes place before the team leaves for the field and continues annually throughout the time the team is on the field. These workshops help keep the team and sponsors working together through each stage of church establishment.

Team Send-off

Each team has a send-off where family, sponsoring churches, and staff from Great Cities meet to pray for them on the day of their departure. Many family members escort the team members and a mountain of suitcases to the airport. It is an emotional moment, a time of great pride, great anticipation, and a tinge of fear of the unknown, but no regrets. Commitment to the mission is palpable.

Crisis Care

Each missionary departs with an "On-field Emergency Packet." This packet contains information for meeting a family emergency or a crisis within the host country. Members of the Great Cities staff attend numerous crisis care briefings and workshops with experts in foreign security. Prior to departure, the team works page by page through the emergency handbook, filling out appropriate papers for family, churches, and Great Cities, in the event of a crisis. The team departs the States with an emergency plan and specific steps for implementation in the event of death, kidnapping, a terrorist attack, or other tragic crisis.

Crisis Care in Action

With the 9/11 terrorist attacks, we experienced a wakeup call to have an on-field crisis care plan. After four decades of ministry in South America, the various governments continue to be more than gracious in allowing Great Cities teams to receive visas and live as residents of South American cities.

The intent of relating the following crisis is not to belittle the nations that have been good to us. Rather, the purpose is to illustrate the need to stand ready for crisis intervention and care in a fallen world. Therefore, I will take the liberty to change names and places of the following event.

Patricia was a bright fifteen-year-old who found Jesus through the church and the mission team. She struck up a special friendship with Sandra, a young American missionary. They both loved the Lord and His church. Tragedy struck one evening when Patricia was on her way to Sandra's apartment. The beautiful young girl was raped, murdered, and disposed of like trash.

The police immediately began to focus their investigation on her friend Sandra and the church. The police could not have been more wrong. There were no charges filed, but they unendingly harassed Sandra. She was being wrongfully accused; the police were not listening and it seemed she would become a scapegoat for the murder.

We consulted with local lawyers and received counsel that Sandra had every right to leave the country. We immediately devised a plan to transport her at night from her city to an international airport. She was safely in the air before the police realized she was gone.

Step Four: Care with Passion

The following morning, Sandra was front-page news as police sought her return and arrest. The investigation then turned to the missionary team and to members of the local church, resulting in court summons for DNA testing. Fear of a corrupt police department reigned throughout the church.

After getting Sandra out of the country, Great Cities put together a five-member response team to go to the city to help the missionaries and the churches deal with fear, anger, legal problems, media relations, and grief over Patricia's death.

Over ensuing weeks, all parties communicated through an encrypted e-mail service. From our on-site response-team member dealing with legal needs and media relations, we learned that the police department and the court judges were known as the most corrupt in the nation. We also learned the murder suspect was most likely the son of a high-profile citizen, thus the need to divert the investigation toward the church. The murder was never solved.

Following legal advice, the quick intervention of our staff spared Sandra from what could have been years of wrongful imprisonment. The church faced the crisis together, and the missionary families remained on the field.

From that experience, a written crisis-intervention policy emerged with specific emergency steps that carefully explain to missionary teams and their supporters how each party should proceed in the event of emergency.

On the Field

Built upon the Stateside relationship, the major—and perhaps the most critical—elements of missionary care happen on the field in the selected team city. Care begins with the arrival and settlement of the new missionary team.

Make Your Vision Go Viral

Missionary Team Settlement

Each missionary family has made a costly commitment that has resulted in years of hard work and expense. Local Stateside churches have committed time and money to help the mission team get ready for departure.

The next important step to secure the investment of time, cost, and effort is to ensure that the team settles well into its adopted city. Great Cities Missions provides experienced personnel to settle the missionary team into the city. Two couples accompany the team to their new city. Everyone is housed in a modern, centrally located hotel to begin the two-week settlement process. From early morning to late evening, the team led by the two Great Cities couples works to accomplish the following:

- Purchase telephones.
- Register each team member with the federal police and the Department of Internal Revenue.
- Obtain official translations of all passports into Portuguese or Spanish.
- Open bank accounts for families and the church.
- Rent a post office box.
- Obtain driver's licenses for each team member.
- Work with team members to select, rent, and cosign legal contracts for all apartments.
- Work with team members to purchase appliances and furniture.
- Work with team members to purchase cars.
- Purchase car insurance.
- Purchase or define medical/hospital coverage.
- Locate a family doctor to provide medical and hospital care.
- Retrieve baggage from customs officials.
- Contract language teachers.
- Provide counsel and reassurance during the first days of settlement and in the weeks to follow.

Step Four: Care with Passion

The settlement process pays huge dividends. The two-week settlement work by the Great Cities staff leaves team members poised to begin their cultural adaptation freed from the minutia of settlement so they can continue to concentrate on language study for the first year. This is one more step to ensuring the long-range success and productivity of the team.

Daily Care and Sustenance

A team of missionaries needs nourishment as individuals and as a collective group to accomplish the assigned task. Like the human body, the team does not always function at peak performance. There are times when it may need a transplant of new personnel. There are times when workers need outside consultation to help solve a problem that blocks the missionaries from the final objective of church establishment.

There are times when the group needs encouragement and emotional support. At other times, their concern is for spiritual and intellectual stimulation. At Great Cities, sustaining has two principal concerns.

First, there is the concern for the spiritual, emotional, and physical well-being of the missionary personnel.

Second is the concern to accomplish the task of the established church with at least 300 members on a recognizable avenue. The function of missionary care is an attempt to address both concerns.

On-field missionary care is as vast and complex as the number of diverse individuals who compose all missionary teams. Each missionary will need a mentor and coach to facilitate caring for multiple families on multiple teams—an extremely complex issue.

Mentor

I make a distinction between a mentor and a coach. Mentors help me grow; coaches help me gain expertise. At the very start of Stateside training in the sixth-month internship at Great Cities, each candidate receives orientation on the importance of a mentor. In the beginning, individuals from the Great Cities staff serve as mentors or they shoulder-tap selective volunteers from the Dallas area.

With current technology, that mentor may continue once a church planter arrives on the field, or the missionary may transition to a new mentor. A mentor helps keep life focused and in balance. From family to team members to new Christians to neighbors and social contacts in the community, there are always multiple relationships to balance. Through focus on Scripture, extracurricular reading, and stimulating discussion, as iron sharpens iron, a good mentor can aid in soul growth.

In 2008, staff member Georgia Freitas designed the Continent Care Connection to enhance the role of mentoring care. The first year was an experiment designed for missionary women. The connection idea encompasses the goal of connecting to God, to other missionary women, and to Care staff.

Georgia began to select trained counselors, former missionary women, and experienced women leaders in the church. This staff was diverse yet rich with experience and wisdom. The aim of the entire experience was to mentor missionary women serving across the continent of South America. Prayerfully, each member of the Great Cities team of twelve was aligned with four missionary women. Each mentoring group agreed to a pact of confidentiality.

The missionary women relished the opportunity to worship and pray together in the English language, not easy to do when working in Portuguese or Spanish. On a beautiful, solitary Brazilian beach, the team designed alone time for women to reflect, pray, and read Scripture.

The twelve Great Cities mentors were there to serve. They carried the baggage of each guest from the bus to the hotel room. Every evening, the guests found presents on their pillows. The vocabulary of the week was one

Step Four: Care with Passion

of encouragement. On the final night, a banquet honored the missionary women. The week was infused with fun and recreation. Each mentor group worked to prepare a presentation in the banquet talent show.

Since missionaries are sometimes perceived—falsely so—to "have it together" as "great servants of God," the team wondered if counseling slots would fill. To the amazement of the twelve women, there was not an empty counseling spot. Doubts, pain, and problems flowed freely. It was as if missionary women were human, facing the same daily challenges as their Stateside counterparts, only they were doing so in an adopted culture through an acquired language without an adequate support network. Many young missionaries shoulder responsibilities carried only by older women in Stateside churches.

The Continent Care Connection received the highest ratings of anything we had ever attempted. For many missionary women it was a life changer, and they pleaded for a repeat of the session the following year. The missionary women began to ask us to provide the same experience for their husbands. So after two years of ministry to the women, the men's Care Connection was offered. Several of the women took the initiative to enroll their husbands.

We have repeated the Continent Care Connection for the past five consecutive years. Sessions for missionary men offered on alternate years see the same positive results. Feedback tells us we are enriching and saving marriages and mentoring in areas of spiritual growth and in parenting. Many of the mentoring relationships continue between the Great Cities mentoring team and missionaries throughout South America, which gives me great pride.

Coach

In the sports world, a coach's important role is obvious. Many in the business world now see the value of a coach. Likewise, churches are beginning to see the merit of expert insight to reach kingdom objectives. Critics may question the validity and wisdom of applying business principles to the church, but I would argue that truth is truth, and God honors truth wherever it's found. Since God is Truth, I would also argue that God and His Holy Spirit use truth as They seek to draw people's hearts to the gift of Jesus' death and resurrection.

The coach's role differs from the mentor's role. Mentors help with a person's growth; coaches help people grow expertise. Some coaching work is done Stateside, but the coach assists most after the team is on the field. In the mission enterprise, the ideal situation for a coach's productivity is regular visits to the teams. It is important to be current. If the Great Cities ministry is to sustain mission teams in South America, the coaches need on-site information. It's vital to understand obstructions faced by mission teams and family units. The coach can often help team members identify strategies to work around barricades blocking progress.

It bears repeating that it is no easy task to move into a foreign country without being a native speaker of its language or without being at home in its culture. The situation is even more complicated by the assignment of church establishment on a main avenue in the city. To complicate the task even more is the fact that mission teams are composed of trained but inexperienced personnel. The missionaries themselves have not started a church in their homeland and have never before established a church on foreign soil. In this setting, many problems and questions arise. From the beginning of Great Cities, coaches have attempted to think in terms of solutions.

The coach has the advantage of personal experience in establishing a foreign church. With each team that arrives on the field and successfully moves toward the goal of the established church, additional experience is gained for the coach to pass on to the next team.

Based on this experience, we see where input, resources, and counsel provided to teams and their supporting churches have been vital to the

Step Four: Care with Passion

project's success. At key junctures, it is the problem-solving aspect of coaching that is the principal ingredient in keeping the project moving toward the goal of urban church establishment.

On-Field Visits

Great Cities' care ministry also encompasses on-field visits. In 2004, Great Cities launched a series of systematic visits to missionary teams. North American teams are visited eight months after arrival on the field, again at eighteen months, and at the three-year point.

Regularly scheduled visits to teams on the field are key to better missionary care and team relationships and are vital to the coach's ability to aid team members in planting larger and healthier congregations.

The first on-field visit at eight months is to make sure that all missionary personnel are doing well and coming out of culture shock. Early identification of team or individual conflicts is vital. If conflicts emerge, then solutions will be proposed and progress toward the implementation of these solutions will be monitored. Should conflict continue, a date is set for a conflict-resolution workshop.

On the first visit, the coach helps the team secure an adequate, well-located meeting place in which to begin its work. Good beginnings help assure good results. The coach serves as a strategy consultant to assist the team in pointing the work in a good direction. A mistake in selecting the location of the beginning church can haunt the work for years.

The second on-field visit takes place at eighteen months. Remember that the coach strives for good strategic beginnings. At this point, team members usually need encouragement and guidance to stay on task. It is important to reaffirm strategic progress and verify that both church plant and evangelism are on target. Once again, team relationships are evaluated and a strategy developed to solve potential problem areas. Should conflicts be present, a six-month plan will be developed with the team, with specific assignments and regular reports to monitor progress. Should conflicts persist without resolution, recommendations may be made for personnel changes in an effort to resolve ongoing difficulties.

The third visit takes place at the three-year mark. At this point, all team members have returned from their first home furlough, should have culture shock behind them, and are starting to function in the new language and culture. Once again, the coach will evaluate strategy progress.

Each family makes a five-year, open-ended commitment to the field when they sign on to the project. At the three-year mark, one of the coach's objectives is to initiate a discussion with team members concerning long-range time commitments to the work and the implications these time commitments have for the team's work strategy. For youth, five years equates to eternity. But on the field, time speeds up. It is not surprising at the three-year mark to see a team yet to face the implications of their five-year commitment being halfway over.

The coach reminds the team of two realities. First, the job is not finished. Second, in all likelihood, some of the team members will be returning home. Those who stayed five years honored their commitment. Some families will be at peace to remain with the work for the near future. At the five-year mark, a congregation of new believers exists to help move the church forward. Like any five-year-old, they still need guidance to grow into a healthy body.

The first family's return home is emotional for the entire team. It is helpful to face this traumatic event two years before it takes place. To face eventual departures openly helps prepare both the church and the mission team for continued progress. It is a great time to evaluate the infant church's growth and to begin a plan to acquire a permanent meeting place. The coach will counsel the team for many months through the property acquisition.

Step Four: Care with Passion

Annual South American Missionary Conference

A great legacy of the Sao Paulo missionaries is the annual missionary conference. I attended my first conference in the city of Anapolis in January 1970. The missionary conference has evolved into another component of Great Cities' missionary care program. A couple from our staff attends the annual missionary conference because it is an opportune time to be available for counseling, encouragement, problem solving, and face-to-face time with individual missionaries. Held in Brazil, the conference serves missionary families from all over South America.

Reentry

Caring with passion includes the entire cycle of the missionary experience, from recruiting to reentry. Teams learn about reentry prior to field departure. However, at the beginning of preparation, missionary candidates lack the experience to decode classroom instruction. Not everything makes sense in the new missionary's mind—concepts can be new and vague.

Anticipating reentry, Great Cities care experts begin to provide information and resources to the missionary family a year in advance. Upon return, each family receives a book to assist with the many reentry challenges each will face.

The staff intercedes with the families' sponsoring churches and supporters to obtain proper reentry support. Since it is difficult to understand the cost and needs of an unfamiliar experience, many churches and individuals will help with the return when specifics are clarified.

Reentry continues to evolve. I hope to see the time when it is routine for trained staff to travel to the field to walk every missionary family through—to an even greater degree than now—the entire reentry process.

We have made huge strides in the reentry process over the past twenty-five years. Those of us who returned to our homeland in earlier years without guidance or emotional and financial support stand amazed at the progress to date.

It's imperative that Great Cities be as methodical in missionary care as in recruiting and training. The care of missionaries is indispensable. Let us support them as they go about the important task of planting churches among the urban Portuguese- and Spanish-speaking people in the great cities of the Latin world.

13

STEP FIVE: BUILD WITH ZEAL

For the first fifteen years of Great Cities, the Central Church of Christ in Amarillo, Texas, and the Golf Course Road Church of Christ in Midland, Texas, funded the ministry. At the fifteen-year mark, Golf Course Road completed its commitment, and Central was in a temporary financial downturn due to the national recession. Dr. Ellis Long was transitioning from the leadership of the Great Cities work.

Three years before, Bob Waldron joined Great Cities. Former missionaries to Guatemala, Bob and Gina, upon their return, served on the faculty of the Bear Valley Bible Institute in Denver. Bob and Gina worked ten years with the Great Cities ministry.

Since the Midland church was underwriting my family and the Waldrons, in June 1991 Bob and I faced facts—we had no income.

The first order of business was to stay in business. We could no longer remain in the College of Biblical Studies at Abilene Christian University, since we would begin to compete with the same base of donors. We immediately went to the school president and the deans to thank them for housing the ministry the previous fifteen years.

The next step was to move to a downtown office and organize as a 501(c)3 nonprofit entity with the Internal Revenue Service. That would make it possible to receive tax-free grants and gifts. Immediately, the search for funding began.

The need for a full-time fund-raiser was obvious. We contracted Dr. Ernest Clevenger, friend and former president of Faulkner University, as the first of three development consultants. My inexperience was the only thing greater than our need. From the first, Dr. Clevenger began to teach us how to raise funds and build a development program. To my dismay, I learned that a consultant is not the same as a fund-raiser. I was hoping fund-raising would be someone else's job. I soon discovered it is the consultant's job to counsel and teach—not to raise funds. Though Dr. Clevenger did bring major funding to the table, his greatest contributions were teaching us fund-raising skills and providing the orientation work to help build a board of trustees. He also gave direction for creating our articles of incorporation and bylaws to become a nonprofit entity under the auspices of the Central Church of Christ in Amarillo.

Our second consultant was James Ravanelli with Abilene's Ravanelli and Associates Fund Raising Counsel. Over many years, Jim helped increase income. Among Jim's many contributions to the ministry, two stand out. First, he led us to stop thinking like missionaries with working funds and begin to think as a nonprofit entity with a formal budget. That is most likely obvious to you, but to missionaries accustomed to controlling personal work funds, that was a revelation. A second major gift Jim offered was his expertise in walking us through a capital campaign to construct the church building in Curitiba.

My third consultant was Dr. Terry Johnson, former president of Oklahoma Christian University. Dr. Johnson served for thirty-two years as an administrator of Oklahoma Christian, including twenty-one years as president and five years as chancellor.

From his broad and deep experience as a university president, Dr. Johnson showed us how to create diverse streams of income to fund the min-

Step Five: Build with Zeal

istry. He taught the value of spending time in "white board" sessions to identify and quantify potential donors. He showed great skill as he worked with me to identify and recruit high-value trustees. Each trustee is selected for the value he or she can bring to the table to complete the mission. I learned to expect trustees to participate with finances. I also learned there is a wealth of gifts needed around the table having nothing to do with money. Terry was a great mentor through his willingness to spend three to five days each month with me on the road to make calls on friends and donors. Like the previous consultants, funds continued to increase under his leadership.

Grant Boone worked with Great Cities as director of development from February 2003 through December 2006. Under Grant's watch, the Nashville donor base increased, major annual donors joined us, and the ministry's national presence increased. As a former broadcaster for the Golf Channel Network, Grant used his God-given skill to articulate the mission. The following year the ministry moved to Dallas, while Grant remained in Abilene, and Kent Allen accepted the director of development role for fifteen months. Kent raised much-needed funding, making the transition possible. Terry Johnson was crucial to both men joining the development effort.

Contracting the right consultant is some of the best money any nonprofit entity can spend. I was blessed to work with three of the best. Each of the three consultants raised the level of our game.

Constant Coffee Contact

After I learned that development consultants do not raise money, Dr. Ellis Long shared with me a tip he learned from Abilene Christian University president, Dr. Bill Teague. The idea was to put together an artist portfolio to tell the Great Cities story and share its financial need. Remember once again, this was prior to Google and the Internet.

Through the years, I made hundreds of presentations over breakfast, coffee, lunch, and dinner. I wore out numerous cars and fake-leather portfolios stained by coffee and ketchup. Hand-to-mouth fund-raising kept our doors open with daily manna.

Competing Lighthouses

One lesson I learned early on is that lighthouses do, in fact, compete with each other. Lighthouses compete for personnel. More often than not, lighthouses compete for the same pool of resources. Funding is not equal from lighthouse to lighthouse. I find this to be another of the areas when I do my best to acquire resources and trust God with the results. Lighthouses often supplement each another, but they do compete.

Building a Granite Mountain with Manna

From day one, funding was a source of anxiety. It was only during the seven years when I was part of the annual budget of the Midland Golf Course Road church, with a free office on the campus of Abilene Christian University, that funding was not an overwhelming concern. For the other twenty-three years, as the ministry grew, funding was always a challenge.

Like the Israelites in the wilderness, God always provided manna for the day, and the doors remained open. There were times when I feared the manna would stop, but upon arrival of manna, my trust in God increased.

When Dr. Terry Johnson began to serve as development consultant in 2002, I heard for the first time his concept of the granite mountain. The goal was to build long-term, solid support from multiple sources into the granite mountain. The granite mountain did not have to be rebuilt each year, since it was composed of long-term committed funds. With the granite mountain becoming part of the daily manna, growth began to occur.

God's Mission

On the staff, wanting to be fully open to cooperating with God in His mission, we often remind each other that it is God's mission, not our own. That

Step Five: Build with Zeal

means when parts of the mission falter, the failure is ours, Satan is creating havoc, or, for reasons we may not understand, God may close a door.

To help discern which of the three is taking place, prayer is a constant, in and out of the conference room. Everything gets a prayer bath. The Great Cities staff is a praying staff—we pray around the conference table, in each other's offices, on the road, and on our own. The truth is though, we do not pray enough. Prayer is like living; it takes a lifetime to begin to unwrap its mysteries and power. As our trust in God grows, our prayer life increases.

Loving the Whole Church

Building a nonprofit ministry has the blessing of difficulty. It cannot be accomplished alone. Nor can it be attained by a small segment of the church.

In the States, we live under the Constitution of the United States of America. I can only assume its writers were in agreement with the final copy. Today, over two hundred years removed from the authors, our nation's vibrancy is closely tied to the vigorous debate of the original intent of justice, free speech, free press, the right to bear arms, the power of the federal government, states' rights, and the promotion of the general welfare of the people.

In the church, Scripture is our holy constitution. About fifteen minutes of conversation with a fellow believer should be enough to understand that no two people are mirror interpreters of Scripture. The apostle Paul loved the Philippian church and commended them for many Christlike attributes. He also loved the Corinthian church, where there was not much to commend. Both were within Paul's circle of fellowship.

I am still learning to love the whole church. I am not there yet, but I am making progress. I do know that to "proclaim Jesus by planting churches in the great cities of the Latin world," we cannot let any faction of the church set the agenda. I must learn to love the whole church and welcome to the table those who will join us to take the Jesus of Scripture to a lost world.

Make Your Vision Go Viral

Congregational Oversight

When we began to build the financial foundation under the Great Cities ministry in June 1991, I knew we would need the Central Church of Christ in Amarillo to continue in its original role of guidance and oversight. At the time money was scarce, yet there was an Amarillo core committed to the future of the Great Cities project. Emerging leaders were open to the idea of Central's continued oversight role, based on their respect for and experience with the older leaders in the church. There were those who were not opposed, but could see the difficulty in one church funding and continuing to oversee what could morph into an all-consuming expense and never-ending detail.

Over the next five years, the ministry continued under the Central church with extra budgetary funding from Central members and their friends and families. The breakthrough to reconnect with the budget and leadership of the Central church came one day over lunch with Central's elder Shelby Stapleton. Expressing his managerial-operations type personality, he stated the problem: "The ministry has grown to the point that when people stop me in the hall and ask a question about Great Cities, I do not know what to tell them." I countered with the idea of establishing a board of trustees, with representation from those of Central's eldership who were active in the project. That way, his response could be, "I do not have a clue, but if you will talk with Al, Bill, Leon, or Warlick, they can answer your question." Fifteen years later, the board of trustees continues to be a great solution, with the Amarillo Central church again playing a strong financial role in the project.

Loving the Trustees

No one could enjoy working with trustees more than I do. It is one of the greatest rewards of the executive director's role. The key is careful selection of the trustees. I scout for godly men and women with diverse expertise,

STEP FIVE: BUILD WITH ZEAL

financial resources, and likable personalities. Over coffee, meals, and meetings we become committed friends. I want the trustees to be generous, smart, willing to express strong opinions, and capable of the push and push-back that is necessary to reach good decisions. I love the trustees for who they are, and I continue to love and appreciate each one long after service as a trustee ends.

Taking Risks

Anyone attempting to lead a church planting ministry should be a man or woman of God. God followers ought to be the ones who are most prone to take risks. When we attempt to join God in His mission, we can be courageous risk takers. I'm not talking about being stupid. Rather, there are times when our best intuition and counsel tells us we need to make a decision beyond our foreseeable resources. It is time to trust God for a result that seems consistent with His nature and His will. As the one in charge, I had no choice but to accept risk to get from broke to viable progress.

At times I met payroll with zero-interest credit card loans. I took some heat for such action, but it was a calculated risk I have never regretted. When your back is against the wall, you act with whatever resources are available.

At this writing, Great Cities has a paid staff of fourteen. Not one of the fourteen was hired with a salary in sight. In each case, there was a job to be done, a risk to be taken. And there are times when risks taken on staff do not work out. It comes with the job.

Each team-recruiting project comes with risk. Some recruiting projects did not succeed; others exceeded beyond expectation. I have always kept a sign on my bookshelf and one on my computer screen. They read simply: Take Risks.

Make Your Vision Go Viral

Being Authentic

Authenticity and transparency are important in building a nonprofit entity. The entity can be built only on trust. Donors can spot insincerity and airs at once. Even if a lack of authenticity is slow to spot, over time it will surface. Being who I am wired to be puts me at total ease when visiting with potential donors, no matter how important their job or position might be. God has used authenticity to rebuild our financial base. Donors must trust the leader of the entity if they are to participate.

Learning from *All* Great Leaders

While building with zeal, I have realized the valuable lesson that it is possible to learn from all great leaders. Through the years, I have become a fanatic connoisseur of books, articles, and lectures across the spectrum of world leaders in business, government, nonprofit management, fundraising, theology, education, and world missions. It saddens me to see leaders who never get beyond the limited circle of their self-created small orbit.

Planned Procrastination

Another concept I use in building is what I like to call planned procrastination. I often say never do today what you can do tomorrow, or you will be wasting time. That drives overstructured people crazy. There are only so many hours in a day, and at the end of the day, the work is never complete. It becomes critical to keep the most important—not necessarily the most urgent—items at the top of my to-do list. That implies there are always items that will wait until tomorrow.

Building a Superb Staff

Unfortunately, experience is seldom a consideration in foreign missions and church planting. In Churches of Christ, church committees or elderships

Step Five: Build with Zeal

hire and supervise missionaries. Those who hire and supervise usually don't have experience with church planting in a foreign nation. Most often, even those who go to do the work don't have experience or specific training in church planting.

Experience matters. I love the statement by Stephen M. Sweatman, president and CEO of Missions Training International. He is fond of saying, "Our staff is our curriculum." At Great Cities, a staff member's training and experience must align with the task for which she or he is hired.

Hire Givers

It is important to hire givers. The nature of the assignment at Great Cities is not contained within a five-day week of eight-hour days. It is necessary to balance a busy schedule of family demands, staff demands, on-field demands, and appropriate down time. Staff members have to give graciously of their time to meet a flexible schedule that some weeks may require forty hours and other weeks may require 168 travel hours.

I also want a staff of generous people. We are a nonprofit entity whose work depends on liberal gifts from our donor base. Generous donors pay the Great Cities staff. How can we expect others to give sacrificially, living from their gifts, while not identifying with them as fellow donors?

Hire Tens and Fire Sixes

A superb staff consists of talented people. Lackluster talent produces lackluster results. Hire perfect tens and fire sixes. The work is too important and too hard to do anything less. Through the years in building the entity, I learned never to hire someone I could not fire. People are the most important asset of any organization. Jim Collins gave the corporate sector, the private sector, and the nonprofit world the vocabulary in the research project *Good to Great* to express this concept. Get the right people on the bus, the wrong people off the bus, and the right people in the right seats on the bus. It is a lesson I wish I had learned fifteen years earlier.

Be the Grease

In building a superb staff, I learned it was my job to be the grease. I want the staff to succeed so the mission will succeed. As the CEO, directions and decisions from my seat can create either ease or difficulty for the staff as they all work to complete their jobs. I am always available to help us all work from the same page and to help in any way I can to promote employee success.

Creating Identity

When Ellis and Doris Long opened the Great Cities office on the Abilene Christian University campus, it was an anomaly in Churches of Christ. As the entity grew and developed, no one knew where it fit. It became obvious over time that it did not fit in an educational institution. The university, with its broad scope of purpose, priorities, and budgetary concerns, is in business for the confirmation of degrees. Their business is not for church planting.

The scope and cost of the Great Cities project was new to churches and did not fit into congregational structure. The 1990s generated conflict around the ministry as we attempted to create an identity and legitimacy for a valid place within Churches of Christ. With the congregation at the center of the movement, no one knew where to place a church-planting mission entity on the scale of legitimacy.

As the twenty-first century began, the storms of conflict passed. The structure with the Amarillo Central church and the new nationwide board of trustees gave legitimacy to the entity.

The next vital step to the creation of identity came in the form of a marketing grant. Bill Johnson, an elder of the Amarillo church and a founding

Step Five: Build with Zeal

trustee of Great Cities, working with Berrylin Houston, a trustee of the Kathleen McGehee Trust of Jacksonville, Florida, together approached the Amarillo Central church and the Frank and Ann McGehee Trust—also of Jacksonville—seeking a one-million-dollar marketing grant to be dispersed over five years. The grant began to place Great Cities on the map, at least within Churches of Christ.

Partnering with Local Churches

While the struggle for legitimate identity decreased, the challenge became how to partner with local churches. In the first fifteen years of the ministry, with few exceptions, we fell into the role of recruiting missionary teams who would, in turn, raise the support for each individual family. The churches were hardly aware of our existence. As strategic problems emerged, we would work directly with the missionary personnel, relying on our field experience to solve problems.

Through workshops with the mission teams' supporting churches, and as our constituency became more aware of our existence, the role of Great Cities slowly became more apparent. We continued to recruit and train each team while building our expertise to play a role in team care and church-planting strategy. The churches began to recognize our specific expertise. At the same time, we attempted to communicate to the churches our total cooperation and willingness to help each congregation be successful.

Team churches filled the role of financial support for a specific family and built a prayer net and a congregational relationship with their missionary couple. Since the financial role and participatory role is unique to the local church, it oversees the missionary family and their work. In these ways, the local church performs a role we cannot fill.

The team also serves a unique role: team members serve on the ground in a foreign nation. They must learn the culture and the language to build relationships that will lead to sharing Jesus.

This model allows the three entities—Great Cities, Stateside churches, and the missionary team—to play to their strengths. It fulfills the old adage of "TEAM: Together Everyone Accomplishes More."

Cooperating Carefully

Throughout the process of building the entity, I was surprised at how often and how intense the pull of cooperation and sometimes merger became. It always seemed to me that such overtures were beneficial to the courting party and detrimental to fulfilling the Great Cities mission of "proclaiming Jesus by planting churches in the great cities of the Latin world."

Upon reflection, the Great Cities mission had clear definition from its inception. It is fortuitous that Dr. Ellis Long, with his focused and structured nature, was the first guardian of that mission. Reading through the Gospels, Acts of the Apostles, and the Epistles, it is apparent that Jesus and His apostle Paul followed well-defined missions.

Once the mission is clear, difficult decisions must be faced to avoid mission drift. Management writings are replete with examples of mission drift in the corporate world. And sadly, many churches are examples of mission drift. Nonprofit entities constantly face the devastation of mission drift as flirtation begins with funding sources that do not match the mission. To chase fads is to kill the mission.

Readers of Jim Collins will quickly identify the concept of preserving the core while stimulating progress. It is perhaps the primary concern of the executive director. I cannot overstate the importance of sticking to the core mission. In our own case, "To proclaim Jesus by planting churches in the great cities of the Latin world" is a mission grounded in the eternal yet contemporary nature of Scripture. We cannot drift from our core purpose and remain true to the inception of the entity.

At the same time, to stimulate progress toward mission accomplishment calls for constant change. By its nature, culture is in constant flux. Com-

Step Five: Build with Zeal

munication is always in a state of change. Language and cultural values change from generation to generation. In a climate of change the CEO of any nonprofit must be vigilant to keep the entity growing and progressing.

One final concept of Jim Collins that gave me vocabulary to describe my role in building with zeal and passion is the concept of clock building. Collins paints the contrast between telling a person the time as opposed to building clocks that can tell multiple people time over multiple decades. That is the joy and satisfaction of those of us who work with Great Cities Missions. When we served as missionaries, we went to Latin America and planted one congregation. By working together as a staff, we have the opportunity to work with multiple teams and see hundreds of churches planted. We take great satisfaction in building our church-planting clock.

Transitioning to Dallas

A decade into the rebuilding process, it became apparent to me that, by virtue of our location in a small town, our financial and staff growth would soon hit a glass ceiling. It also was obvious that missionaries were not in furlough contact with us due to our out-of-the-way location. We would need to relocate close to an international airport in a city with a multimillion-population base. That was not a decision I reached without major personal struggle. It would take seven years before we could pack the moving vans.

A strength the staff brings to the mission is the luxury of daily life in the presence of the mission. We live and breathe the mission twenty-four hours a day. In Abilene, we repeatedly discussed the pros and cons of moving to a different city. I assigned research projects to the staff. Reluctantly, I knew what we should do and determined to move forward.

In the beginning, the question of relocation was difficult for the trustees. To be fair, they did not have as much simmering time as the staff. It was also a difficult decision for trustees who were members of the Amarillo Central church. In their defense, Amarillo had stood by the Brazil work since 1958. If the ministry moved, their preference was to see it move to Amarillo. I saw a move to Amarillo as not answering any of the reasons for leaving Abilene. We would still be in a non-central location with a limited funding population. The growth advantage was just not there.

Discussion continued. In a meeting of the board of trustees in Glorieta, New Mexico, in October 2004, the motion passed unanimously to move the ministry to the Dallas/Fort Worth Metroplex.

Over the next twenty-four months, we faced several major issues. We were in the process of integrating five new trustees, a radio-television ministry asked us to consider a merger request, and we were trying to determine if we had the support base to launch a capital campaign. We were in dire need of filling three important staff positions; the team pipeline for recruiting, training, and care was at full capacity; and we were in the process of launching our first pilot study of using teams of national workers.

Money was tight, partially due to donor caution provoked by the major issues just cited and partially due to the 2004 presidential election year. We are not immune to the financial restraints in the years surrounding any presidential election when policy direction begins to be uncertain and potential donors hold on to their funds waiting to deal with the reality of a new president.

In October 2006, at the board of trustees meeting held in Jacksonville, Florida, the trustees moved and approved with unanimity "to move to the North Dallas target area as soon as feasible in three phases: with 'beachhead' office, short-term lease, then either build or buy—depending on what is best."

A transition committee of eight trustees, a staff member, and our development consultant, Dr. Terry Johnson, executed the move. Among the many talented trustees, Retired Army Brigadier General Jim Brickman of Norman, Oklahoma, served as chair of the Transition Committee. General Brickman, exceptionally gifted and highly trained in logistics, led the

Step Five: Build with Zeal

Transition Committee and met multiple times in Dallas over a period of six months until every detail was covered.

The office was leased in North Dallas and readied on January 1, 2007. My family moved to the Metroplex in early February to help open the Dallas office. Kent and Phyllis Allen of Edmond, Oklahoma, joined us for fifteen months as they applied their remarkable talent to the transition.

Ron Freitas took responsibility for closing the major portion of the Abilene office and moving its contents to Dallas in June. Likewise, Bryan Gibbs was a key player in moving the Abilene office, while retaining a portion of the Great Cities office in Abilene for an additional thirty-six months.

Transitioning to New Executive Leadership

Only three of us made the transition from Abilene to Dallas. Calvin and Linda Henry were already in the Metroplex. Kent Allen was hired from Edmond, Oklahoma, during the last quarter of 2006 as director of development. We went about the work of filling vacant positions to get the staff back to a functional level.

While living in Abilene, in anticipation of the move, Ken Lewis and I traveled to Brazil and Chile in April 2006 to shoulder-tap experienced people to fill anticipated vacancies on the Great Cities staff. While in Chile, we visited Kelley and Julie Grant, who had joined the Great Cities Santiago team a decade before. They were happy in the Santiago work and chose to remain for the near future. I hoped one day to turn the executive director job over to someone with Kelley's capabilities. He had been on my radar screen for a number of years.

Fifteen months after the move to North Dallas, Kent Allen returned to the call of Oklahoma Christian University in Edmond, Oklahoma. It was time to inquire of Kelley with renewed urgency.

At the time, two thoughts were dominating my mind. I was beginning to witness in various arenas people my age and older who had settled into their daily routine assignment. To me it seemed obvious that their hard work and effectiveness of previous years brought the assignment to a level they could no longer handle. The job now required higher energy levels and greater technical skills found in younger people. I believed in the mission so much that I determined I would not become the proverbial cork in the bottle, blocking the flow of the healing oil of the Spirit.

The second ever-present thought in my mind was pain. With age, the multiple exostoses I'd been diagnosed with caused painful arthritis. The chronic pain in my legs that started a decade earlier continued and made travel increasingly difficult. I no longer had the endless energy I knew throughout the first sixty years of my life. Deep within my soul, I knew it was time to begin the transition from the leadership role of executive director.

Once on the phone, Kelley listened patiently to my plea. E-mails and phone calls continued for eight weeks. Kelley agreed to attend the April meeting of the board of trustees as a guest speaker. It would provide a week for him to meet all the staff, to meet the trustees, and to set the stage for the trustees to interact with him. I shared with the executive committee my desire to begin a transition.

The board of trustees could not have shown more support or handled the consequences in a more professional manner. At the trustee meeting of October 2008, Kelley had not yet decided to leave the work in Santiago, nor had the trustees made an offer to him. Upon the request of the full board of trustees, the executive committee agreed to do a comprehensive search for a new executive director. The first step was to interview and vet Kelley. They would then make a recommendation to the entire board before proceeding to seek other candidates.

Step Five: Build with Zeal

Kelley, still not sure about leaving Chile, agreed to meet with the executive committee in January 2009. The executive committee chairman arrived early and prayed over every chair, asking God to give wisdom to the trustee that would occupy the seat. The important decision would set the direction of the ministry for the future.

I was reminded anew of the power of prayer as I witnessed all parties depending on God to act. On January 27, 2009, with all parties in agreement, the board of trustees met via conference call and unanimously approved the following resolution:

> Resolve that Kelley Grant be approved as the next executive director of Great Cities—the transition begins when Kelley Grant concludes his current mission to Chile and returns to the United States in January 2010 and Kelley assumes the executive director's position in January 2011. Furthermore, that the concept for Gary Sorrells's transition to retirement on his 66th birthday on January 2, 2013, be approved with the specific details of the transition to be developed by the executive committee with Gary Sorrells's and Kelley Grant's involvement and concurrence.

On April Fool's Day 2010, Kelley arrived at the office to prepare for his new assignment. I was pleased to see it was not a joke when he returned to the office on April 2.

For the next nine months, we met together, traveled together, and worked together on special events and fundraising. He spent time with the staff to get to know each person and the basic details of each one's assignment.

We traveled together to meet individually with each trustee to continue to build relationships that had begun in April 2008. We began the process of identifying and eventually inviting additional trustees to the board from the support network he created during eleven years of working in Santiago.

We traveled together with trustees of a foundation as we visited teams and cities in Peru and Brazil.

We worked together through the vetting, hiring-and-firing process of a potential employee—nothing at all pleasant but a valuable learning experience for the new executive director.

We walked through the process of creating a budget and a funding mechanism for the following year when Kelley would begin to lead the ministry.

We designed and implemented a plan to move Kelley into my slot with the Amarillo Central church. I wanted to do everything within my power to keep this great church on board with the ministry.

On December 31, 2010, the process of building with zeal was complete.

From my darkest hour of ministry setback in June 1991, when faced with a fifteen-year-old team-recruiting ministry and the immediate evaporation of all sources of funding; through the process of renewing the strong relation with the Amarillo Central church; to the formation of the board of trustees; to laying a growing financial base; to building a staff; to seeing various pilot projects turn to reality; to moving ministry offices from Abilene to North Dallas; and finally to the transition of executive leadership; a great sense of humble satisfaction settled over my soul.

God is good.

Part 3

LOOKING BACK—
LOOKING FORWARD

14

CELEBRATE TEAM ARRIVALS

Excitement was palpable as the first teams started arriving in South America. No one was more aware than Ellis Long, Alaor Leite, and Allen Dutton of the obstacles that were overcome to make new teams' arrivals into their adopted country of Brazil a possibility.

Having moved to Brazil in 1969 and returned to the United States in 1977, I knew the complexity surrounding an international move. But not even I knew the total story of the depth of prayer, the toll of stress, and the expended energy given by these three men over multiple years in opening the issuance of missionary visas by the Brazilian government. Yet, as one who loves the people of Brazil, I joined in their elation.

1980s Teams Arrive

During my tenure at Great Cities, twenty-nine teams moved to great cities of the Latin World. Twenty-seven went to South and Central America, one moved to the Caribbean, and one to Hispanic Fort Worth. This chapter will place the greatest focus on the first ten teams. We owe a great debt to the men, women, and children of these teams for paving the way. The success or failure of current missionary teams is largely dependent on the degree to which each one heeds—or rejects—the principles discovered through trial and error in the 1980s, as we learned from the success and failures of the first ten teams.

Recife

Director Cline Paden's handpicked team from the Sunset International Bible Institute in Lubbock, Texas, arrived in Recife, Brazil, on August 15, 1980. The six families of Phil and Pattie Grassie, Joe and Linda McKinney, Mike and Peggy Palk, Mike and Aureni Pruitt, Randy and Kathy Short, and Charles and Terrie Taylor fulfill Jesus' description of being the salt of the earth and a light on a hill.

Dennis Downing, from Abilene Christian University, moved to Recife in 1988 as a single missionary. There he met Germana. God continues to use the Downing family to reach unchurched people with Jesus' love.

In Recife, these men and women have influenced those in the state capital and fifth largest metropolitan area of Brazil. As an Atlantic port city, it is northeast Brazil's most important commercial region.

The Recife team have brought thousands of Brazilians to Jesus from across the northeast. The team's work resulted in twenty-five churches planted in greater Recife and another fifteen planted in their state.

A wonderful serendipity of their effort shines from Joao Pessoa, capital of the Brazilian state of Paraiba. Upon university graduation, three children of Joe and Linda McKinney, with Hunter Hagewood, an MK (missionary kid) from Sao Paulo, and other college friends moved to Joao Pessoa to plant a church. For the past several years, I thrill to read week after week of the kingdom good they are doing. They join their parents by following in the steps of Jesus.

Brasilia

The South National Church of Christ in Springfield, Missouri, assumed the responsibility in 1977 of a church plant in Brasilia, the federal capital of

Celebrate Team Arrivals

Brazil. Collaborating with Great Cities, South National's first missionary families, Gary and Inez Curro, arrived in 1979, and Jerry and Gail Heiderich followed in September 1980.

Brasilia typifies the pioneering spirit of that nation. In 1955, Juscelino Kubitschek became president of Brazil. President Kubitschek made the creation and construction of Brasilia the symbol of his administration. The idea of a centrally located federal capital dates back to the end of the seventeenth century. The president recruited urban planner Lucio Costa and architect Oscar Niemeyer. Their efforts culminated in a work of national pride that emerged from the red savannah soil. Brasilia formally became the national capital on April 22, 1960, and in 1987 it received the designation by United Nations Educational, Scientific and Cultural Organization (UNESCO) as a World Heritage Centre.

My first visit to Brasilia was in January of 1970 after a thirty-five-hour train ride from Sao Paulo on trains reminiscent of the *Butch Cassidy and the Sundance Kid* movie. In 1970, ten years after the city's inauguration, its red dirt was still dominant. The wide boulevards, designed not to need signal lights, seemed like overkill for the smattering of cars in the city. Today, brilliant green grass covers the red soil, and the overly wide streets of 1970 bulge with bumper-to-bumper traffic.

Through the first teams, we began to identify critical mistakes to avoid in church plants. Since we were a competing voice with supporting churches and the members of the missionary team, it was easier to identify the mistakes than it was to correct them.

Mistakes

Staggered arrivals created a problem in strategy completion. With the arrival of the Curro family in 1979, the Heiderichs in 1980, Bob and Donna Carpenter in 1981, Ron and Carla Prater in 1983, Basil and Rachel McClure in 1989, and Mark and Ellen Abshier in 1989, it was difficult for everyone to unite and work in unison. The result was a lack of united focus on the church planting goal.

The second critical mistake was the strategy or game plan generated by the South National church. Following the golden rule of "whoever has the gold rules," the South National plan, conceived by people without experience, won out over the strategy designed by those with expertise gained from working in South America's great cities. Following a rural mission model for a world-class city guaranteed failure. The South National policy outlined unrealistic growth goals and a series of negatives that limited assistance to the project. The goal was admirable in wanting the Brazilians to be self-sufficient. The reality is, though, an infant church—like an infant child—needs help and assistance to succeed.

By 1988, after a decade, the South National church was weary. The Brasilia church had moved over a dozen times. Everyone was frustrated. But South National agreed to launch a building program with the Brasilia congregation—reinforcements were on the way.

The next year, the Park Plaza Church of Christ in Tulsa, Oklahoma, sent Basil and Rachael McClure to join the team. The same year, their Abilene Christian classmates Mark and Ellen Abshier arrived to join Bob and Donna Carpenter who continued to work on the project. The La Mesa Church of Christ in La Mesa, California, assumed oversight responsibilities for the Abshiers.

Jerry and Gail Heiderich were in Abilene to complete master's degrees. They agreed to return to Brasilia. Ellis and Doris Long committed to working on funding for property and a building. Jerry Heiderich would join Ellis in fundraising prior to returning to Brasilia. Allen Dutton and Alaor Leite agreed to lead the land search. Once property was located, Brazilian architect Walfredo Thome, Ellis's close friend, agreed to construct the building. Since the area zoned for churches was limited, Dr. Thome accepted responsibility to work with the city government to change zoning

Celebrate Team Arrivals

laws for the first church building construction outside the original church zone perimeter.

The Lord blessed the work of the Duttons, Heiderichs, Leites, Longs, and Dr. Thome with the purchase of a strategically located school in 1992. The following year, churches and friends raised the first $100,000 toward the construction of a worship center. Fundraising continued until Stateside churches earmarked $160,000 for the building.

I remember well the beginning of 1995. Major League Baseball was on strike, the playoffs and World Series canceled. Baseball Commissioner Bud Selig was hard at work to get players and owners back to work.

That same year, churches hit a snag on the building project. Park Plaza church leaders balked at the idea of building in a foreign country. They froze their building account. The South National church began to have second thoughts, and they, too, froze their building fund account.

I began to negotiate with the stuck churches. I wanted to see our players get back to work. I saw it as important for the nation of Brazil to keep the Brasilia project on track. Interested parties had given $160,000 through the two churches toward the construction. The amount was the proverbial drop in the bucket compared to the cost of building in the federal capital. But it was a significant beginning for the fund-raising. Through a series of negotiations, we reached agreement to send the Brasilia land funds to the Amarillo Central church.

In January, Jerry Heiderich and I met in the Sao Paulo home of architect Walfredo Thome and his wife, Janir. It was one of the most inspirational and informative meetings I have ever attended. I have come to expect to be enlightened and inspired in the presence of this godly architect. We were attempting to figure out what it would take to build the building, and Dr. Thome inquired as to the amount of money on hand. We informed him of the $160,000. His immediate response was the teachable moment. In his enthusiastic but somewhat squeaky voice, he loudly responded in the form of a question with animation and arms flying up, "Why don't you get started—don't you know people are being lost while you are messing around?"

He went on to declare that in order to be successful, it was important to build the roof first. By having enough funds to erect the structure and complete the roof, if worse came to worse, members not trained in structural engineering could lay bricks, build walls, and install windows and doors at a slower pace.

On September 10, 1995, the groundbreaking took place. In December, Jerry and I met with Dr. Thome in Sao Paulo to finalize the move of his work crew to Brasilia. In January 1996, with the leadership of Jerry Heiderich and the aid of a group of leaders from the Brasilia church, Jerry began to oversee the initial stages of the building project.

By 1997, only the Heiderichs remained in Brasilia. The McClures and the Abshiers were living in the States. Ron Prater, who had left Brasilia in 1987, planned to return. Ellis and Doris Long moved to Brasilia in 1997 to help complete the building and to aid in the further development of church leaders. Dr. Thome and Ellis had worked together to build the beautiful Nove de Julho church building in Sao Paulo in the 1960s. Only God knows the degree these two men have influenced the growth of the kingdom in South America. Once again they would work together to build a church building for the glory of God.

For four intense weeks in April and May of 1999, Jerry Heiderich and Ellis Long returned to the States to finish fund-raising. The Lord blessed their efforts by finding the Prestoncrest Church of Christ in Dallas to take over the support of the Heiderich family. Jerry and Ellis also raised three hundred thousand dollars to complete the building project.

The renewal effort culminated on November 11, 2000, with the inauguration of a beautiful worship center in Brasilia. The building was a great contribution and one of the things we did right. It fit in perfectly with the beautiful architecture of the federal capital. A gift to the city of Brasilia, it testified to God's presence in the city.

Campo Grande

The team to Campo Grande entered Brazil on January 19, 1981. Its members included Jeff and Pam Burton, supported by the White Station Church of Christ in Memphis; Jeff and Suzanne Custer, supported by the Madison, Tennessee, Church of Christ; Eugene and Karen Goudeau, supported by the Golf Course Road Church of Christ in Midland, Texas; and Billy and Kathy McLain, supported by the Church of Christ in Fayette, Alabama. The team was trained at Harding University in Arkansas and at Harding Graduate School in Memphis, Tennessee.

Campo Grande, the state capital of Mato Grosso do Sul, is located in the west central region of Brazil. The state shares western borders with the nations of Bolivia and Paraguay. It is the twenty-third largest city in Brazil, with a population of eight hundred thousand. Home to six universities, Campo Grande is a multinational city.

Upon arrival, the team settled into an apartment building of four floors, no elevator, and one family on each floor. After spending the day together in intense language study, families jokingly tell about taking off their shoes at night to climb the stairs without alerting their colleagues, in an attempt to gain emotional space for the evening. Another lesson learned. In the settlement process, multiple neighborhoods make happy team members.

The Golf Course Road church in Midland played an important role as a "prime mover" congregation, adding grease to the wheels when needed. They walked with the team and the new church from team arrival, through each step of congregational maturation, through the building project, and finally to the appointment of elders, deacons, teachers, and evangelists. Long after the church was firmly established, the two congregations maintain a special relationship as they continue joint projects on behalf of Brazil.

Another reflection worthy of note is that the team had a good balance of leaders and doers as well as a good balance of gifts for task accomplishment. There is no substitute for high-quality personnel.

The Campo Grande team was the first to compose a strategy document and adhere to it from arrival to departure. As the tenth year arrived, the team was still using the strategy document as a blueprint to build a work that would stand the test of time. The result was an established church that now has a thirty-year history and sees its role in touching a nation. The creation of a strategy document is now included as a standard tool in team training at Great Cities.

Manaus

Manaus, established in 1669, is the state capital of Amazonas. Its two million residents make it the eighth largest city in Brazil. The city, located 900 miles inland from the Atlantic Ocean, receives ninety inches of rain annually and is home to twelve colleges and universities.

The Manaus team members were missionaries—*real* missionaries. The rest of us were just evangelists. The heat and humidity of living on the Amazon River in the heart of the Amazon Jungle is not for the faint of heart. The first three times I visited Manaus, I left sick from heat dehydration. On one occasion, after two downward-spiraling days in a hotel, it was time to flag a taxi and head for the hospital. The hospital stay included two days of intravenous hydration and a missed flight to Sao Paulo. I went to the airport directly from the hospital. Since the flight was full, the airline graciously gave a free upgrade to first class on the Boeing 747. The only time I ever sat in first class on the largest aircraft of the time, I was so sick that I just moaned and groaned while my seatmates enjoyed their multicourse lunches.

Manaus team members Paul and Cheryl Dawson, Rick and Denise Hayes, and Daniel and Carol Morgan moved to Manaus on February 7, 1981. Tim and Amanda Kuenstler arrived on November 3, 1988.

Celebrate Team Arrivals

The Lord had many people in the city with receptive hearts for the grace of Jesus. It was an exciting time. The baptismal towels were always damp and difficult to dry in the humid Amazon climate. Together, new believers were grafted into the body of Christ—the church.

Building a Worship Center

Like other churches in the great cities, lack of urban space for the church to meet quickly became a barrier. Churches are like families. They need a place to call home.

During the financial downturn of 2008, the U.S. media covered many stories of laid-off working families displaced from millions of homes. Featured stories highlighted the difficulties of families staying together without a home. Some remained together by living in their cars and using convenience store bathrooms to prepare children for school. It was possible for a time, but was not a long-term solution. Far too often, the mission church attempts to function without a home.

The first-century Jerusalem church started its life meeting at the temple for mutual encouragement and continual teaching. Like in the first century, churches today need space. When churches grow beyond a house-group size without adequate meeting space, it's difficult for them to enjoy the interaction with fellow believers and witness elders, teachers, deacons, and evangelists evolve. The Manaus church was no different. Its story of property acquisition illustrates the challenge in solving the need of a meeting place for a church in the great cities.

In August 1985, the church reached a worship attendance of 270 in temporary quarters. The opportunity was at hand to acquire the residence of a former governor. There was sufficient land to construct a worship center on the property. In September, a down payment was made on the historic property located on Seventh of September Avenue near the heart of the city. It took twelve months to complete the necessary documentation.

Make Your Vision Go Viral

The Westover Hills Church of Christ in Austin, Texas, and the White's Ferry Road Church of Christ in Monroe, Louisiana, worked with the Manaus church to supply funding. An architect from Manaus designed the construction plan and submitted it to the city, and the churches set about to raise the projected $350,000 dollars. By 1987, documents ground to a stop inside the maze of bureaucracy. The fund-raising reached a plateau of $200,000—short by $150,000.

In 1987, the missionary team found itself in transition. The Ricky Hayes family was on a U.S. study sabbatical. The Dan Morgan family announced plans to return to the States in December. The Paul Dawson family planned to leave Manaus to join the work in Fortaleza, Brazil, in mid-1988. Great Cities was working with Tim and Amanda Kuenstler to acquire visas so they could join the Manaus work in November 1988.

A critical meeting took place at the Abilene Holiday Inn in December 1987. Ricky and Denise Hayes, Tim and Amanda Kuenstler, Ellis Long, and I spent the afternoon determining steps to implement the building project. Together, we decided to present a plan to the churches to scale back the Manaus construction to the amount on hand: $200,000. The Hayes family would return to Manaus within six months to submit a modified building plan to the city. The Tim Kuenstler family would join the Hayes family in Manaus six months later in November 1988.

David and Kay Rose, former missionaries to the state of Sao Paulo, were members of the Westover Hills church in Austin. David played a key role in moving the project forward through the Stateside churches. Construction began in July 1989, and the Manaus church first met in their new worship center on January 28, 1990. The church inaugurated the 450-seat building with a full house on March 24, with city and state dignitaries present for the historic occasion.

In the summer of 1996, North Americans Bryan and Jacqueline Bost, who worked with the Sao Paulo team, moved from Sao Paulo to Manaus for a five-year commitment to continue the maturation process of the church and to help the congregation appoint leaders. On December 5, 1999, the church appointed five Brazilian elders and six deacons.

Manaus Medical Campaign

One of the fun—and complex—projects was the 1994 Manaus Medical Campaign. Great Cities consultant Jim Ravanelli and I spent many hours together designing our first medical mission trip. We determined that we would need four groups to make the effort work.

First, we would seek the cosponsorship of the Amarillo Central church and the Austin Westover Hills church. The Amarillo church was vital to our own sustenance, so we continued to discover new ways for our sponsoring church to participate in the Great Cities work. The Westover Hills church had served as the primary mover church for the Manaus project since the beginning in 1981.

Second, we would need the cooperation of the church in Manaus. They would be essential in making necessary contacts within the city. The church would serve as the legal entity responsible to the city so that we could receive authorization by officials to conduct the medical campaign. Church members would be among local personnel playing foundational, onsite roles for success.

Third, we would seek the cooperation of the Brazilian government. Without the Ministry of Health, the Brazilian Customs Agency, and city officials, the medical campaign could not take place.

Finally, we would need to recruit personnel for the campaign. We would need medical doctors trained in different specialties including ophthalmologists, dentists, and nurses. We would need translators who knew both English and Portuguese. In addition, we sought a variety of assistants to serve as aids to the pharmacy and the eye clinic, and for crowd organization. We would also need teachers and assistants to help with children.

The Central church and the Westover Hills church agreed to sponsor the effort. David Rose, Westover's coordinator of the Manaus work, agreed to lead the campaign. Manaus missionary Ricky Hayes agreed to handle Manaus logistics.

We quickly became aware we were involved in a "God thing." Medicines and eyeglasses began to flow into the Great Cities office. Fifty-seven North American volunteers, including nineteen medical specialists, prepared for the trip. Fourteen Brazilians from Sao Paulo, including ten Christian doctors and a dentist, joined the effort. Fifty workers from the Manaus church dedicated full-time service during the six days of the campaign. Doctors and nurses from Manaus agreed to work with the clinic and provide the oversight needed for U.S. medical personnel to practice in Brazil. The total of volunteers reached 125.

Televised opening ceremonies featured the vice governor of the state of Amazonas, the minister of health, the mayor, and other government officials giving their support for the project. The city offered the twenty-acre site of the Manaus Coliseum for the clinic.

The first morning, the line began to form at 5 a.m. On the final day of the clinic, three thousand people from Manaus and surrounding towns—many having rowed local rivers in small boats for hours—lined up in hopes of receiving medical care. By week's end, five thousand of Manaus's poorest people received medical care, and two thousand pairs of glasses were distributed.

Let me share one behind-the-scenes story. At the Great Cities offices, volunteers had packed fifty Rubbermaid tubs of medicine and supplies. When the travel group reached Miami, the airline refused to take the medicine without permission of Brazilian officials, so the group left for Manaus without the medicine. Early the next morning, I called Brasilia, asking to speak to the minister of health. To my complete surprise, he agreed to speak with me over the phone. Speaking Portuguese, I explained our pre-

Celebrate Team Arrivals

dicament, and he agreed to prepare a letter authorizing me to enter Brazil with the medicine. I caught the first flight to Miami, presented the papers from Brazil's minister of health—and the fifty tubs and I were on our way.

Upon arriving in Sao Paulo, Customs officials informed me the letter gave me permission to bring the medicine into Brazil, but there was no permission to send medicine across state lines to the city of Manaus. After two hours of negotiation, officials agreed to send the medicine to Manaus and let a Customs official there make the decision to release or not release the medicine. I was on my way, again.

Because of the number of tubs, the airline placed the medicine on the last flight of the evening to Manaus. At midnight, I accompanied David Rose, Ricky Hays, the lawyer who represented the Manaus church, and some able lifters to Manaus's Brigadeiro Eduardo Gomes International Airport to receive our cargo.

Intentionally, I stepped to the front of the baggage conveyer belt to receive the first crate of medicine. On the lid was taped an envelope. I slipped the envelope into my jacket pocket and went directly to the lawyer. He read the letter, placed the envelope in his suit pocket, and told me, "This envelope needs to disappear." He understood the need to avoid the red-tape bureaucracy of those hoping to receive extra money. The Sao Paulo Customs official had sent a wire to Manaus to tell them to look for the letter. The letter disappeared, and Customs released the medicine without further difficulty.

The Manaus medical campaign was the highest-profile event ever presented by Great Cities Missions. Lost people met Jesus. Hurting people received His compassion through His church. And city officials invited us to repeat the event the following year.

In the meantime, the Manaus church invited a new evangelist to work full time. Many good things happened under his leadership. The church selected elders, deacons, teachers, and evangelists received training, the church grew, and other congregations were established. Unfortunately, the new evangelist felt the medical campaign would be overly distracting from developing the local congregation. We honored his preference and did not return the next year. That was a shortsighted decision on my part. In hindsight, facing a wide-open door from the city, I should have done more to repeat the medical effort.

I have only praise for the people and the churches who have worked in Manaus. Living in the Amazon demands that people be wired for the task. Not everyone can adjust to the heat, humidity, massive rain, and isolation. Sure, there is a wonderful international airport, but a casual glance at a Brazilian map attests to the seclusion of the city.

The Manaus team was composed of risk-taking, goal-focused activists. They did not move to Manaus to relax. Heaven will include residents from the Amazon because members of the Manaus team accepted God's call to serve as ambassadors for His mission to Manaus.

Fortaleza, 1981

Fortaleza, located in northwest Brazil, is a desired Brazilian vacation destination because of its pristine beaches. The state capital of Ceara, Fortaleza is a great city with 3.4 million people and home to thirteen colleges and universities. As a professional soccer base, it is one of the host cities of the 2014 FIFA World Cup Soccer Tournament. The 1981 mission team, recruited from the Harding Graduate School of Theology in Memphis, Tennessee, selected this sports city as the destination of its church plant.

A five-family team made the move to Brazil on September 21, 1981. Joe and Jenny Carr, Duane and Debbie Jenks, Roger and Teddy Copeland, Rod and Tina Chisholm, and Terry and Jenny Lawson settled into the city, enrolled in Portuguese language study, and began to make friends with neighbors, merchants, and others encountered in day-to-day living. Team members Ken and Liz Lewis, former members of the Sao Paulo team,

Celebrate Team Arrivals

arrived in April 1985 and served through December 1991. David and Babi Ingram moved to Fortaleza from Sao Paulo in January 1988. David later served as one of the church's first elders.

On April 1, 1982, the missionary team conducted its first worship service in the Portuguese language. The congregation serves the city and its state from its worship center on University Avenue. Once again, Sao Paulo architect Dr. Walfredo Thome built a beautiful building in 1989 on a forty-four-thousand-square-foot lot at the center of three primary streets, among multiple bus routes, and only three blocks from downtown. It is wonderful to see churches meeting in South America on well-known streets with phone numbers and websites making them easily accessible.

Because of the work of the Fortaleza team, churches now meet in nine permanent locations, two temporary meeting places, and at least a dozen house churches.

Belo Horizonte, 1982

The 1982 Great Cities team to Belo Horizonte had its genesis through student evangelistic campaigns and the influence of the 1967 Belo Horizonte team of missionaries.

The explorer Joao Leite da Silva founded in 1701 what would become a spectacular city. I never fail to feel the vibrating pulse of the city each time I visit. Its expanded metro population is now home to more than nine million Brazilians. Situated in southeast Brazil, as if at the center of a clock, four other strategic Brazilian cities—Vitoria at three o'clock, Rio de Janeiro at six, Sao Paulo at seven, and Brasilia at eleven—make Belo Horizonte a hub city.

F. H. and Becky Gates, Eddison and Lajuana Fowler, Randy and Vicki Matheny, Glenn and Nancy Robb, Jamie and Tammy Richardson, and Mike and Melody Ford built with respect and joy upon the initial work started by the Operation 68 team.

Mike and Melody Ford were my students at Lubbock Christian University, and the remainder of the team did undergraduate work in Tennessee at Freed-Hardeman University. The entire team did graduate work at Abilene Christian University.

The work in Belo Horizonte produced thirty congregations, with three elderships. A prime location in the downtown area for a one-thousand-seat worship center, the Seminario Biblico Nacional school of theology, a culturally relevant television program, and a well-developed Christian camp are just a few of the many ways the Lord has used this godly team.

Rio de Janeiro, 1982

The Queen Jewel Cities of South America are Rio de Janeiro and Buenos Aires. From the beginning of the Great Cities mission, they were at the top of the list for mission team recruiting. With the arrival of a missionary team in Buenos Aires in 1972—through a cooperative but independent effort—the pressure lessened for Buenos Aires, so Rio de Janeiro became a primary target city.

Rio deserves its "Marvelous City" nickname. Its wealth, beautiful mountains, beaches, harbors, and architecture stand in stark contrast to its poverty, violence, and slums. With all of its pluses and minuses, Rio is definitely a marvelous city. I never tire of ascending Pão de Aucar at sunset to watch the lights appear over the city of multimillions. Rio is a city that never sleeps. So many times, looking down from the mountain above the beautiful harbor, I have prayed in the darkness for this heavenly city threatened by the mouth of hell.

In the summer of 1976, now author Max Lucado, Bryan Gibbs, and three Abilene Christian University colleagues—Mark Aldriedge, Kim Carver, and Marty West—spent three weeks with our missionary team in Sao Paulo. (Bryan served ten years on the Rio de Janeiro team. Since 1994, he continues his work with Great Cities Missions). Everyone recognized the heart and talent of the five young men and recruited hard.

Celebrate Team Arrivals

Before returning to the States, the students requested a meeting with Howard Norton. The young university students met until late one night at his Nove de Julho church office. Howard encouraged them to recruit a team of friends and return to Brazil to plant a church. After thoroughly discussing teamwork, Howard told them it would be good to leave them alone so they could visit at ease about their future. Later that evening—actually in the wee hours of the morning—they decided among themselves to form their team and return to Brazil.

It would be difficult to name a person who loved Rio more and worked harder on her behalf than Dr. Ellis Long. The summer of 1976, when the four Abilene Christian students were in Brazil, was the summer Ellis and Doris Long returned to the States and opened the Great Cities office on the campus of Abilene Christian University. Ellis lobbied hard for Rio.

The five summer visitors returned to Abilene and began to recruit a team for Rio de Janeiro. After marriages and extensive recruiting, the membership of the team was firm. Its members, Marc and Sue Curfman, Bryan and Becky Gibbs, Keith and Bryn Kreidel, Max and Denalyn Lucado, Ron and Janine Morgan, Paul and Debbie Reding, Tony and D'anna Roseberry, Lloyd and Tracy Stewart, Marty and Angela West, and Larry and Connie Zinck, needed to finish school, raise their funds, and prepare for the move.

In pondering on the success of the Rio de Janeiro team of the 1980s, it is necessary to reflect on the 1980s, as described in chapter 7. The ACU Rio team exemplified the skepticism and independence of the 1980s generation that had witnessed the coverup of the Vietnam War and the Watergate scandal by elected officials. Not heeding experienced counsel, the ten couples followed their own staggered arrival schedule, beginning in 1980 with the final couple arriving in 1986. Over the seven-year arrival period, no two couples arrived at the same time. In 1987, three families returned to the States after completing their five-year commitment. Thus, there was always someone arriving and adapting while others were closing down and departing. With such transience, the team was unable to agree on a unified strategy and had difficulty maintaining a core of families on the field at the same time with the same focus on a game plan.

The Rio success was not exactly how Ellis and I envisioned it. Those of us who are task-oriented tend to see failure when the way we envisioned the task does not reach fruition. In this case, that would have been a large church near the Maracana Stadium and the grand commercial center of the city map.

It looked different from what we envisioned, but the Rio team was successful. The team planted congregations in outlying areas of Sao Gonçalo, the Ramos neighborhood, and in the growing area of Jacarepagua, the fourth largest neighborhood of Rio de Janeiro. There is a congregation in the Baixada Fluminense and two churches in the city of Macaé, a city that has flourished in the past twenty years because of its proximity to the large oil deposits that are being pumped off the cost of Rio.

Maria Jose lived in Rio de Janerio. Life had been tough on her. Her husband was the foreman of a large ranch three hundred miles north of Rio. While separated from her husband over a marital spat, a tragedy occurred. Lumber-thieving murderers ambushed and killed her husband and their twenty-year-old son on a deserted road of the ranch.

Her guilt over alienation from her husband and her grief over his death and the death of her youngest of four sons was unbearable.

A mutual friend introduced her to Max Lucado. The following evening, Max listened to her story over pizza. From the pizza place, they walked next door to the School of the Bible. Max began to lead her in her quest for God through his risen Son. Max and Denalyn Lucado and other team members continued to befriend her.

Late one night, she could wait no longer. She had to put on Jesus in baptism for the forgiveness of her sins. Maria was afraid to go through one more night without being completely obedient to Jesus. She was ready to trust him

Celebrate Team Arrivals

for the rest of her life. Max Lucado and Ronnie Morgan took her to the home of Larry and Connie Zinck. Though it was late and bitter cold, she went down into the water of the swimming pool and Ronnie Morgan buried her in the water of baptism and raised her through the power of Christ to walk a new, grace-filled life. Maria Jose remembers the intense cold of the evening, the freezing water, and, in her words, the warmth she felt throughout her body, a sign that she was in Jesus, after she came up from the water.

Maria Jose began to open her home for Bible study. Max Lucado went on to study with and baptize her daughter. Maria Jose served as a delightful receptionist for visitors at the School of the Bible in Rio de Janeiro.

I first met her in her home city of Vitoria, Brazil, where she returned to her roots seven hours north of Rio to serve as secretary—as well as mother and grandmother—to the young, newly arrived mission team to Vitoria.

This morning as I visited with Maria Jose over the telephone, she could not stop speaking of her thankfulness to Max Lucado who introduced her to Jesus and to her many teachers and friends on the Rio team. Maybe there was not a big church left near the Maracana soccer stadium, but across Brazil, lost people still feel the impact of the Great Cities Rio de Janeiro team of the 1980s.

Salvador, 1984

Just below the most eastern coastal projection of South America is located the "Capital of Happiness," Salvador, the center of Afro-Brazilian culture and state capital of Bahia. The happy citizens take pride in their arts, music, dance, soccer, and spectacular beaches.

On February 8, 1984, a team composed primarily of graduates from the Sunset International Bible Institute in Lubbock, Texas—Ron and Bev Bontrager, Tim and Janet Brumfield, Charles and Cynthia McKinney, and five team children—departed for their new home in Brazil. They were met by Great Cities' representatives Allen and Maria Dutton, and Alaor and

Miriam Leite, to help the team with documentation, home rentals, furniture purchases, automobiles, and enrollment in Portuguese study.

Being new arrivals, team members carefully scripted Sunday services and slowly read their worship assignments in Portuguese. The first baptism took place on July 22, 1984, and the church started to grow as it followed relationship lines of family and friends.

In 1985, the little congregation moved to a larger location near downtown. The team removed walls to seat seventy-five people, and recorded attendance reached 195.

Church planting is never simple.

The Salvador church, with the aid of Stateside churches, purchased a prime lot in October 1987. As the church started to develop the land, an unscrupulous city official claimed he owned the land and hired a judge to evict the church's construction workers.

But God is in control.

Two years later, an archenemy of the corrupt official purposefully bought the land from the church for its full value. It was his opportunity for their ongoing game of business chess. The corrupt official was about to hear "checkmate," and the church was about to have a place to meet.

With the cash from the sale and help from supporting churches, the Salvador team purchased main-avenue property in the prime area of Bonoco. The property included a building to house the growing church.

The Charles McKinney family returned home on May 2, 1987. Ron Bontrager and his family returned to the States in June 1988. Monty Huffman, who was raised in Belo Horizonte, and his wife, Melody—one of my students from Lubbock Christian—joined the work in Salvador in December 1989. As the Huffmans adjusted to Salvador, their young son Matthew tragically died of spinal meningitis in August 1991. Heartbroken, the family returned to the States.

The church purchased adjacent property to the Bonoco building in

1992 to add additional space. By October 1994, 392 Brazilians had entered the baptismal waters. Each person represented a young Christian plant in the rich soil of Brazil. A small orchard was beginning to take root.

Tim and Janet Brumfield and their two children continued in Salvador through 1996. Working with Brazilian Christians, the power of Jesus changed lives of new acquaintances. In addition to Bonoco, congregations now meet in Cajazieras, Feira de Santana, Itinga, Mussurunga, Murituba and in the capital city Aracaju in the state of Sergipe. May God's grace flow abundantly throughout the state of Bahia.

Curitiba, Brazil, 1986

In 1967, as a transfer to Abilene Christian, I was impressed with a fellow transfer student who graduated from the two-year Bear Valley Bible Institute in Denver and came to Abilene to continue his studies. He made me aware of the Denver school.

After joining Ellis Long in Abilene and completing the writing and design of a new recruiting brochure, it was time to schedule recruiting trips. I made a list of schools and remembered Bear Valley. Leonard Gray, a former missionary to Africa, was directing the school and Bob Waldron, former missionary to Guatemala, was teaching Missions.

In March 1982, after speaking in chapel at the Bear Valley School, I began to meet the students. The commonality of our western U.S. culture and our blue-collar backgrounds placed us at ease.

Numerous receptive hearts from Bob's class responded. A team for Curitiba, Brazil, emerged with Ron and Georgia Freitas, John and Sherena Langley, Alan and Ree Nalley, and Rod and Linda Nealeigh as its members. I challenged them to be church planters in the Brazilian city of Curitiba, boasting a population of 1.3 million.

The capital of the state of Parana, Curitiba roots go back to 1693. Prior to achieving statehood, the providence in southeast Brazil was formed in

1853 and populated by immigrant waves of Germans, Italians, Poles, and Ukrainians. Curitiba's European heritage continues strong.

The team bonded on their Brazil survey trip in 1983. What fun it was to introduce them to the Brazilian culture in Rio de Janeiro, Sao Paulo, and Curitiba. The Freitas, Langley, and Nalley families boarded the plane in August 1986 for their new home.

In January 1987, while attending the Brazil Missionary Conference in Belo Horizonte and seeing all of the young, talented missionaries, I thought of Rod and Linda Nealeigh. Knowing they were exceptional people, I regretted they were not in Brazil.

Immediately, I wrote Rod and Linda, who were in their fifth year of work with a church in Gillette, Wyoming, and encouraged them to revisit their decision and take steps to join their team in Curitiba. The church in Brazil needed outstanding leaders. The following year, they reunited with the Curitiba team and served for twenty-three years.

Two other couples served with the Curitiba team: Antenor and Phyllis Gonçalves (1990–1995) and Enio and Becky Latorre (2003–2010).

Every member of the Curitiba team contributed to the success of the project. Through the years, Ron and Georgia Freitas served as Curitiba team liaisons, in constant contact with me at Great Cities.

The great spirit of the Curitiba team made it receptive to guidance. They had a good balance among gifted evangelists, team leaders, and teachers. They were open to assistance in executing a church planting strategy.

In the early days of my work with Great Cities, I came across a video titled *The Church Alive*. The video advocated an urban church planting strategy designated "Encounter with God." What was remarkable was its systematic likeness to the strategy our team developed in Sao Paulo and continued to tweak through the work with Great Cities. Independently, we reached the same conclusions on church planting strategy in the Latin city.

The video told the story of the Encounter with God growth in the

Celebrate Team Arrivals

city of Lima, Peru, through Christian and Missionary Alliance churches. Beginning in the Lince neighborhood with 120 members in 1973, the LeTourneau Foundation, led by the large-equipment, earth-moving firm of Roy LeTourneau built an education center and a one-thousand-seat worship center on a main avenue in Lince. Using a team approach, the church was filled in one year. By 1993, following the same strategy, thirty-two churches were established with several numbering into the thousands.

The primary difference between the Encounter Strategy and the Great Cities Strategy was the upfront funding provided by the LeTourneau Foundation to build a one-thousand-seat worship center and then to fill it.

Committed to the strategy learned in Dr. Ellis Long's course on Urban Evangelism, the Curitiba team was stuck at the property acquisition step. In the spring of 1989, Bob Waldron and I encouraged the team to travel to Lima and see what they could learn. It was a lesson in seeing God work through strategy and funding to reach a city.

Over the next four years, the team attempted to raise funds, but the effort reached a plateau at $65,000. With the backing of colleagues, Ron and Georgia Freitas traveled to the States in 1993 to work full time on funding.

Parallel to the Curitiba fundraising, in 1994 and 1995 Great Cities raised $127,000 to develop a manual for urban church establishment that would include sections on how to conquer the property barrier in a world-class city. Jim Ravanelli was working with us as a fundraising consultant. He agreed to work with me on three church funding projects to create the handbook. The first project was to team up with Ron to solve the Curitiba property dilemma.

On Thanksgiving Day 1994, eleven years after the Curitiba team survey trip, the church purchased property near the center of the city. The congregation sacrificially contributed to the entire endeavor. In a two-step process—first building an education/parking building—the Curitiba church of 300 members proudly inaugurated a beautiful 700-seat worship center with an attendance of 902 on November 4, 2000.

God blessed both Great Cities and the Curitiba church to plant a congregation of Christian teachers, evangelists, elders, and deacons in a beautiful building on a main avenue of a capital city. May they touch the city for eternity.

Florianopolis, Brazil, 1987

The final 1980s team to arrive in Brazil formed at Harding University in Searcy, Arkansas. Great Cities missionaries Ken and Terrie Graves with Galon and Sharon Jones served as the backbone for the church plant in Florianopolis. Each couple spent over a decade in Brazil, growing and raising their families and the church.

Alaor and Miriam Leite and Allen Dutton met the families on November 17 to settle them into the city. By the end of the month, both the Graves and Jones families had moved into homes, purchased furniture, and gotten their documents in order.

Their chosen location was the southeastern city of Florianopolis. The beautiful coastal metropolis boasts forty breathtaking beaches and a population springing from a rich German, Italian, and Portuguese heritage. Over half a million people live in this capital of the state of Santa Catarina.

God honored the work of these families, and a church continues to shine the light of Jesus for the inhabitants of the city.

The '90s Teams Arrive

The Rodovia dos Imigrantes (Immigrants Highway), a modern feat of engineering, connects Sao Paulo to the Atlantic Ocean. Descending the mountains over forty-four viaducts and seven bridges, the motorist also encounters eleven extremely long tunnels. Imagine the difficulty of digging mile after mile through solid rock to complete each tunnel.

Celebrate Team Arrivals

There is no better analogy to describe the 1980s: a completed tunnel—through solid rock—serves as a conduit for Jesus' love to the Brazilian people. After fifteen years of work begun by Ellis and Doris Long in 1976, the 1980s ended, and Ellis and Doris Long and Midland's Golf Course Road church were transitioning out of the ministry. Bob Waldron was transitioning in. He and I would continue to follow the familiar format of missionaries by serving as codirectors.

The 1990s were building years for Great Cities Missions to establish itself as an Internal Revenue category 501(c)3 nonprofit entity under the sponsorship of the Amarillo Central church. We spent a huge amount of time and effort in the 1990s focused on building a diversified financial base to posture for future growth. It was a decade of adding personnel and a decade to begin recruiting teams for national capitals of Hispanic South America.

While building the Great Cities entity for the future, God blessed our effort to recruit six teams. Departing for South America in the 1990s were three teams to Brazil and three to Spanish-speaking capital cities.

Vitoria, 1992

With its bay, bridges, beautiful beaches, and conical mountaintops, Vitoria is reminiscent of a mini Rio de Janeiro. As the capital of the Brazilian state of Espirito Santo, the city serves a metropolitan area of six surrounding cities. Vitoria, Espirito Santo, translates as Victory, Holy Spirit. What a great place in which to make the Spirit of Jesus known.

I launched the Vitoria recruiting project in May 1986, meeting with a student group from Oklahoma Christian at the Lar Belem in Campinas, Brazil. The team for Vitoria solidified with members Taylor and Connie Cave, David and Barbara Duncan, Terry and Kelli Fischer, and Rick and Monika Sandoval. Sao Paulo team families living in Edmond, Oklahoma—Howard and Jane Norton, John and Catherine Pennisi, and Don and Carol Vinzant—played key roles in preparing and encouraging the Vitoria team.

In January 1992, with college complete, team members were ready for the research trip to South America as a Great Cities team. Great Cities supporters Dub and Nell Henderson, Al and Pat Smith, and Bill and Marjorie Strawther accompanied us as we went to Buenos Aires, Argentina, and to Brazilian cities Sao Paulo, Rio de Janeiro, Campo Grande, Curitiba, and Vitoria.

The Oklahoma Christian team moved to Vitoria in November 1992. Teston and Jo Gilpatrick, who worked with our Sao Paulo team, joined the work in Vitoria in 2000 and served with the Vitoria church plant until their return to the States in 2009.

On November 9, 2003, the Vitoria church inaugurated new classroom space and a five-hundred-seat worship center across the street from the Federal University of Espirito Santos on a main avenue connecting the airport to the downtown area.

Montevideo, Uruguay, 1993

Bob Waldron took the lead to recruit our first team for a South American Spanish capital city. Three couples from Abilene Christian University committed to go as a Great Cities team to Montevideo. Team members Bryan and Larisa Elliott, Warren and Danna Roane with daughter Adriana Nicole, and Greg and Ann Sparks with daughter Emily Ann made a solid and talented team.

At the same time, two additional factors came into play. Three veteran missionary families initiated a joint work in Montevideo: Dan and Elise Coker, Ronnie and Beverly Rama, and Jack and Beatrice Walker.

Second, the Southern Hills Church of Christ of Abilene accepted the challenge of Dan Coker and Ellis Long to take the lead in raising funds for a multistory building in downtown Montevideo. The El Chana Tea

Celebrate Team Arrivals

Company had owned the distinguished building with its clock tower. The purchase would allow a place to develop a congregation and to train and evangelize the city.

Instead of starting a parallel effort, the new Abilene team elected to join the veterans. The joint work did succeed in leaving a congregation with elders, teachers, deacons, and an evangelist at a principal location in Montevideo.

Buenos Aires Team Merger, 1990

In 1972, the University Church of Christ in Abilene sent a team of three families to Buenos Aires. The on-field team averaged five families through 1989. The effort resulted in a dozen small congregations meeting in distant neighborhoods away from the city center.

On April 11, 1980, a team of leaders from Freed-Hardeman University arrived on the south side of Buenos Aires to begin a church plant. After language study and cultural adaptation—just as the teamwork was to begin—the 1982 Falkland-Malvinas Island War entered front and center on the world stage. When the Americans sided with the British, the Argentine contempt for the American position caused an anti-American sentiment to saturate the nation.

The war and its aftermath resulted in a slow start for the new American team in Argentina. By the close of 1989, the south side Buenos Aires team could point to only two small church plants.

With the input of Drs. Clyde Austin and Ellis Long, the University Church of Christ in Abilene reviewed its mission in 1986 and focused on a plan to implement in January 1987. The plan included moving their missionary families toward the center of the city with a ten-year timeline to plant a primary avenue congregation.

Thirty months later, with missionary relocation complete, church planting progress was still slow.

In the summer of 1989, I was wearing two hats. As a member of the University church, I was working on the Argentina subcommittee, and my work continued as a director of Great Cities. With twenty years of team and urban church planting experience, I launched a proactive plan to jump-start the downtown church plant. I made a list of people to contact and lobbied each one in order of the list. My goal was to merge the remnant of the two teams in Buenos Aires and to encourage a plan to purchase property and build a worship center at a strategic location.

By November 1989, the idea was growing among Stateside supporters, so Bob Waldron and I flew to Argentina to present the plan over several days to both groups. By early 1990, after assessment and a team integration workshop, a united team of Jay and Cathy Abels, Steve and Lynette Austin, Joel Banks, Glen and Kathy Henton, Jim and Katherine Holway, Reece and Jacquie Mitchell, Yancy and Lanette Smith, Steven and Diane Teel, and Craig and Rhoda Webb signed on to meet the goal.

Working closely with Kris Southward, a CPA and a deacon of the Abilene University church, step by step a temporary meeting place was leased in 1990 and strategic property was purchased at the corner of Anasco and Bacacay in December 1993 next to a subway line and a city park. In October 1997, a beautiful center designed by Sao Paulo architect Dr. Walfredo Thome opened for worship. The Caballito congregation met with incredible joy in its own center for worship.

Natal, Brazil, 1995

Natal is located on the northeast coast of Brazil at the point where South America is closest to Africa. Brazil, as a U.S. ally during World War II, allowed the American air force to used Natal as a departure point for North Africa en route to Europe.

The Great Cities missionary team of Bryan and Jannet Carruth, Verlan and Telma Manor, Mike and Julia Martin, and Kelli Pearson arrived in its

Celebrate Team Arrivals

chosen capital city in March of 1995. As with the church in Manaus, the Westover Hills congregation of Austin played a key role in church establishment by taking the lead in providing centrally located property for the work of the Natal church.

The Natal team planted two congregations. Both churches continue to progress.

After the work crossed over into the twenty-first century, key leaders from the church in the city of Porto Alegre, Brazil, moved to Natal. They are doing an admiral job building on the foundation laid by the American missionary team and the Westover Hills church.

Bryan Gibbs on Staff

In December 1992, Bryan and Becky Gibbs and their four boys returned to Abilene from Rio de Janeiro. After a decade of service to Brazil and a year spent in reentry, Bryan joined the Great Cities staff as a recruiter. His first assignment was to recruit a second team for Rio de Janeiro.

At Bryan's invitation, former teammate Max Lucado spoke at a recruiting dinner in Oklahoma City in 1994. The recruiting of Rio team two was off to a good start.

Rio de Janeiro, 1998

Corcovado Mountain is the site of the 130-foot Christ the Redeemer statue. The symbolic Jesus stands with open arms for the people of Brazil. Peering through the clouds below, I saw skyscrapers, cemeteries, shantytowns, and signs of humanity clear to the horizon. It would be foolish to think of the work of Jesus as complete. On top of Corcovado Mountain, standing at the base of the Christ statue, I felt as a mere speck as I looked over the city below. The enormous need eclipses the enormity of the monument.

To plant another group of Christ followers in Rio de Janeiro, the first members of the core team, Gordon and Ila Dabbs, Kevin and Debra Reynolds, Scott and Sharla Reynolds, and team children arrived in Rio November 8, 1998. Dan and Kirsty Baird, the remaining team members, arrived twenty-nine months later on May 1, 2001.

The team got off to a good start with twenty-two baptisms after its settlement process. Through one-on-one teaching, worship services, group classes, and a citywide television program, the church enjoyed growth.

The Lord blessed the team with two significant accomplishments in leaving an established church for another vibrant section of Rio de Janeiro. On Sunday, June 25, 2006, the assembly of 407 people inaugurated a spacious center for worship and Bible study. In November 2009 the church appointed Brazilian leaders to lead the congregation into the twenty-first century.

Ken Lewis on Staff

Having worked in Brazil many years with Ken and Liz Lewis, I knew Ken had the right stuff. As Bob Waldron was leaving in April 1998 to lead the new Missions Resource Network, it was good to have Ken join us to work with Bryan Gibbs in recruiting. Together, Bryan and Ken recruited nine teams for capital cities of South America while simultaneously teaching, preparing and providing onsite care for these and other Great Cities teams.

Santiago, Chile, 1999

Prior to Bob Waldron's departure, he was the prime mover for the first Great Cities team recruited from students of a public university. With a son at Texas A&M, Bob learned of the spirit that permeated every nook and cranny of Aggieland, producing bright graduates with a can-do attitude. In addition, thousands of Aggies for Christ, past and present, loved their inspirational leader, Bob Davidson. Davidson demanded the can-do spirit be present in Aggies for Christ.

Celebrate Team Arrivals

Mark and Denise Dean, Scott and Holly Emery, Kelley and Julie Grant, Jill Grove, Jeff Hatcher, Keith and Michele Kilmer, and Elizabeth Riley signed on to plant a main-avenue church in Santiago, Chile.

Even among the modern megacities of South America, Santiago stands out in its own right in its setting among the Andes Mountain chain. I will forever remember the plane window view painted by the moon, the stars, the mountain peaks, valleys, and the bleached-white, sparkling snow of the Andes as the LAN Chile flight locked in on the Santiago de Chile International Airport.

Sent by Great Cities, Allen Dutton and former Chile missionary Roland Bowen arrived in Santiago on April 13, 1999, to begin team settlement. Twenty-two months later, committed to the church planting project, Aggie Zane Perkins and his Harding University wife, Tae, with their two children joined the team. Team member Jeff Hatcher, who arrived in Santiago as a bachelor, did some recruiting on his own, and his bride, Penny, was a late but valuable addition to the team.

Chileans began to hear of the grace of Jesus and His offer to hit the delete button on a sin-filled life and insert the promise of eternal forgiveness. One by one, family by family, the body of Christ was growing. On Sunday, March 19, 2006, the Providencia congregation, with 360 in attendance, inaugurated their new worship center and classroom wing. On a main street, in front of a city park, with land for future expansion and a Chilean leadership, the Providencia church will be a fountain of grace flowing to the people for generations yet to come.

The Teams of 2,000

To continue the analogy of the highway through the mountain range between Sao Paulo and the Atlantic coast, additional roadbed laid in the 1990s gave Great Cities legitimacy as a recognized entity. By the end of the

'90s, sixteen church-planting teams recruited and placed through Great Cities were living in South America.

Ron and Georgia Freitas on Staff

Jesus promises His followers, "No one who has left home or wife or brothers or sisters or parents or children for the sake of the kingdom of God will fail to receive many times as much in this age, and in the age to come, eternal life" (Luke 18:29–30). The fulfillment of Jesus' promise becomes obvious in foreign mission work. Colleagues like Ron and Georgia Freitas are as close as family to me. It was a pleasure to see them become members of the Great Cities staff in 2001. As recruitment of teams continued at a pace that challenged the capacity of the ministry to train and care for a growing number of teams, Ron and Georgia, while aiding in recruiting, shouldered an increasing amount of training and on-field care.

The decade from 2000 to 2010 proved strategic. Key additions to staff and trustees, and the move from Abilene to Dallas, set the future direction. Team arrivals continued. Six North American teams arrived in South American cities. At the same time, the Hispanic and Latin church became a new recruiting ground for missionary teams. Six teams of Hispanic Christians and one team of Brazilian Christians moved to capital cities.

Buenos Aires, Argentina, 2001

Mike and Carol Dotson, Chris and Alessandra Kelley, Glen and Kathy Henton, Eric and Erika Henton, and Steve Atkins planted a new church in the Vila Urquiza area of Buenos Aires.

A unique feature of the Buenos Aires team was the membership. Recruiting from established resources, one team member was a second generation Christian from Brazil, while another couple was former members of the previous Buenos Aires team, and still another young man was an MK, having grown up in Argentina and then joining a mission team with his wife and young daughter.

Porto Alegre, Brazil, 2002

Porto Alegre, capital city for the state of Rio Grande do Sul, is on my personal list of favorite Brazilian cities. The city hosts a large number of immigrants from Germany, Italy, and Poland. As a port city with an urban population of four million, and its borders with Argentina and Uruguay, Porto Alegre is a key city for advancing the gift offered through Jesus.

The families of John and Samantha Jewell, Kevin and Benay Blume, Kyle and Leslie Klein, Paul Morrow, Matt Rehbein, and Sascha and Jennifer Terry took on the challenge of a new church plant for Porto Alegre.

Asuncion, Paraguay, 2003

Asuncion is one of the oldest cities of South America. The founding of the city occurred forty-five years after Christopher Columbus first reached the Americas. It serves as the seat of the federal government, the principal trade hub for the nation, and the industrial and cultural center of the country. A warm memory I have of the city is attending a downtown Asuncion theater watching the newly released movie *The Mission*, the story of the Jesuits' attempt to protect a South American Indian tribe from Portuguese slave traders.

A team of students formed on the Freed-Hardeman University campus in Henderson, Tennessee. Chris and Vickie Fry, Ethan and Ashley Hardin, Vanessa Heady, and Enoch Rinks answered the call of this great city of two million residents.

Salvador, Brazil, 2005

Great Cities' first mission team to Salvador in 1982 encountered a gigantic city of people open to Jesus. The success of the 1982 team deemed worthy a second effort.

Team members united at the six-month Great Cities internship. Coming from Canada, Alabama, Oklahoma, and Texas, they were ready to leave for Salvador on March 13, 2005.

Matt and Mary Virginia Mabery, Keith and Stacy Parker, Randy and Jennifer Porter, Russell and Valerie Quirey, and Travis and Alicia Sass arrived in Brazil ready to give a minimum of five years to planting a church in a new location in Salvador.

Niteroi, Brazil, 2008

To live in Niteroi and look across the bay to Rio de Janeiro must be one of the great views of the world. We were late arriving in Niteroi. This city of a million people is a city that deserved the attention of a mission team long ago. The reward of living in Niteroi with its beautiful beaches, sparkling sunshine, world-class shopping, and warm Brazilian people is unsurpassed.

Recent graduates from Oklahoma Christian University trained in the Great Cities Dallas internship. Membership of the Niteroi team is Wes and Carrie Gotcher, Zane and April McGee, Brent and Jill Nichols, Ben and Juliana Roberts with their children, Daniel and Jonah, and Nathan and Sara Zinck. Following the precedent of other teams, five new babies were born to team families since their arrival.

Cusco, Peru, 2009

Cusco is a great old city. As the historic capital of the Inca Empire between the thirteenth century and 1532, it is now, since 1983, designated as a UNESCO World Heritage Site. Built at an altitude of 11,200 feet, Cusco receives two million visitors annually as a tourist stop before the rail trip to the Inca city of Machu Picchu.

Machu Picchu, designated in 2007 as one of the New Seven Wonders of the World, merits the trip. However, Cusco is a grand city in its own right. With a population of four hundred thousand, the Peruvians are open to learning of the living Jesus who takes the place of the often depicted, dead, frail, statue Jesus hanging from a cross.

Matt and Charla Cook with daughter Gabriela, Barton and Allison Kizer with son Cole, and Gary and Jenifer Reaves with sons Logan and Brody, are the right team members for the task. The team formed on the Freed-Hardeman University campus and excelled in the Great Cities internship prior to arrival in Cusco in October 2009.

From a remodeled downtown theater, the team works to show Jesus to city residents and to adjacent communities.

Expanding the Mission through National Teams

The Baxter Institute of Biblical and Cultural Studies operates its modern campus in Tegucigalpa, Honduras. The school's beginnings date to its opening class in Mexico City in 1964. It moved to Honduras in 1978. The four-year Bible college, recognized by the Honduran government, places graduates throughout North, Central, and South America.

With the beginning of the new millennium, Sao Paulo team member Dr. Howard Norton was on campus as a guest lecturer on team missions. Baxter President Calvin Henry, having followed Dr. Norton's work in team missions and his history with Great Cities, inquired as to the possibility of Great Cities Missions recruiting teams from the Baxter campus.

I was skeptical but willing to explore the idea. I knew the teams would need support from North American churches. Philosophically, this was not a problem. Through the years, I have witnessed both good and bad support situations with national Christians. I have also witnessed both good and bad support situations of North American churches supporting North Americans.

There was no doubt in my mind as to the students' quality and ability. My skepticism focused on two basic concerns.

First, North American team members raised their own support. For Baxter students who spoke only Spanish and lacked a relationship with the

North American church, the burden of finding support would add to the already unmanageable load carried by the Great Cities staff.

Second, more often than not, when North American support of a national evangelist fails to work, the national evangelist is the one hurt. Because of language and relationship limitations, it is seldom possible to find another supporting church among North American congregations. At the same time, their former careers pass them by, making it difficult to reenter the work force.

After multiple conversations with Calvin Henry and numerous exchanges over the Great Cities conference table, we were ready to accept a pilot project by training and sending a team of Baxter students to Bogota, Colombia.

The next step was a trip to Baxter Institute to visit with the Baxter board of trustees and the students. Representing our own board of trustees, I accompanied staff member Ken Lewis, trustee Don Vinzant, and our board chair Larry Vinzant to Tegucigalpa in November 2001. The two boards agreed to the pilot project.

Bogota, Colombia, 2003

Like Brazil, Colombia has an impressive list of great cities. At the heart of the nation is its capital, Bogota, with over nine million residents. Its twenty districts form a powerful economic and industrial base. Both city and nation merit hundreds of church plants.

Around our table, the staff designed the pilot project for our first all-Latin team as we interfaced with a group of students from Baxter who had Bogota on their hearts. The project design included four basic tenents:

- The candidates for the team were to follow the Great Cities assessment model.
- Upon the team's arrival in Bogota, we would follow a seven-year timeline.

Celebrate Team Arrivals

- Great Cities would underwrite the cost for Calvin and Linda Henry and the team to come to the States to raise funds.
- The team would follow the Great Cities' training model, including Team Missions, Culture and History, and Urban Church Planting Strategy.

The first team selected from Baxter Institute in Honduras was Luis and Claudia Betanco, Raul Chumbile, Samuel Diaz, Luis and Damira Garcia, Carlos Ingles, and Marvin and Gisela Tercero. In May 2003, the team arrived in Colombia.

Colombians selected Alfonso Guevara and Ailton Hoyos to serve as elders of the congregation on March 6, 2011. With the task complete in just under eight years, the team went on to new assignments.

Calvin Henry on Staff

In 2004, Calvin Henry relinquished the presidency of Baxter Institute after seven years to take on the role of director of Latin Teams at Great Cities. Calvin and his wife, Linda, have worked in Latin American missions since 1977. In addition to Honduras, they served in Costa Rica for eleven years and in Colombia for three years. Calvin has degrees from Abilene Christian University and Harding Graduate School of Religion.

Based on the initial success of the Bogota team, we felt confident to move ahead with team formation among Latin leaders. The next six years continued to validate that decision.

Santiago, Dominican Republic, 2006

The second Baxter Institute team, resulting from the Henrys' work, was a team to an important city in the Caribbean. Santiago de los Caballeros pays tribute to the thirty caballeros (gentlemen) who signed the original city charter. The two million residents of Santiago live in the second largest city of the Dominican Republic.

The capital of Santiago Province receives major economic benefit from its adjacent farming and livestock ranches. The city is moving toward the future with an impressive telecommunication industry. One of its valuable exports for baseball fanatics is its impressive list of over thirty Major League Baseball players, including Jose Lima, Jose Cabrera, and Tony Pena, Jr.

Missionary team members Jose and Sara Alvarez, Cristian and Ana Cruz, Dimas and Sandra Lopez, Omar and Aracelis Odalis, and Omar Rodriguez arrived in the city on January 17, 2006, and experienced an inspiring inaugural worship service on May 21, with forty-eight visitors from the city.

Barranquilla, Colombia, 2006

Located on the Caribbean Sea at Colombia's northern border is the city of Barranquilla. It is the most important coastal city in the nation. Six hundred fifty miles north of Bogota, it, too, is a strategic location for church planting. The population of 1.6 million provides many opportunities for introducing Jesus.

Calvin and Linda Henry recruited Henry and Oralia Duarte, Hermes and Maria Castillo, Olyden and Leonela Jimenez, and Manuel and Elsa Lopez from the Baxter school. The team candidates went through the Great Cities assessment process and training and then arrived in Barranquilla in September 2006, holding their inaugural worship service on May 6, 2007.

Four Team Types

Seeing the success of Latin teams, the plausibility of Hispanic teams for North America's cities with large Spanish populations moved toward reality. At the same time, we started to realize, with third- and fourth-generation Brazilian Christians, we also have an opportunity to form church planting teams from among the Brazilians.

Celebrate Team Arrivals

For the first time, Great Cities now has four pools of talent from which to recruit:

- We will continue to form teams of North American Anglos.
- To that, we added Spanish-speaking Christians from Central America.
- We would now add Hispanic Christians aimed at planting churches in North America.
- And we would recruit from within the Brazilian church to increase church planting in Portuguese-speaking Brazil.

Hispanic Fort Worth, Texas, 2008

Just as Calvin Henry focused on recruiting Latin teams, Ken Lewis focused on recruiting Hispanic teams for North America. For years, we dreamed about initiating a Hispanic church plant within driving distance of the Great Cities office. Such a plant would provide a practical training ground for future teams.

During the transition from Abilene to Dallas in 2007, a Fort Worth church signed their building title over to the ministry for the express purpose of planting a Hispanic church in an area of town that was 95 percent Hispanic.

The team of Manuel and Yvina Calderon, Manuel and Nancy Gonzalez, Javier and Karla Leon, and Luis and Jessica Rosas came together after the Anglo church closed and the ground lay fallow for over a year.

On April 5, 2009, the work officially opened. Over the first sixteen months, there were forty-eight baptisms, and Sunday worship attendance averaged 145.

Brasilia, Brazil, 2009

In April 2006, Ken Lewis and I traveled to Santiago, Chile, and Rio de Janeiro, Brazil, putting out feelers to select people to join the Great Cities staff.

Bryan Gibbs met us in Brasilia after we left Santiago and before our interviews in Rio. Ellis and Doris Long had set a date to depart Brasilia for their deserved retirement in Abilene. Our desire was to be helpful in the transition. In a meeting called with the Brazilian leadership of the church, the conversation moved toward the future. The proposal of the Great Cities men was to recruit a team of Brazilians with university educations to lead the congregation in the nation's capital. The decision was unanimous.

I asked staff member Bryan Gibbs to dedicate his full-time effort on the Brasilia project. That meant recruiting a team and coordinating the team assessment package, the training, the funding, and the integration of the team into the Brasilia church.

Team members raised the first 20 percent of their support in Brazil. Bryan expressed the attitude and philosophy of the Great Cities staff:

> The Brasilia Project is the future of missions. A true partnership between the church in Brazil and the church in North America, it allows the church in Brazil to do what it does best: evangelize its own nation. It also allows the church in North America to do what it does best: equip, assist, encourage, and provide a portion of the financial resources that the Brazilian church is not yet capable of providing.

Three couples recruited from the Sao Paulo churches moved from Sao Paulo to Brasilia in January 2009. Team members Otavio and Alessandra Calegari and their two children, Augusto and Ester; Renato and Carol Pereira and their two children, Vitor and Catarina; and Junior and Patricia Lira arrived to lead the Brasilia congregation into the future.

Cartagena, Colombia, 2008

Calvin and Linda Henry started working with a group of Baxter students set on serving in Cartagena, Colombia. Besias and Deisy Desil, Gary Hall, Sebastian and Raquel Jimenez, and Luis and Schalee Sanchez, with team children, make up the team. Cartagena is another of the jewels of South America. This Caribbean Sea resort is the fifth-largest city in Colombia. Established in 1533, the original two hundred residents grew to today's population of one million. A World Heritage Site is eighty-two miles south of Barranquilla, making a convenient networking distance for former Baxter students.

The team finished its Great Cities internship on January 25, 2008, departing on their research trip prior to their move to the chosen city in April 2008.

Mexico City, 2009

I agree with Calvin Henry's assessment of Mexico City, that "this great city is too large and too important to ignore." The game plan is to place multiple teams in strategic areas of one of the largest cities in the world.

Former Sao Paulo team member Dr. Howard Norton—after a multi-decade tenure as a Bible professor at Oklahoma Christian University then Harding University—became president of Baxter Institute in Tegucigalpa, Honduras, on June 1, 2009. With a heart for church planting, the Baxter Institute continues to produce candidates for missionary teams.

On August 29, 2009, Baxter Institute graduates Luis and Lesbia Mendez, Frank Meza, Luis and Abby Navarrete, and Ramon and Maria Elena Ramirez, arrived in Mexico City. From the previous research trip with Calvin and Linda Henry, the team located in the municipality of Izcalli.

Izcalli is twenty-five miles north of Mexico City's center. Created in 1973, the municipality is one of 125 making up greater Mexico City. Izcalli has over a half-million residents.

These twenty-nine Great Cities teams, with a total membership of 279 missionaries plus a tribe of missionary kids, moved to great cities of the Latin world from 1980 through 2010. It is my prayer that God will bless them, their supporting churches, supporting families, and friends, all who have worked on the board of trustees, donors, staff of Great Cities Missions, and the thousands of new Brazilian and Hispanic Christ followers. May God multiply these humble beginnings into a kingdom harvest beyond our wildest imagination.

15

TEN LESSONS

On our success graph, it has not all been up and to the right. For thirty-five years, I witnessed God's blessing the Great Cities church planting efforts by missionary teams. There are things He has not blessed, when we as human vessels failed to let Him use us as His instruments. At other times, we have witnessed Satan's enormous destruction. It was as if we stood on the sidelines, unable to intervene.

Like daily living, church planting must always be an exercise bathed in prayer and submission to God. With that being the overarching principle coloring every act, I want to share ten solid principles of church planting I learned in the trenches.

INCLUDE THE GIFT OF EVANGELISM

God's desire is for each of us to grow and serve in the kingdom as it shines light into a dark world. Evangelism is like other gift sets; not everyone is an outstanding communicator of God's grace. There seems to be a high correlation between a team's number of gifted evangelists and the number of people they reach with God's message. Teams without gifted evangelists make less of an impact on their city.

Evangelism must continue to be modeled throughout the life of the church. It is always an outward act. It is the very definition of evangelism to reach out with the gospel message. Healthy churches arrive at a wholesome balance of following natural networks of new believers for building a church and reaching out to distant points to help new believers understand God's heart for a lost world. The Recife team is an example of what Jim Collins calls "preserving the core while stimulating progress." The team members and new Christians focused on building a church as described in Ephesians 4. Simultaneously, as the team had some gifted in evangelism, they and their new converts planted thirty-nine additional congregations. Without gifted evangelists, it is difficult to build a growing church.

God Blesses Tenure

God blesses the long-term tenure of the team families. The continuity of a ministry that unfolds over decades blesses multiple generations. At least sixty-eight of the Great Cities missionaries who arrived as members of the first eighteen teams spent ten to thirty years on the field. That number does not include the last eleven teams that started church plants less than ten years ago. Team churches in Belo Horizonte, Campo Grande, Curitiba, Fortaleza, Recife, Salvador, and Sao Paulo are strong in part due to the long tenure of missionary personnel.

Staggered Arrivals Undermine Mission

Few actions undermine meeting the objectives of a missionary team like staggered team-family arrivals. The very nature of team missions calls for the presence of the missionary personnel on the team. It goes back to recruiting the right people for the right seats on the bus, and encouraging all of them to be present on the bus at the same time.

Ten Lessons

Staggered on-field arrivals are not the only way "staggerdness" harms a team. Late arrivals to a team—through marriage or the recruitment of friends who make last-minute decisions to join the team—always damage the togetherness of team training. At best, it is disruptive to the team mission. At worst, the late arrival fails to fit in as a team member and distracts from the team objective.

Beware of Competency Extrapolation

It took me awhile to identify the vocabulary to describe a phenomenon that caused team breakups prior to field arrival and undermined team strategy. Just because people might be brain surgeons, astronauts, missionaries in an unrelated part of the world, or theologians does not make them the brightest bulbs in the room. Bright people can undermine the mission through competency extrapolation.

Experts in their discipline are not necessarily experts in church planting or in designing mission strategy. Be it an academic missiologist, an experienced African missionary, or a competent business executive, expertise in one's own area of experience does not translate into church planting in the great cities of South America.

Many of my own personal failures in helping teams plant urban churches in the Latin world was due to my early lack of experience in being unable to work around the self-anointed experts. In the end, CEOs of a multimillion-dollar enterprise may provide specific insight into various aspects of church planting, but they should never gain control of a church planting strategy. It is a mistake to believe you can direct competency as a CEO into a working skill and insight for a cross-cultural urban church plant.

Observe the Window of Opportunity

Beginning with Brasilia and afflicting the past thirty years of church planting is the challenge of getting the resources of supporting churches, the mission team, and Great Cities on the same page for the first ten years of the church planting project. Supporting churches reflect the short attention span of North Americans. Supporters are thrilled and excited with the project for the first three years. By year five, they are beginning to yawn.

The mission team grows in language and culture skills for the first three years, hitting its stride in both only during year five. Often by year five, there are one or two hundred Christ followers and nowhere to house them within the scarce, expensive space of the megacity.

At year five, the window of opportunity starts to close. The supporting churches are tired and see new fields as ways to excite their people. Some on the missionary team begin to think about returning home. We at Great Cities view the whole mission, knowing what needs to happen to leave an established church, but see the resources evaporating.

An important key is to form a tight relationship between supporting churches, Great Cities, and the missionary team prior to field departure. This provides the greatest assurance that all parties agree on the objective and can reach agreement on what it will take each party involved to declare the mission accomplished.

Never Short-Circuit Team Assessment

Many of the first teams helped us learn the value of a comprehensive team assessment. At first, Great Cities let the teams down in the area of team assessment prior to field service. Neither the supporting churches nor Great Cities Missions understood the value of team assessment. When Ellis Long recruited the first five teams, the idea of prefield missionary evaluation was not on the radar. In the fellowship of Churches of Christ, assessment metrics went unused for both missionaries and staff hires at local congregations. Dr. Clyde Austin first implemented multiple instruments for psychological assessment with team number six, the young men and women preparing to move to Rio de Janeiro.

Ten Lessons

In 1992, I was visiting one of the first teams as a missionary marriage was coming apart. Two wonderful people who had stepped forward in faith over a decade before to plant a church were now in intense pain and confusion. I have often wondered, if they had gone through the levels of assessment available today, perhaps remedial intervention would have prevented a horrible family tragedy. It's stories like this that make me a committed believer in prefield assessment and missionary care.

Another of the first five teams was composed of highly talented leaders. But family of origin issues, interpersonal relations difficulties, and a divorce were Satan's way of attacking the team. These early team experiences continued to add to the body of growing evidence of the need for rigorous prefield assessment. After assessing hundreds of individuals, with only one exception, every time we followed a shortcut or made an exception, it has always been detrimental.

Build with Family Units

In 1986, the Golf Course Road Church of Christ in Midland, Texas, graciously endorsed six months in Brazil for our family in an effort to reinforce our children's identity of dual nationality. We wanted to maintain strong family ties with Brazil.

A part of my assignment during those six months was to research new target cities and to learn from experiences of newly arrived teams to Brazil. One trip took me to the city of Fortaleza. Each member of the Fortaleza team owned a newly invented, first-generation Radio Shack computer. I remember the team members showing me a computer printout of one page listing initial converts.

When looking at the list, to their surprise they saw no complete family units. With a change in strategy, page two began to show a long list of family converts, where both husband and wife made commitments to follow Jesus. From that point forward, Ellis and I made sure we were teaching new teams to study with family units. Remember, we are attempting to plant and establish churches that will last as lighthouses to all the people. The church is open to all. But without the stability of family units, it is difficult to build a congregation of believers that will last over time.

Remember the Power in Continuity

A primary lesson the Belo Horizonte team taught us is the power of continuity. The 1982 Belo team did not arrive in the city oblivious to the work of the previous group, nor did it arrive feeling the need to reinvent the wheel. Rather, they sought to work to build continuity. They built on the foundation and helped to complete walls and rooms envisioned by the original builders. At the same time, there was freedom to add to the building ideas never imagined by the original team. Due to the continuity that extends from 1968 through more than four decades, the church in Belo Horizonte is strong.

Observe the Importance of Pace

It is important for the team to pace itself and not begin the work too soon after arrival on the field. In one case, the *Open Your Bible* radio program from Sao Paulo created a backlog of contacts in the city. Instead of taking sufficient time to settle into the culture of the city and create space for intensive language study, the new team began to teach correspondence course contacts immediately upon arrival. People came to Jesus, and overnight there was a church needing care. By getting quickly drawn into the work, the team placed at risk the possibility of speaking outstanding Portuguese that would have enhanced a long-term, productive future in Brazil.

A new team is excited about planting a church. If a team is evangelistic, it is not uncommon for the missionary team to baptize one hundred thirty people and see the church approach a Sunday attendance of two hundred by the end of four years. The fast work pace in a tropical climate can cause burnout to set in. Missionaries, like other task-oriented people, must take care to take days off, honoring vacation and battery-recharging time if they are to last through the long haul.

Document a Key Strategy

One key to success in team missions is to reach agreement on the main objective and the steps it will take to see the goal accomplished. Teamwork requires different skills, yet it also requires everyone to be on the same page. Assuming that everyone has the same understanding of the goal places the mission in danger.

Only by making the time and effort to sit around a table and record a written strategy will a team be able to reach agreement and share a common expectation with all supporters. Teams that have shelved the strategy document upon field arrival return home with little to show for a great expense and the trust placed in them by supporters, not to mention the missed opportunity to make God's grace available to hurting people. Of the twenty-nine teams that departed for the field through Great Cities from 1980 through 2010, the teams who discarded their strategy document experienced the least success.

Planting a church with beloved team members can be a climactic experience remembered warmly and celebrated with gratitude throughout life. The wise team will do everything within its power to apply the ten principles outlined in this chapter. By doing so, the likelihood increases exponentially of hearing the words, "Well done, good and faithful servant."

16

MISSION AND PAIN

As I begin this chapter, I don't know if I have the guts or, for the refined, the courage, to include what I am about to write in the book. Here goes for what I anticipate will be a tough walk down memory lane.

I am overwhelmed with God's grace. My hope is this chapter will not come through as an exercise in false humility. I am extremely grateful God allowed me to be a participant in the Great Cities story.

My first plane ride in Brazil as weight for Carl Henderson and his instructor while practicing stalls on a hot Sunday afternoon became a prophetic symbol for life. For a while, the journey was a nice, smooth, steady climb. Then the bottom would drop out and the plane would go into rapid-fall mode. The only time I felt a remote sense of relief was each time the aircraft "hit bottom," and I regained a slight feeling of normalcy during the subsequent climb—only to know it would not be long before the bottom would drop out again.

The plot of the Bible is God's perfect creation, spoiled by sin, its ongoing restoration, and a final, perfect state. In the midst of the chaos of sin and imperfection, Scripture teaches, "I am fearfully and wonderfully made."

You created my inmost being; you knit me together in my mother's womb. I praise you because I am fearfully and wonderfully made; your works are wonderful, I know that full well. My frame was not hidden from you when I was made in the secret place, when I was woven together in the depths of the earth. Your eyes saw my unformed body; all the days ordained for me were written in your book before one of them came to be. (Psalm 139:13–16)

I must admit at first reading, the "wonderfully made" is not the me I know. I hurt. Sometimes I have a hard time giving God an A+ on the construction of my earthly temple.

In 1948, as a toddler I moved with my family to House, New Mexico, for two years. They were to help with the family farm. I was an active little guy. My memories of the toddler years are few, but I remember the thrill of chasing the chickens and the cats. I remember sand was everywhere, and corncobs littered the ground. I thought they were for the pigs to eat; only later did I learn the pigs left the cobs after devouring the corn.

On the farm was my first initiation on how to use the big hole in the outhouse, always being careful not to fall in. To be ready for Sunday morning church, we took our Saturday night baths in an old iron tub with water heated with a wood fire in the bathhouse. From those days through my Carlsbad years, the Saturday night bath took place after shoes were shined for the next morning's worship.

It was on the dry-dirt farm in House where I experienced my first encounter with the medical system. I am sure one of my teenage uncles must have left a can of kerosene on the front porch. Obviously, a little farmer needs to stop and quench his thirst from time to time. I remember none of this. As family lore has it, in haste, they transported me the fifty miles to the hospital in Tucumcari, New Mexico, located on famed Route 66, for a rapid stomach pump procedure.

Mission and Pain

My earliest feeling of hurt and desperation took place at the University of New Mexico Carrie Tingley Children's Hospital in Hot Springs, a town later named Truth or Consequences (or T or C, New Mexico, for the convenience of the residents and the Chamber of Commerce).

My parents took me there from Artesia, New Mexico, where we lived after the farm and prior to the Carlsbad return. It was the beginning of a lifetime of hospital and surgical intervention. Six decades ago, state sponsored hospitals were sparse and frugal operations. The child-friendly concept was galaxies away from the practice of the day. My bed was in a ward with who knows how many other children. As a three-year-old, I forgot to count my fellow little sufferers.

What I do remember was my iron bed with sidebars as high as I was tall. My parents followed hospital regulations and placed me behind the bars as I cried in utter desperation when I saw them walk from the room. Alone for the first time, I did not know what was happening. I do not remember the reunion with my parents. It must have meant super reassurance for a little boy who had just experienced his first hospital trauma.

During the first few years, the doctors misdiagnosed my condition as Ollier disease. At the age of five, I returned to Carrie Tingley Hospital for my first bone surgery on my arms. I will always remember the smell of the ether they used to anesthetize me. With more research, over the next decade the disease was identified as multiple hereditary exostoses (MHE). The two unusual diseases are similar in many ways but different, with MHE having less risk of bone cancer. As a rare disease, only one in every fifty thousand people contract it. The condition produces benign bone tumors and shortens and bows the bones. It causes numbness from nerve compression, nerve damage, tendon and muscle irritation, weak bones, and risk of bone cancer in later life. It results in pain, fatigue, and mobility problems throughout life.

My journey with MHE has not been easy. Seldom did a day go by during my six years of grade school without someone asking, "What is wrong with your arms?" Thankfully, as I entered junior high, kids started to pick up social norms and didn't utter every thought and question that passed through their minds.

My first surgery at age five was the beginning of thirty bone surgeries in multiple hospitals in North and South America while living with pain that turned chronic at age fifty-three.

Nine months after the death of our son Jay in September 1998, I went to Amarillo for a few days' work with the Amarillo Central church. I was tired and in a hurry, so I drove the five-hour trip without a break. When I stood up in Amarillo, I had excruciating pain in my right ankle.

Each day and evening, I made my scheduled calls and return to the hotel to get off my ankle. My assumption was a bone was inflamed but it would settle down if I could stay off my legs.

I continued to work the following week. Our son Michael was in Lubbock, attempting to live on his own. Due to his tuberous sclerosis complex (TSC), he could not focus sufficiently to hold a job. So once again, I was on my way to Lubbock to help him locate another job and a new place to live. The pain was now in my leg and growing worse. The following week, I had an appointment with a student as a member of his doctoral dissertation committee. I met the appointment and went from there to my bone doctor.

When Dr. Shannon Holloway saw my leg, he sent me directly to the hospital. A blood clot had migrated from my ankle to my groin area, postured for the last part of the journey to my lungs.

Two weeks later, I was able to check out of the hospital. The goal was to get out in time to meet our daughter's vacation schedule for a daughter, mom, and dad trip to San Antonio. The three of us had planned the trip in anticipation of her marriage.

Mission and Pain

We put a bed in the Chevy Astro van so I could extend my leg and took off for the River Walk in San Antonio. After the boat ride on the river, a walk through the shops, and an evening dinner, my leg once again swelled like a balloon. With chronic pain in both legs, the next morning it was back to Abilene and straight to Hendrick Medical Center for another week in the hospital.

After five days at home in my recliner, the pain only got worse. To my utter frustration, as I started to move about one afternoon while dragging a storm branch from the backyard to the alley, I fell and broke my hip. There I was again, spending another two weeks in the hospital, with an additional two weeks living at a rehabilitation center. I could see this aging thing called the "golden years," even though I was only fifty-three, was not all it was reputed to be.

Over the next five years, I underwent five more surgeries, traveled to Scott and White Medical Center, the Texas Tech University Health Sciences Center's Pain Clinic, the University of Texas Southwestern Medical Center in Dallas, and the Institute for Chronic Pain relief at Abilene's Hendrick Medical Center. I was desperate enough to begin a nationwide search, so I sought out the Mayo Clinic in Jacksonville, Florida, and MD Anderson Hospital in Houston. I was open to any and every lead I could find in an effort to relieve my chronic leg pain.

I also sought out alternative approaches to mainstream medicine. Nothing worked. By 2003, it was obvious the pain medications were not the solution. I worked my way off all prescription medication and determined to move forward. The pain was not solvable, and God sure was not answering my prayers according to my personal preference.

An article in the May-June 2005 *Journal of Pediatric Orthopedics* reported a pain study conducted among a worldwide population of people dealing with multiple exostoses. To their surprise, 84 percent of the 293 persons completing the questionnaire alleged to live with chronic pain.

Although I was determined not to be defined by my disease, as I grew in my understanding of life, the question finally crossed my mind: how can I possibly make sense of my being "wonderfully made"?

I reached an answer that works for me. What is me is not just my body. Stay with me. I am not talking about the Gnostic heresy of the early church. Some falsely claimed you could sin with your body since it was not your spirit. There were those in the early church who found a nice excuse for enjoying all the enticements of sin while claiming their spirits exempt from their unruly bodies.

However, my claim is different. I'm claiming that as an untarnished aspect of God's perfect creation, God breathed into me the breath of life and gave me His perfect essence in my soul—which is uniquely me for all eternity.

God did in fact "create my inmost being; knitting me together in my mother's womb." To be clear, I am formed in wonderful fashion. I just happen to be living the result of man's satanic fall. By the act of man's fall, I find myself living in a diseased house. My earthy dwelling is just one of the negative results created through the transgression of God's first man and God's first woman over a piece of holy fruit. My reality is, it's my soul that is the eternal me, not my body. This dysfunctional body will be traded in for a brand-new one that works to perfection with an eternal guarantee (1 Corinthians 15:42).

Even in its fallen state of the present, the body is a remarkable creation. The writer Philip Yancey coauthored three books on the marvels of God's creation—the human body—with the late Dr. Paul Wilson Brand, including *Fearfully and Wonderfully Made*.

Dr. Brand was born on July 17, 1914, to missionary parents working in India. Part of what is remarkable about Dr. Brand's work is his lifetime spent compassionately treating those in India with leprosy. Practicing medicine for nineteen years in Vellore, India, he treated bodies damaged by the disease of leprosy. Listening to patients' complaints and viewing their malfunctioning bodies, he reacted by compiling a ninety-page manuscript marveling at what God had made even in the face of dreaded disease. From his deep friendship with Philip Yancey, the old, yellowed manuscript became the book *Fearfully and Wonderfully Made*.

While living in Galilee, Jesus often healed those with diseased bodies. God's creation was both spirit and body. Body and spirit are connected. Jesus received a new body after His resurrection. It still enjoyed a good fish fry (John 21:12) along with the ability to appear and disappear through walls at will (John 20:19).

In 1 Corinthians 15:35–55, Paul tells us of the new bodies we will receive at our resurrection. Once again, our spirit will be at home in a body.

Discovering this import understanding of Scripture was not a conclusion I reached at the beginning of ministry. The truth be told, in my early years I did not think a lot about trying to reconcile a perfect God with the imperfections of life.

Even arriving at an intellectual understanding of the fall of man does not make life a trek through the bluebonnets in the Texas Hill Country. Living with the pain of incurable disease is not easy.

Surviving the Pain of Death

In chapter 8, I observed that while living in Lubbock we began to understand more deeply that a tenacious trust in God was our only option to survive life. It was there that the diagnoses of tuberous sclerosis complex for our twin sons became an everyday reality for the remainder of our lives.

What we could not have known at the time was the role TSC would play as the bookends to the thirty years of recruiting, training, and caring for missionaries through the Great Cities ministry. We worked tirelessly to proclaim Jesus by planting churches in the great cities of the Latin world. From day one in the Great Cities missionary recruiting ministry, my baby boomer work ethic kicked in. I was determined to do a good job.

Cut from reflective cloth, it is easy for me to think of life like a bookcase. The bottom shelf displays the books of my growing up years. Shelf number two contains the books of my college years. The third shelf is replete with the books of my Brazil years and transition back to the U. S.

On the left end of bookshelf four is a large bookend marked "Tuberous Sclerosis Complex." The bookend stands tall. It signifies the beginning of thirty-three years of books placed one after the other. No matter the subject, TSC colored each book and its chapters for the entire thirty years of work with the church planting ministry.

In the early years, I would spend my free time at the library of the Texas Tech School of Medicine to learn all I could about the disease. If only the invention of the personal computer had arrived twenty years earlier. Laboring through the card catalogs and roaming within the endless aisles of medical journals, copying article after article, we slowly began to acquire a basic knowledge of the disorder.

For twenty-one years, throughout Jay's life, God taught us a deeper compassion and trust. He taught us how to love when it's impossible to receive love back. On September 16, 1998, Jay left this earth for eternity to await his new and perfect body at the return of Jesus. His brain, along with every system of his body, was full of disease. His soul remained pure from the day of his birth. Although I had twenty-one years to prepare for his death, to stand by the bed and see my son expel his final breath was the greatest pain I had ever encountered.

Jay's twin, Michael, was full of life. The disease had not damaged his brain. His curious mind and the speed of his legs kept us constantly on full alert. How he loved to learn to read the book *Curious George*. Readily he identified with the main character of the story. With the camera, we

Mission and Pain

chronicled his life from first steps, to tricycles, to bicycles, to scouts, to school, to his job, to the purchase of his red Dodge truck. We camped, we fished, and we picked opposing sports teams to experience the good-natured competition of a father and a son.

With each passing year the disease would stake its claim throughout a little more of Michael's body. Just after celebrating his thirty-third birthday, and following a lifetime of medical appointments, multiple surgeries, and medical procedures, Michael died in his sleep of renal failure. We had now lost both sons and felt reduced totally to trust God tenaciously.

In six months, my assignment as the chief executive officer of the Great Cities Missions would end. The timing of Michael's death served as the final bookend during my leadership with Great Cities. No pain in life has been greater than the sudden death of Michael and the subsequent preparation of his funeral.

The lessons taught to me as a child return to memory. Just as God provided manna for the Israelites, He can still be trusted to provide for me now. Just as He stood by His prophets, He can stand by me now. Just as the God of Scripture could be trusted to move obstacles beyond the comprehension of those facing impossible odds, He can move obstacles that rise up to challenge my trust in Him.

Here is what I know. I haven't survived. I am *surviving*. I choose to trust God with my life that remains.

God is aware of my life circumstances and He is not panicking. Each of us lives in the face of real life. Our task is to trust Him and do the best we can under any circumstance to be faithful to whatever assignment He has given us. I'm often reminded that Paul the apostle said that it is by God working through weak and imperfect people that His glory shines through all the more brightly.

After fifty-plus years of God working through imperfect people, there should be no doubt that Great Cities Missions is a God project.

17

GOD OF THE FUTURE

It's difficult to wrap our minds around the eternal God. God is not bound by time. He was present before Creation, during Creation, and at the fall of man. He was present as He began to recreate man through Noah and through Abraham. His grace and patience stood by the children of Israel, from Egypt until their deportation to Babylonian captivity. Still, His presence was with a remnant He would use to place Jesus upon the earth. He witnessed the crucifixion and the resurrection of his Son. He was with the early church as they started to move the redemptive mission toward eternity. God is still present. He is God of our present and God of our future.

GREAT PAST

The ministry, with its roots in the vision of thirty-one college kids from Abilene Christian College in 1957, has experienced a great past, with hundreds of missionaries planting hundreds of churches. A donor base consisting of individuals, foundations, churches, elders, trustees, and staff members of the past have played vital roles in bringing the ministry to its present state.

Make Your Vision Go Viral

The Great Cities mission is firm and on track. Due to the degree of difficulty and complexity, there will always be one or two steps backward for every three steps forward. I stand grateful for the historic and continual backing of the Central Church of Christ of Amarillo. I will be eternally grateful for our trustees and the quality, vision, and expertise each brings to the table. The staff of today is a team of high quality, exceptional experience, and an eternal commitment to God and His Son, Jesus. The financial base, although not where I would desire it to be, is strong and growing. Teams are in the pipeline training for the field.

It is easy to reflect on the past and see the hand of God. I see the hand of God on my life from the New Mexico desert to the present day. I see the hand of God at work through the lives of thirty-one college kids in 1957. I see the hand of God at work from the first articulation of the Great Cities concept to the results of the present day. Over my last five years as executive director, God brought the ministry through the deepest economic recession since the Great Depression. In tribute to the power of God, during the same period the ministry made its greatest strides forward. I marvel at the past but am astounded with the opportunities for the future.

The Latin World

One out of every ten people on the face of the earth speaks Portuguese or Spanish. Only Mandarin and English are more widely spoken. At difficult junctures in the Great Cities work, some have inquired as to a timeline projection of "mission accomplished." The best I can tell, that milestone will appear with the return of Jesus. From a human perspective, the need of reaching lost people in the Portuguese- and Spanish-speaking world increases every nanosecond.

I frequently visit South America. For the past forty years, never have I been in South America without being impressed with the growth of its cities. Since arriving in Brazil in November 1969, the metro area of Sao Paulo has grown from eight million to thirty million residents. Across the South American Continent, fifty cities have populations greater than one million and another fifty cities host from 350,000 to one million residents.

Among the seventy-seven million Spanish speakers of Central America and the Caribbean Islands, there are at least ten great cities. Churches still need planting in that region.

Mexico, our neighbor to the south, offers endless opportunities for planting churches. The most striking need is Mexico City. The greater Mexico City area is among the top two or three cities in the world, with an estimated population exceeding thirty-five million. Ten other cities exceed a population of one million, with the next thirty cities serving as home to between 500,000 and 936,000 Mexicans. Great cities of Mexico merit hundreds of church plants.

In our own homeland, fifty million Hispanics live and work. Here in the United States are ten cities with large Hispanic centers that each serve as home to a million Spanish speakers. Churches still need planting in Chicago, Dallas, Denver, El Paso, Houston, Los Angeles, Miami, New York, San Antonio, and San Diego.

Portugal is the motherland of Brazil. Brazilians love their autonomy and national success. They love to poke fun at the Portuguese people. In spite of the humor, many still have family and historic connections to the homeland, explaining the strong emotional tie to the nation.

Portugal's population of ten million resides in 149 towns and cities across twenty provinces. The national capital of Lisbon, with its 545,000 residents, and Porto with 237,000, are the largest cities. Nine other cities have populations exceeding 100,000. Portuguese-speaking churches still need planting in that nation.

Spain intrigues me. Two of its cities—Madrid and Barcelona—each exceeds five million city dwellers. Fifteen other provinces would be candidates for church plants in their cities.

The five African nations of Angola, Cape Verde, Guinea-Bissau, Mozambique, and Sao Tome and Principe speak Portuguese.

In Asia, Portuguese is spoken in East Timor; Goa, Daman, and Diu in India; and Macau in China. It is one of the official languages of East Timor and Macau.

The task is one of planting churches in hundreds of cities for one-tenth of the world's population on five continents where the population speaks Portuguese or Spanish.

God Power

The storyline of the Old Testament is God with His people. In the New Testament, after the crucifixion and resurrection of Jesus, the storyline becomes God *in* His people.

Let me quickly get in line with all those of the past two thousand years who do not understand the intricacies of the Trinity. Somewhere between God the Father, Jesus the Son, and the Holy Spirit, being one yet being separate, answers get foggy in the limited human mind.

Just prior to Jesus' death, He told His closest followers He would send an advocate to live inside of them (John 14:16–17). He went on to say, "Because I live, you also will live. On that day you will realize that *I am in my Father*, and *you are in me*, and *I am in you*" (John 14:19–20; emphasis mine).

When Jesus encountered Saul on his way to Damascus to harm Jesus-followers, He identified himself to Saul as the One who Saul was persecuting (Acts 9:5). Jesus lives inside of each persecuted Christian. So by harming Christ followers, Saul was harming Jesus.

After his encounter with Jesus, Saul described the power of God's Holy Spirit and the Holy Spirit of Jesus living in the body of believers who submit to the life empowered by Christ:

GOD OF THE FUTURE

You, however, are not in the realm of the flesh but are in the realm of the Spirit, if indeed the *Spirit of God lives in you*. And if anyone does not have the Spirit of Christ, they do not belong to Christ. But if *Christ is in you*, then even though your body is subject to death because of sin, the Spirit gives life because of righteousness. And if the *Spirit of him who raised Jesus from the dead is living in you*, he who raised Christ from the dead will also give life to your mortal bodies because of *his Spirit who lives in you*. (Romans 8:9–11, emphasis mine)

The apostle Paul told the Corinthian church, "We are the temple of the living God. As God has said: 'I will live with them and walk among them, I will be their God and they will be my people'" (2 Corinthians 6:16). During the first century, Gentile readers of the New Testament letters would recognize a temple as the dwelling place of the gods. Jewish believers would readily identify the temple as the dwelling place of Jehovah God.

Two other insights given by inspiration to the apostle Paul shed light on the way God works. Paul said, "We are God's handiwork, created in Christ Jesus to do good works, which God prepared in advance for us to do" (Ephesians 2:10). God's design is to do His work through His creation.

Paul then showed the partnership between man and God in undertaking the challenges of recreating a fallen world. So Paul told the Philippian church in chapter three: "Continue to work out your salvation with fear and trembling, for it is *God who works in you* to will and to act in order to fulfill his good purpose" (Philippians 2:12–13, emphasis mine). Paul said it is God at work in us to make good things happen that fulfills His own purpose.

Author Philip Yancey in his book *Prayer: Does It Make Any Difference?* strings together various statements by the apostle in an attempt to explain one way God chooses to work:

Work out your salvation with fear and trembling, for it is God who works in you to will and to act according to his good purpose.

I worked harder than all of them—yet not I, but the grace of God that was with me.

I no longer live, but Christ lives in me.

For we are God's workmanship, created in Christ Jesus to do good works, which God prepared in advance for us to do.[1]

Yancey then draws the logical conclusion: "The partnership binds so tight that it becomes hard to distinguish who is doing what, God, or the human partner. God has come that close."[2] It is a sobering idea to reflect that God is working with me to the extent that I do not know if it is I or God, because we are doing it together.

When I reflect on the challenge of planting churches across the face of the Latin world in an effort to proclaim Jesus among Spanish- and Portuguese-speaking people, I must conclude that God stands ready. He stands ready to work through specific, redeemed people. The church planting needs of the great cities of the Latin world will go unmet until individual Christians who possess the Holy Spirit of God at the heart of their souls step forward and accept the Lord's offer of a working partnership.

Let me describe possible ways to unleash the power of God in an attempt to join with Him in His work.

A Financial Engine

For Great Cities Missions to be a serious player on the world stage in reaching the great cities of five continents where Portuguese or Spanish is spoken, financial resources must be available. There is the need to create a financial engine to supplement income received from individuals, churches, and foundations.

Nonprofit entities need multiple streams of income to survive and thrive. A financial engine has potential to be greater than a small stream of income. It could be a large tributary flowing in to feed the River of Mission.

Traditionally, giving to missions comes from honorable, sacrificial sources and from less than honorable—good enough for missions—castaway motives. Seldom is there enough money to be creative and to undertake major objectives in reaching lost people with the living Jesus.

The church does not lack for money. God, the giver of all good gifts, anoints people within the church with the gift to make money. I am talking about people who get as much fun and satisfaction from putting together deals and making money as I get from landing a hooked rainbow trout. There is nothing easy about finding rainbow trout in a mountain stream. It requires long hours, walking up and down mountains and riverbanks, sweating, fighting bugs, often being soaked by rain, and burned by sun. What exhilarating fun.

There is nothing easy about making money. It takes long hours confronting storms, sweating bullets, pacing up and down, having a mind that will not shut off, being soaked by unforeseen setbacks, and burned by unethical people. But for the person wired to make money, what fun and satisfaction they receive.

Now for the what-if: What if two or three business types have already made all the money the family could possibly use, but the thrill of the game is still present because of God-given wiring? Would it be possible for two or three entrepreneurs to form a business for the sole purpose of working with Great Cities Missions to fund church planting in the great cities of the Latin world? These people could collaborate in a major way with God by recognizing once again their God-given gift. As a working partnership with God, their spiritual gift and expertise of a lifetime could build a financial engine that would supply millions of dollars to reach the great cities of the Latin world.

Working with foundations, churches, and individuals has many upsides. A downside is, by nature, the way funding is determined. Instead of concentrating funds toward a set number of entities over a long period, often funds are in small amounts spread among many entities with the intent of communicating to the entity that it cannot depend annually on the same source.

What we are missing is the piece of the puzzle that would apply the same God-given gift of entrepreneurship used to build megabusinesses. Were the same expertise applied to build the kingdom throughout the major cities of the world, millions of dollars could be generated annually by those accustomed to working in the business arena.

Five Visions

Needs and opportunities abound around the world. Accepting God as living in us and being our partner in the implementation of good works, Great Cities can be a world player if we take hold of five visions. Each has the potential to become reality. To wrap a layer of feasibility around what some would conclude as outlandish and audacious dreams, it will take the cooperation of individuals who are willing to believe that God within them can accomplish one or more doable steps to reach kingdom goals.

1. Multiple Continents

I dream of our God doing increasingly great acts among Portuguese- and Spanish-speaking people. This is not a recent desire. This burning in my soul was ignited long ago. I envision great and effective churches planted on five continents of the world. These churches—with reproducing DNA—will have a critical mass large enough to grow mature elders, teachers, deacons, and evangelists. Such a vision seems entirely aligned with the will of God. I reach this conclusion based on the entirety of Scripture condensed into five statements, each expressing the same truth. Salvation is found only through Jesus.

The apostle Peter makes the first statement, shortly after the Resurrection. A few days before, Peter saw Jesus ascend through the clouds, returning to God the Father. In defending his act of restoring a man's legs by the name of Jesus, he declared, "Salvation is found in no one else, for there is no other name under heaven given to mankind by which we must be saved" (Acts 4:12).

The apostle John makes the next four statements. In his record of the Gospel, he said what he learned to be true about God:

> For God so loved the world that he gave his one and only Son, that whoever believes in him shall not perish but have eternal life. For God did not send his Son into the world to condemn the world, but to *save the world through him*. Whoever believes in him is not condemned, but whoever does not believe stands condemned already because they have not believed in the name of God's one and only Son. This is the verdict: Light has come into the world, but people loved darkness instead of light because their deeds were evil. Everyone who does evil hates the light, and will not come into the light for fear that their deeds will be exposed. But whoever lives by the truth comes into the light, so that it may be seen plainly that what they have done has been done in the sight of God. (John 3:16–21; emphasis mine)

He then cited two direct quotes of Jesus: "I am the gate; whoever enters through me will be saved" (John 10:9) And Jesus reaffirms His identity to the apostle Philip: "Don't you know me? . . . Anyone who has seen me has seen the Father" (John 14:9).

The apostle John wrote to the churches, "We have seen and testify that the Father has sent his Son to be the Savior of the world" (1 John 4:14).

Based on Scripture, the assumption that God wants all humankind to be saved and that salvation comes through His Son is firm ground on which to stand. The vision to plant churches across the cities of five continents among Spanish and Portuguese speakers is aligned with the will of God. To play a greater role in the fulfillment of the vision, we need gutsy people—people who will allow God to work in them and with them—to join with us to see lost people saved in these great cities.

Module upon module, while continuing to work in South America, the ministry can undertake this task in North America, Europe, Africa, and Asia. Our only limitation is our own lack of willingness to join with God and align with likeminded workers to build upon a history of expertise and success. Together we can see a great vision realized throughout five continents.

2. Endowments

I have often heard it said that there will be two types of universities in the twenty-first century: the extinct and the endowed. Universities realize the difficulty of annually raising operation funding.

After thirty-five years of existence, Great Cities Missions has no endowment. Each year on January 2, after a New Year's Day holiday, the treadmill starts to roll again. Annually, funding must be raised once again for continued operation. We often forget world missions as families leave estates and trusts for the next generation. One nice estate gift could open the doors for the ministry to move into Spain or Portugal or to accelerate missionary team training. The drawing board is stacked high with grand visions.

3. A Center for Missionary Team Training

To be effective in planting churches on five continents among Portuguese and Spanish speakers, a third vision, the creation of a center for missionary team training, is imperative.

God of the Future

This is a hard idea to sell. It is a dream that requires the leadership of well-resourced visionaries. If we are ever to be a major player in sharing Jesus through church plants across the globe, now is the time to make a major modification in our funding strategy to ensure the future. God has granted this ministry success. As we look to the future, immediate attention should be focused on long-range funding. To address long-range funding we must establish perpetuity through permanence and grow endowment funding.

An atmosphere of permanence needs to be created to directly affect giving and attracting endowment funds and long-range estate acquisition.

People have a right to expect that Great Cities Missions will have an effective and permanent future, making it possible to honor the intent of the donor who gifts an estate built over a lifetime. It is only through building permanence that sizable gifts will be attracted to fund vital aspects of the mission. The possibility of Harvard or the Mayo Clinic going out of business never crosses a donor's mind. Donors know these institutions are permanent. Donors need to know that Great Cities is in business for perpetuity.

Many components of the ministry must be endowed to get off the annual treadmill of survival. The foundational piece to make this possible while creating a lasting future will be the Great Cities Missionary Recruiting and Training Center.

As you approach the center, your eye will focus on an impressive globe surrounded by flags of Portuguese- and Spanish-speaking nations. The center will house offices and include a state-of-the-art theater where prospective missionary candidates can view a hurting world via a wraparound screen.

Equipped with the latest technological advancements, live conferencing will connect to mission teams from around the world. This will increase the potential to recruit, train, and support the needs of missionary teams with up-to-the-minute data.

The training center will house language labs, classrooms, areas for relationship and team building, and serve as a resource hub for church planting in the Latin world. Access to technology, a great teaching center, and an urban curriculum that includes a continued emphasis on prayer and trust in God will make it possible to prepare highly trained missionary teams.

The training center will house the Center for Missionary Team Women to prepare women for daily life and ministry in a foreign country. Experienced missionary women will instruct their young counterparts on issues common to those living in a foreign culture. The center will support women in all stages of life. Great Cities is committed to making the Center for Missionary Team Women a first-rate program to recruit, train, and care for missionary teams' courageous women who accept God's call to the challenges of sharing the hope found in Jesus.

Unique to the building will be a Mission Kids Training Center, where needs and interests of children will be met in preparation for a move to a foreign nation. They will be able to read age-specific books and watch age-specific movies on their chosen country. A scaled-down children's kitchen will allow the kids to prepare simple foods of their new culture.

The design of the entire ambience will facilitate relationship building. Prayer gardens, sitting areas, coffee nooks, and fireplaces will all point to the importance of preparing the team to work effectively as a unit. The most exciting result will be a significant increase in bringing people who speak Portuguese and Spanish to Jesus.

Is it possible that God is scanning His radar looking for individuals He is dwelling in to work with Him to bring this vision to fruition? Could you as a reader of this book be a person chosen by God for this purpose?

4. Increase Expertise in Providing National Work Teams

A fourth vision centers on the development of another valuable resource. Across the nations of Central America, Mexico, Hispanic South America, and Brazil, the children and grandchildren of third and fourth generation churches make up a rich resource pool of national Christians ready to take their place on missionary teams. Using their native language, combined with the DNA of growing up in a mission church from day one, national Christians bring to the table the language, zeal, and experience of bringing others to Jesus.

In 2003, we initiated a pilot project recruiting team members from Baxter Institute of Biblical and Cultural Studies in Tegucigalpa, Honduras (see chapter 14). From Baxter Institute, the Great Cities Missions has been the recipient of high-quality, well-trained personnel filling seven team rosters for the cities of Bogota; Barranquilla; Cartagena, Colombia; Santiago, Dominican Republic; Mexico City; and Fort Worth, Texas.

The first team into Bogota, Colombia, established a church with national elders, teachers, deacons, and an evangelist in just over seven years.

In 2008, we started a similar pilot project in Brazil, recruiting teams for the federal capital Brasilia. Three talented Brazilian couples and their children with a supporting financial partnership of family, the Brazilian church, and churches from Oklahoma and Texas joined the project. Their success creates confidence in this growing resource.

The area of mission teams staffed with national workers is one with a bright future. Calvin Henry, with his wife, Linda; Ken Lewis, with his wife, Elizabeth; and Bryan Gibbs, with his wife, Becky, have led the recruiting, training, and care for our pilot work with Hispanic national and Brazilian national teams.

We are in the work deeply enough to see that the weak link in the chain is limited funding. Three couples are not physically able to multiply themselves sufficiently to cover all of the bases of recruiting, training, routine and crisis care, interpersonal relations, and seeking financial and strategic support for a growing list of teams. They need additional help.

Teamwork among Latin leaders, like teamwork among Anglos, comes with difficulty. There is still a lot to learn to enhance teamwork on Anglo teams. For Latin leaders, the learning curve is greater. I would argue that Anglo teams—as a heritage from the Second Great Awakening—have more exposure to democracy and an awareness of the strength of teamwork's roots in Judeo-Christianity. Ecclesiastes 4:12 speaks of the threefold cord not being easily broken. Proverbs 15:22 tells of the value of listening to many advisers for plans to succeed. In earlier chapters, I referenced to the use of teamwork in the New Testament. In addition, for the last decades we in the United States find teamwork incorporated into business models, educational models, family life, and churches.

Our Latin friends have centuries of authoritarian models in government, churches, education, business, and family. Holy Scripture has not been as readily available in Latin homes. In contrast, what Anglos gain by osmosis gives them a head start in learning teamwork. The good news is the Hispanic people are intelligent and driven by desire for a brighter future. They are personable and group oriented in social settings. They can learn to work as a team. With the Hispanic head start on language and culture, I would argue a Latin team that has learned to work together could be most effective.

The vision is to be able to learn how to better equip Latin team members to work together to plant churches. An important component of the dream is to better equip the Great Cities staff with increasing expertise in understanding crossing cultural barriers and to know how to incorporate native Brazilian and Hispanic caregivers to join with us to care for these outstanding team men, women, and children.

5. On-going Building of Highly Talented Staff

A fifth vision for Great Cities Missions is to continue to hire optimum talent to fill staff positions. The ministry should always have a staff recognized as a highly valuable component. Assuming potential staff recruits will come from a pool of experienced people, success is tied to capability. As one who spent six decades dealing with the medical system, I have always been aware that one-half of all doctors graduated in the lower half of their class. Before selecting a doctor, I do my research to determine if Dr. Potential graduated from a renowned medical school, and, if possible, I seek to determine class ranking. In every case, when I failed to hire highly capable staff members, their tenures were short and their contributions were limited.

Going Forward

Our Great Cities Missions owes abundant gratitude to thirty-one college kids who arrived in Sao Paulo, Brazil, in June 1961 as a team with a vision. Their deep friendship allowed them to remain united on the field long enough to implement a vision ignited a decade before for South America—moving missionary teams to great cities.

We serve the God of creation, of history, of the present, and of the future. The cities of the Latin world are growing at an accelerated rate. One-tenth of the world's population speaks Spanish or Portuguese and spreads across five continents of the globe.

I have referred to the research of Jim Collins. A third insight drawn from his work is what his research group tagged the "Hedgehog Concept." The hedgehog is a little animal genetically created and programmed to roll itself into a ball and stick out its quills to protect against attack.

Collins uses the analogy of the hedgehog's ability to do one thing well to compare it to an organization. The Collins research revealed that enduring and great organizations know their passion, are better than others at their proclaimed expertise, and have a financial engine to power the mission. Where these three converge is an organization's "hedgehog."

Make Your Vision Go Viral

We are passionate about proclaiming Jesus by planting churches in the great cities of the Latin world. We excel in building teams, but we still struggle with the financial engine.

The answer to our financial engine is to see that God lives inside His children and desires to work with and through them to restore fallen humankind back to Himself. God has gifted some of His children with entrepreneur vision and the gift to make money. These men and women are vital in playing key roles as they realize God's desire to work with and through them as a partner in turning five visions into reality.

Accepting God as living in us and being our partner in the implementation of good works, Great Cities will be a world player when we take hold of these five visions.

Hundreds of Portuguese- and Spanish-speaking cities across the world need the grace God offers through Jesus. Building endowments is important to longevity in reaching the five continents. I believe the creation of our Missionary Recruiting and Training Center is the key to addressing the endowment need and to increase recruiting and training of missionary teams needed to reach the great cities.

A vital part of the overall picture is to recognize the important role of national teams and to increase our own expertise in partnering with our Hispanic and Brazilian brothers and sisters.

Finally, it is always important for Great Cities to be conscious of the need to build its own staff with highly capable people.

May God grant these visions, and may heaven overflow with wonderful people around the globe who can only know Him through the Portuguese or Spanish language. With God's help, we can make our vision go viral.

Notes

Chapter 1

1. Palmer Harsough, "Jesus Is Calling." Public Domain.

Chapter 10

1. Stan Lindquist, "Is the Psychological Test Worth It?" *The Evangelical Missions Quarterly* (April 1983): 114, 116.

Chapter 11

1. Charles A. Weitz and Elmer S. Miller, *Introduction to Anthropology* (New Jersey: Prentice Hall, 1979), 329.
2. Roger Greenway, *Guidelines for Urban Church Planting* (Grand Rapids, MI: Baker Books, 1976), 17.

Chapter 17

1. Philip Yancey, *Prayer: Does It Make Any Difference?* (Grand Rapids, MI: Zondervan, 2010).
2. Yancey, *Prayer*.

About the Author

D<small>R</small>. G<small>ARY</small> S<small>ORRELLS</small> is a New Mexican by birth in the desert of New Mexico. He is an heir of a family with deep faith and a long Christian heritage. From childhood he followed God's call to a life with a mission.

At the invitation of a team of Abilene Christian College graduates, he arrived in Sao Paulo, Brazil, in 1969. For the next forty years, he focused on the proclamation of Jesus by planting churches in the great cities of the Latin world.

As a resident of Latin America for eight years, he directed the Institute of Biblical Studies, Camp Mount of Olives, and planted the South Metro Church with a team of coworkers. Today national elders, deacons, teachers, and evangelists lead the church.

Upon his family's return to the United States, Gary served three years as a member of the Bible Faculty of Lubbock Christian University, and eleven years as a member of the Mission Faculty of Abilene Christian University.

Gary's formal education includes B.A. and M.A. degrees in Bible from Abilene Christian University and an earned Doctor of Ministry degree from Abilene Christian University in 1994. In addition, he studied at Lubbock Christian University, Texas Tech University, Trinity Divinity School, and Northeastern University in Burlington, Massachusetts.

About the Author

Between 1980 and 2011, Gary worked with a vision of the Sao Paulo, Brazil, missionary team and the Central Church of Christ in Amarillo, Texas, to plant churches in capital cities of Latin America. As the vision grew, the trustees appointed Gary as executive director of the not-for-profit entity Great Cities Missions in 1990. He became director emeritus in 2011.

Gary is the author of *God Reflection* at GodReflection.com where for the first time he brings the totality of his God walk with family, the church, academic training, work experience, life scars, and accrued wisdom to reflect systematically on God. It is as if all of the trails of life cross at this point to explore what God means for our daily lives.